POETS, SAINTS, AND VISIONARIES
OF THE GREAT SCHISM,
1378–1417

POETS, SAINTS, AND VISIONARIES
OF THE GREAT SCHISM,
1378–1417

Renate Blumenfeld-Kosinski

THE PENNSYLVANIA STATE UNIVERSITY PRESS

UNIVERSITY PARK, PENNSYLVANIA

Library of Congress
Cataloging-in-Publication Data

Blumenfeld-Kosinski, Renate, 1952–
Poets, saints, and visionaries
of the Great Schism, 1378–1417 /
Renate Blumenfeld-Kosinski.
        p.   cm.
Includes bibliographical references (p.   )
and index.
ISBN 0-271-02749-5 (cloth : alk. paper)
1. Schism, The Great Western, 1378–1417.
2. Church history—Middle Ages, 600–1500.
3. Catholic Church—History.
I. Title.

BX1301.B53 2006
282'.09'023—dc22
2005024077

The Pennsylvania State University Press
is a member of the
Association of American University Presses.

It is the policy of The Pennsylvania State
University Press to use acid-free paper.
This book is printed on Natures Natural,
containing 50% post-consumer waste, and
meets minimum requirements of American
National Standard for Information Sciences—
Permanence of Paper for
Printed Library Material,
ANSI Z39.48–1992.

CONTENTS

ILLUSTRATIONS

1. The pope leaves behind the Babylonian woman (the Roman church) and departs for Avignon. Plate VIII from the Pope Prophecies, ed. Pasquilino. Venice: H. Porrus, 1589. (Author's collection)

2. The two-headed monster from the *Ascende calve*. Vienna, Österreichische Nationalbibliothek, MS 13648, folio 8v. (Courtesy Bildarchiv d. ÖNB, Wien)

3. Frontispiece of Bovet's *Arbre des batailles* showing popes Clement VII (left) and Urban VI (right) and their armies on the upper level. Two figures are debating to the left of the bottom of the tree. Paris, Bibliothèque nationale de France, fr. 1266, folio 5r. (Courtesy Bibliothèque nationale de France)

4. Frontispiece of Bovet's *Arbre des batailles* showing Popes Benedict XIII (left) and Boniface IX? (right; with Pope Urban VI's arms) and their armies on the upper level. A group of clerics is debating to the left of the bottom of the tree. New York, Pierpont Morgan Library, MS M. 907, folio 2v. (Courtesy The Pierpont Morgan Library, New York)

5. Two popes on one throne in Christine de Pizan's *Livre de la mutacion de Fortune*. Paris, Bibliothèque nationale de France, fr. 603, folio 109r. (Courtesy Bibliothèque nationale de France)

6. The "terrible beast" often depicting Pope Urban VI. Plate XV from the Pope Prophecies, ed. Pasquilino. Venice: H. Porrus, 1589. (Author's collection)

7. Pope and crowned beast. Plate XXX from the Pope Prophecies, ed. Pasquilino. Venice: H. Porrus, 1589. (Author's collection)

8. Pope Urban VI identified as a beaver. Plate XV (details) from the Pope Prophecies. Cambridge, Corpus Christi College, Parker Library, MS 404, folio 95r. (Copyright Master and Fellows of Corpus Christi College Cambridge)

9. The "terrible beast" with the empty tunic. Plate XV from the Pope Prophecies. New York, Pierpont Morgan Library, MS M. 402, folio 8v. (Courtesy The Pierpont Morgan Library, New York)

10. Winged demons "seduce" prelates and rulers to the Schism. The *Libellus* of Telesphorus of Cosenza. Paris, Bibliothèque nationale de France, lat. 11415, folio 131v. (Courtesy Bibliothèque nationale de France)

11. Toads emerge from the mouth of the false prophet. From a French translation of the *Libellus* of Telesphorus of Cosenza. Paris, Bibliothèque nationale de France, fr. 9783, folio 9r. (Courtesy Bibliothèque nationale de France)

12. The Avignon cardinals pull away the Church's veil and capture Pope Urban VI's papal keys with a lasso. The manuscript caption reads *Primus actus schismatis* (the first act of the Schism). From Antonio Baldana. *De magno schismate* (1419). Parma, Biblioteca Palatina, MS 1194, folio 2r. (Courtesy Biblioteca Palatina, Parma, su concessione del Ministero per i Beni e le Attività Culturali)

13. Pope Martin V weds the reunited church at the Council of Constance. The emperor Sigismund officiates. From Antonio Baldana, *De magno schismate* (1419). Parma, Biblioteca Palatina, MS 1194, folio 13v. (Courtesy Biblioteca Palatina, Parma, su concessione del Ministero per i Beni e le Attività Culturali)

14. Four popes of the Schism years peacefully united in one frame. Clockwise: Urban VI, Clement VII, Benedict XIII, and Boniface IX. From Hartmann Schedel, *The Nuremberg Chronicle*. Nuremberg, 1493, folio 232v. (Author's collection)

Maps

Map 1 The rival obediences, 1378–1409. From R. N. Swanson, *Universities, Academics, and the Great Schism*. Reprinted with permission of Cambridge University Press.

Map 2 The rival obediences, 1409–18. From Swanson, *Universities*. Reprinted with permission of Cambridge University Press.

ACKNOWLEDGMENTS

One of the pleasures of scholarship is sharing one's ideas with others. This book profited from many such moments of sharing and intellectual stimulation. Barbara Newman was the first to help me see the possibilities of a wider study of the *imaginaire* of the Great Schism and has been a patient and inspiring conversation partner along the way. She also answered many queries, as did Robert Lerner, Hélène Millet, David Nirenberg, Joelle Rollo-Koster, Laura Smoller, and André Vauchez. I am very grateful to all of them. For help in obtaining articles from far-flung journals, my thanks go to Danielle Bohler and Bernard McGinn. I enjoyed the many conversations about this project with Kevin Brownlee, Dyan Elliott, Brian McGuire, Nancy Regalado, Bruce Venarde, and Lori Walters. My dear friend and intellectual sparring partner, the late Rona Goffen, played a big part in the conceptualization of this book and in the pleasure of writing it. Gábor Klaniczay read several chapters of this manuscript, and I profited from his incisive and helpful comments and suggestions. Claire Sahlin and Michael Hanly generously sent me the manuscripts of their books before publication.

I would also like to thank the institutions that gave me the opportunity to present parts of this book to challenging and knowledgeable audiences: Cambridge University, Indiana University, the Institute for Advanced Study, the University of Lausanne, the University of London, New York University, the University of Pennsylvania, Princeton University, and Rutgers University.

For generous financial support, my thanks go to the University of Pittsburgh and to the National Endowment for the Humanities, whose research grant for 2003–4 enabled me to finish this book. Most of this book was written while I was a visiting fellow in the Department of French and Italian at Princeton University in 2000–2001 and 2003–4. My thanks go to Marie-Hélène Huet and François Rigolot for their hospitality and helpfulness. The Richard D. and Mary Jane Edwards Endowed Publication Fund of the University of Pittsburgh generously paid for the photos and permissions.

A small part of Chapter 3 appeared in a different form in *Mystics Quarterly* 25 (1999). I thank the editor, Alexandra Barratt, for permission to use this material. A different version of Chapter 1 appears in Mathilde van Dijk and Renée Nip, eds., *Saints, Scholars, and Politicians: Gender as a Tool in Medieval Studies*, Festschrift in Honour of Anneke Mulder-Bakker on the Occasion of Her Sixty-Fifth Birthday (Turnhout: Brepols, 2005).

As always, this book is dedicated to my husband, Antoni Kosinski, who heard more about the multiple popes and the ensuing troubles and anxieties than any mathematician should have to hear.

POPES DURING THE GREAT SCHISM

Gregory XI (1370–78)
(Pierre Roger de Beaufort)

Avignon Line   *Roman Line*

Clement VII (1378–94)   Urban VI (1378–89)
(Robert of Geneva)   (Bartolomeo Prignano)

Benedict XIII (1394–1423) Boniface IX (1389–1404)
(Pedro de Luna)   (Pietro Tomacelli)

                           Innocent VII (1404–6)
                           (Cosimo Gentile de'Migliorati)

                           Gregory XII (1406–15)
                           (Angelo Correr)   *Pisan Line*

                                                  Alexander V (1409–10)
                                                  (Pietro Philargi)

                                                  John XXIII (1410–15)
                                                  (Baldassare Cossa)

Elected at the Council of Constance

Martin V (1417–31)
(Ottone Colonna)

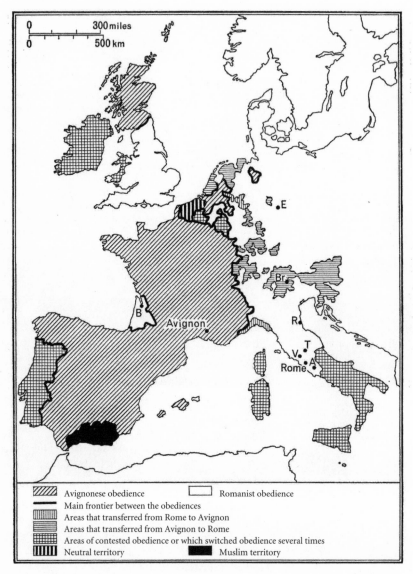

MAP 1. The rival obediences, 1378–1409. Towns in Romanist areas which recognized the Avignon pope: A=Anagni (to 1386); Br=Brixen (to 1389); E=Erfurt (to 1380); R=Ravenna (to 1386); T=Todi (to 1386); V=Viterbo (to 1386). B=Bordeaux, which accepted the Avignon papacy from 1380 onwards. N.B. Portugal was Romanist after 1385; Naples was Romanist from 1400.

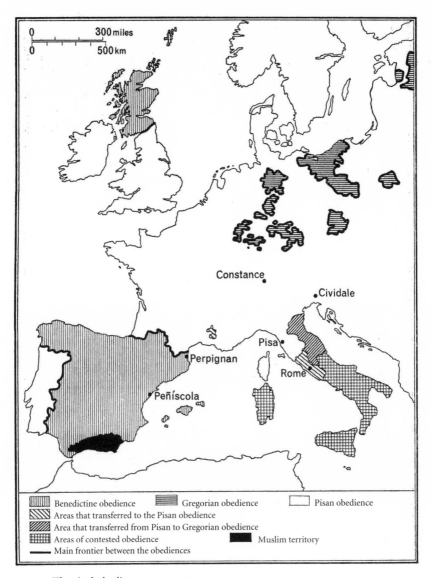

MAP 2. The rival obediences, 1409–18.

INTRODUCTION

E tutti li altri che tu vedi qui,
seminator di scandalo et di scisma
fuor vivi, e però son fessi così.
—Dante, *Inferno* 28:34–36

Dante's "cleft schismatics," forever carrying their intestines or heads in front of them, lived in earlier times, but his image of the damage done by schismatic discord is especially appropriate for the later fourteenth century, a period often referred to as the "calamitous" century. For most readers this term evokes the plague or the Hundred Years War.[1] The Great Schism of the Western Church, although a profound crisis that lasted almost forty years (1378–1417), has not captured the imagination of a modern audience to quite the same extent. But at the time it generated staggering amounts of writings in a large variety of genres. The hostile coexistence of two and finally three popes also created a more

Full citations for all abbreviated titles can be found in the bibliography. For most foreign language quotes the originals will be cited. Biblical quotes come from the Revised Standard Version, with passages from the Vulgate supplied whenever necessary.

1. "The Calamitous Fourteenth Century" is the subtitle of Tuchman's *Distant Mirror*. Graus subtitles his book (*Pest—Geisler—Judenmorde*) "The Fourteenth Century as a Time of Crisis," but he concentrates mostly on the plague, flagellants, and the killing of Jews, though he does have a brief chapter on the crisis of the church (2:3). By contrast, Kaminsky in "From Lateness to Waning to Crisis" claims that none of the late medieval crises were "per se morbid," but rather "disposed on a prefrabricated crisis grid" by modern historians (p. 121). His view of the Schism (p. 121) as an exclusive "crisis of the papacy," presumably not affecting ordinary Christians, is not supported by the evidence, as I shall show in this study.

general anxiety among Christians.[2] The uncertainty about who was the right pope undermined people's confidence in their ecclesiastical leaders and could be felt even at the lowest levels of pastoral care. In this study we shall encounter a large cast of characters, all of whom in one way or another gave expression to their anguish and frustration in face of the divided papacy and attempted to offer hope and solutions. They did so in letters, allegorical and polemical texts, prophecies, and images. Among them we find charismatic saints and visionaries, professional poets, wily diplomats, committed clerics, mysterious prophets, and stubborn, power-hungry popes.

But why did the Great Schism produce more literary, visionary, and prophetic activity than previous schisms?[3] How did it differ from the more than twenty earlier schisms? How was this particular crisis conceptualized? Did medieval eyewitnesses and historians see it as one continuous event or rather as a succession of disconnected turns of fortune? In this Introduction I first give a brief outline of the major events between 1378 and 1417 (more details appear or reappear in later chapters as appropriate) and then provide a preview of the book as a whole and some methodological reflections.

A Brief History of the Great Schism

The Great Schism became "great" only in a retrospective evaluation, of course. No one in 1378 could have anticipated that two and then three popes would fight over the right to the papal throne and thus divide Europe for more than a generation. Indeed, as a historiographical problem the Great Schism did not appear as such until the late seventeenth century, when Louis Ellies Dupin wrote the first chronological history of this event. As François Fossier puts it: "Lived as an event of uncertain contours by the historians of the time, [the Great Schism] becomes more and more blurred in the historical consciousness to the advantage of the description of heresies, which emerge as the most significant marker in the religious history of this period."[4] Yet, between 1378 and

---

2. On the atmosphere of this period, see Mollat, "Vie et sentiment religieux au début du Grand Schisme."

3. Throughout this book the capitalized word "Schism" refers to the Great Schism only.

4. Fossier, "Rapports Eglise-Etat," p. 29. Dupin's work was the 1694 *Histoire des controverses ecclésiastiques* (see Fossier, p. 25). For reflections on how an event or a series of events takes on narrative contours, see the recent excellent introduction by Rathmann to his *Geschehen und Geschichten des Konstanzer Konzils,* which also contains a cogent evaluation of the debates of the last few decades on the narrativization of history.

1417 we find an almost frantic production of texts pro or contra one or the other pope.[5]

Who were these popes? In the early fourteenth century the papacy had moved to Avignon and was dominated by French popes. In the 1360s a number of saintly figures like Saint Birgitta of Sweden (1303–73) and fr. (friar) Pedro of Aragon (1305–81) began to exert pressure on Pope Urban V (1362–70), a French Benedictine from Lozère, to return the papacy to Rome. Urban complied in 1367 but returned to Avignon just before his death. The same saintly personages, to whom we can now add Saint Catherine of Siena, then went to work on Urban's successor, Gregory XI (1370–78), another Frenchman, from the Limousin area. We shall explore the details of their strategies and results in Chapter 2. Suffice it to say here that Gregory finally made the perilous journey to Rome and arrived there in January 1377.

Richard C. Trexler's analysis of Rome just before the Great Schism shows us a "murderous city" where a "deep-seated chauvinism" had prepared the ground for a schism even before Gregory XI's death.[6] This death occurred on March 27, 1378, and set the stage for the tumultuous events that led first to the election of the Neapolitan Bartolomeo Prignano, the archbishop of Bari, as Urban VI (1378–89) and then to that of Robert of Geneva, a relative of the French king Charles V, as Clement VII (1378–94).

According to many eyewitnesses, the conclave where the cardinals gathered to choose Gregory's successor was surrounded by the Roman populace, many of them armed and chanting "We want a Roman or at least an Italian"—or else.[7] When the mob entered the conclave they at first thought that the aged cardinal of Saint Peter (a Roman) had been made pope, something some of the frightened cardinals apparently wanted them to believe until they had a chance

---

5. A convenient time line of the Schism's major events and the polemical texts produced each year can be found in pp. xxxix–lx in vol. 6 of Jean Gerson, *Oeuvres*, ed. Glorieux. See also my list titled "Popes During the Great Schism."

6. Trexler, "Rome on the Eve of the Great Schism," pp. 492, 506.

7. Much of the following brief history is based on Delaruelle, Labande, and Ourliac, *L'Eglise au temps du Grand Schisme*, 1:3–200. For the early years, see also Ullmann, *Origins of the Great Schism*. The account of the April 8 election is based there on a contemporary document, the *Factum Urbani*. The indispensable detailed history of the Schism is still Valois's four-volume *La France et le Grand Schisme d'Occident*, a fascinating read, based on primary sources. Delaruelle et al. offer a huge bibliography of both primary and secondary sources. For a focused account of the early years, see also Bernstein, *Pierre d'Ailly and the Blanchard Affair*. For Spain, see esp. Seidlmayer, *Die Anfänge des grossen abendländischen Schismas*, and for England, Perroy, *L'Angleterre et le Grand Schisme d'Occident;* Harvey, *Solutions to the Schism;* and Palmer, "England and the Great Western Schism." For briefer overviews, see Kaminsky, "The Great Schism," and Millet, "Le Grand Schisme d'Occident."

to return to their safer quarters. Eventually the presumed pope enlightened the multitude that in fact Bartolomeo Prignano had been elected. He was hiding in the "most secret room" of the palace until the vote was made public. According to a curial document telling of these events, the contemporary *Factum Urbani*,[8] and many other chronicles and eyewitnesses, there was a general atmosphere of confusion, fear, and panic during and after the election. The canonist Gilles Bellemère, for example, a rather timorous individual, was so frightened by the tumult in Rome (and especially by the constant ringing of bells) that he took off his clerical garb so as not to become a target for the mob.[9] But other witnesses, such as the Urbanist Alfonso of Jaén, the confessor of Saint Birgitta of Sweden, her daughter Catherine, or the chronicler Dietrich of Niem, disputed this account. Already shortly after the election there were no more disinterested witnesses, for it was exactly these emotions—fear caused by intimidation and outright threats—that would soon become the major argument for the cardinals' rejection of Pope Urban VI. An election under duress would not be canonical and hence invalid.

But why reject Urban VI so quickly after what seems to have been a unanimous election? The answer can be found in his character and behavior. Denouncing immediately the luxurious way of life of the cardinals, he apparently lost all self-control in his vituperations and even bodily attacked a cardinal. Many instances of his private and public displays of anger show a man who replaced all his previous humility and circumspection with self-righteousness and fury after his elevation to the papal throne.[10] The cardinals, who, under the pretext of seeking a more healthful climate, had left Rome for Anagni, summarized their troubles with Urban in a letter to the French king on September 10, 1378, calling Urban an oppressive monster, struck by *truculenta rabies* (combative rage or rabies).[11] Deciding that the first election had been invalid because of the fear occasioned by the Roman mob, the cardinals, now in Fondi and under the protection of the count (whom Urban had alienated by refusing to pay a debt incurred by his predecessor), proceeded to elect Robert of Geneva, closely related to the French royal family, as Clement VII, an act that earned them the scorn of many. Catherine of Siena immediately

---

8. See Ullmann, *Origins*, pp. 11–25, for a translation of the most dramatic passages.
9. Coville, *Recherches sur quelques écrivains*, p. 77. His fascinating testimony was delivered at Medina del Campo on the occasion of the Spanish inquiries into the circumstances of the conclave (November 1380–April 1381).
10. See Ullmann, *Origins*, chap. 3, "The Storm," for a number of anecdotes illustrating Urban's temper.
11. Delaruelle et al., *L'Eglise*, 1:16.

denounced the cardinals as liars and idolaters.[12] Thus, the Great Schism was inaugurated. It was the first time that the same college of cardinals had elected two different popes within a space of five months.[13] Urban would soon establish himself in Rome, while Clement, after a dramatic trip to Naples and futile military efforts, moved his papal court back to Avignon.

The chronicler Jean Froissart (ca. 1337–ca. 1404) labeled the Schism as "a great beginning of pestilence that broke into the church" (un grant commencement de pestilence qui se bouta en l'eglise), thus linking the scourge of the mid-fourteenth century to this new scourge, one that was as nefarious to Christians' spiritual health as the Black Death had been to their physical well-being.[14] For Nicolas de Clamanges (ca. 1363–1437), one of the great theologians of his time, the evil cardinals were at the origin of this "execrable plague of the schismatic division," which he also referred to as "this very cruel beast, laying waste, consuming, and destroying everything."[15] For Pierre Salmon (d. after 1427), counselor to kings and dukes, there was a close relationship between Charles VI's madness and the Schism.[16] For Christine de Pizan (ca. 1364–ca. 1430) the Schism was a pestilence, "painful, poisonous, a contagious plant that was thrust into the bosom of Holy Church at the instigation of the devil." It was a scourge, "a painful calamity, and a purulent wound."[17] The plague, both in the sense of an epidemic and the open wounds it causes, and the beast, especially various beasts of the Apocalypse, became frequent metaphors for the Schism.

In somewhat different metaphorical terms, the church was also seen as being adulterous or alternatively as having been raped by one of the popes, adumbrating the double perspective of the church as the guilty party or victim that will become a staple of many Schism texts.[18] The popes were compared to two rival suitors, while the first election of April 1378 was interpreted as "spiritual matrimony" that the cardinals made legal by "cohabitation" with Pope

12. See Denis-Boulet, *La carrière politique de sainte Catherine de Sienne*, p. 168.
13. For the tumultuous double election of 1159, see Chapter 1. But there the circumstances were quite different, especially because of the involvement of Emperor Frederick Barbarossa.
14. Froissart, *Chroniques*, 9:46. For links between eschatological thinking and the black death, see Lerner, "The Black Death and Western Eschatological Mentalities."
15. See his 1401 *Traité de la ruine de l'Eglise*, p. 67.
16. This was especially clear in the first version of his *Dialogues* (1409). See Hedeman, *Of Counselors and Kings*, pp. 1–28.
17. *Le Livre des fais (Charles V)*, 2:155–56. On Christine and Nicolas de Clamanges and the Great Schism, see Margolis, "Culture vantée, culture inventée," esp. pp. 299–304.
18. See also my fig. 12 from Antonio Baldana's 1419 chronicle of the Schism. Here the Church is attacked by the Clementine cardinals, who violently pull off her veil while Urban looks on helplessly and has the keys of Saint Peter forcibly removed from his tiara. See Guerrini, "Le illustrazioni nel *De magno schismate* di Antonio Baldana," p. 385.

Urban. The cardinals, according to the Florentine chancellor Coluccio Salutati, "had acted like women, taking favors from the man they now denounced."[19] This kind of language did not bode well for an early compromise.

After the second election furious diplomatic activity began for both camps: the Urbanists and the Clementists. Ambassadors were dispatched to all the European powers with the goal of persuading them to adhere to their pope. In almost all cases the adherence to one or the other pope was bound up with already existing or developing political conflicts. Thus, the French and English attitudes toward the divided papacy, as well as their repeated efforts at union, cannot be separated from the vagaries of the Hundred Years War. But it would go too far in the context of this Introduction to analyze the myriad political considerations that entered in a given country's decision-making. Some of these factors will be taken up, however, in the different chapters of this book.

Soon after September 1378 the Emperor Charles IV and then his successor Wenceslas joined Urban's camp, as did England, where the representatives of the "rival claimants arrived simultaneously, both legations asking for help against the anti-Christ and intruder."[20] This choice of words is a preview of the strong vocabulary eventually used by all Schism polemicists: over the years the popes were labeled as traitors, heretics, and antichrists. In England, Clement's hapless representative was arrested and the benefices of the Clementist cardinals were confiscated.

In Italy the areas north of the kingdom of Naples for the most part adhered to Urban, while Naples changed allegiances several times, opting mostly for Clement under Queen Joan of Naples but after 1400 changing back to the Roman obedience. Flanders was Urbanist, except for some divided cities. Scotland went for Clement, while Poland, Hungary, and the Scandinavian countries became Urbanist. The Iberian kingdoms entered into a long phase of neutrality (the famous "indiferencia") pending detailed inquiries into the circumstances of the double election, held at Medina del Campo between November 1380 and April 1381. They finally declared for Clement, though not all at the same time.[21] Portugal flip-flopped several times, as a result of problems of succession and Castilian threats, but eventually became a strong supporter of Urban. France almost instantly became a bastion of Clementism, a

---

19. In his *Quantam cordis amaritudine* of September 1378 (see Harvey, *Solutions to the Schism,* pp. 38–41). See also Rusconi, *L'attesa della fine,* pp. 166–67, for this kind of metaphorics in previous schisms and the Great Schism. These images will reappear in almost all the following chapters in various contexts.

20. Ullmann, *Origins,* p. 104. See his chap. 7, "The English Reaction," for details.

21. For details, see Ivars, "La 'indiferencia' de Pedro IV de Aragón en el Gran Cisma de Occidente."

move for which Charles V was later criticized.[22] Louis of Anjou was an especially strong supporter, having hopes for Italian conquests.

But this dividing up of territories adhering to different obediences was less neat than it seems, for on the microlevel there were a number of dioceses that had two rival bishops who would attack each other "by mutual sentences of excommunication and interdict" and thus undermine their flocks' confidence in their ecclesiastical leaders.[23] In cities like Wroclaw, Constance, Liège, or Basel two competing bishops were in charge, designating each others' masses as blasphemy and sacrilege. Similarly, many monastic houses were led by two abbots or priors, each adhering to a different pope. As for the ordinary citizen, Walter Ullmann puts it like this: "The spiritual salvation of the common people was determined by the attitude of their rulers and superiors, guided as these were by motives far enough removed from the spiritual, religious or moral." Whom to believe? This was by no means clear, and the result was "one of indescribable mental confusion."[24] The great theologian Jean Gerson (1363–1429) addressed this confusion in a 1398 treatise on how ordinary Christians should confront the problem of the Schism. He argued against mutual excommunication by the different obediences, and especially against "terrifying the laity" by claiming that one set of sacraments would be invalid.[25] What counted were the good intentions of the local priests, whom people should trust. Yet, all the while everyone should strive for the unity of the church for the lack of which the popes alone were responsible.

But this unity proved elusive. After the positioning of the major powers a period of entrenchment and enormous polemical literary activity commenced.[26] In these early years we find such important texts as Giovanni de Legnano's *De fletu Ecclesiae* (On the tears of the church; August 1379); Heinrich of Langenstein's 1379 *Epistola concilii pacis* (Letter on the peace council); Konrad of Gelnhausen's 1380 *Epistola concordiae* (Letter on concord); and Saint Vincent Ferrer's 1380 *De moderno schismate* (On the modern schism), a detailed defense of Pope Clement using the scholastic method. Such great thinkers as Pierre d'Ailly (1350–1420), Jean Gerson, Nicolas de Clamanges, and many other

---

22. See Map 1 for the period between 1378 and 1409. See Swanson, *Universities, Academics, and the Great Schism,* chap. 2, on the quick acceptance of Clement.

23. Ullmann, *Origins,* p. 96.

24. Ullmann, *Origins,* pp. 98–99. See also Morrall, *Gerson and the Great Schism,* p. 45: A quarter of the population of Bruges went to Ghent for Easter in 1393 to worship at an Urbanist church.

25. McGuire, *Jean Gerson.* Gerson's text is *De modo se habendi tempore schismatis* (*Oeuvres* 6:29–34). It was probably written for the faithful in the divided city of Bruges.

26. See Bliemetzrieder, *Literarische Polemik zum Beginn des grossen abendländischen Schismas.*

theologians and intellectuals began contributing their ideas and theories on the Schism, and they did so for the most part until the Council of Constance (1414–18). Outside the high-level clerical establishment of the university and the papal courts, other voices lamenting the Schism could be heard, as in a poem on the Great Schism authored by an anonymous cleric in 1381,[27] as well as works by the many poets, prophets, and visionaries we shall encounter in the pages of this book.

Meanwhile, the two popes established their obediences with full colleges of cardinals and the financial arrangements that supported their administrations. Urban VI became embroiled in several notable conflicts with the kingdom of Naples and his own cardinals, several of whom plotted against him and were imprisoned, tortured, and finally killed on his orders while he took refuge in Genoa.[28] Urban's power waned while his unpopularity grew. When he died in October 1389, an annalist from Forli called him "the worst man, cruel and scandalous" (vir pessimus, crudelis et scandalosus). Few mourned his demise. His successor, who would reign for the next fifteen years as Pope Boniface IX, was Pietro Tomacelli, young and good-looking yet "feeble and uncultivated."[29]

The fact that now a second Roman pope had been elected into the Great Schism dashed the hopes of those who had wished that the death of one or the other pope might put an end to the division of the church. While Boniface had enormous political and financial troubles in Italy, in France discussions of an armed descent to Rome were revived, especially after the coronation of Louis II of Anjou as king of Sicily in 1390. The University of Paris became more and more involved in the discussions of the different *viae* (ways) of solving the Schism: the *via facti*, or armed conflict; the *via cessionis*, the abdication of both popes; and the *via concilii*, the summoning of a General Council. It was this latter idea that preoccupied many significant writers of the time, who worked on the conciliar theory that eventually resulted in the Council of Constance.[30] The principal question debated in this context was who had the right to convene a General Council: the pope (but which one?), the cardinals, or the secular rulers? It would take another twenty-five years to resolve these questions.

In France the movement of trying to get the two popes to abdicate gained in popularity. Being in the Avignon obedience, the French concentrated their

27. See Meyer and Valois, "Poème en quatrains."
28. This episode will reappear in a number of contexts throughout this book.
29. Delaruelle et al., *L'Eglise*, 1:66–67.
30. On the development of this concept, see Tierney, *Foundations of the Conciliar Theory*. For a study of conciliarism especially in our period, see Brandmüller, *Papst und Konzil im grossen Schisma*.

efforts on the Clementine papacy. In January 1394 a solemn poll was taken at the University of Paris, and of the ten thousand responses the majority supported the *via cessionis*. Apparently the Parisian scholars thought that if the Avignon pope abdicated the Roman one would follow.[31] But they had not anticipated the developments that followed the death of Clement VII on September 16, 1394.

Although the French king Charles VI immediately dispatched messengers urging the Avignon cardinals to wait with electing a successor to Clement (as did the king of Aragon) in the hope of ending the Schism then and there, the cardinals entered the conclave on September 26 and elected the Spanish cardinal Pedro de Luna as Pope Benedict XIII. He became the most tenacious of popes and hung on to what he considered his rightful papal throne until long after the Council of Constance had deposed him. A skillful diplomat, he had been instrumental in getting the Spanish kingdoms to opt for Pope Clement VII. In the conclave Pedro had taken a solemn oath to abdicate if necessary, but he clearly had no intention of doing so. The next few years were dominated by many French attempts to force him to make good on his promise, all of them futile. Finally, in July 1398 the third council of Paris voted to withdraw obedience from Benedict, which put him in a difficult financial and political situation but did not lead to the desired result.[32] Even when he was abandoned by his own cardinals and besieged in the papal palace in Avignon he did not waver. Because no overt political allies declared themselves, the French eventually had no choice but to restitute obedience to him in 1403, with the strong support of the dukes Louis of Orléans and Louis of Anjou.[33] The conflicts between the Orléans and Burgundian factions were exacerbated by this episode, especially because the bouts of madness of King Charles VI, which first manifested themselves in 1392, often created a power vacuum.[34] Furthermore, the deposition and death (1400) of the English king Richard II, with whom the French were close to an agreement, ruined any chances at a joint action to try and end the Schism.[35] Under the new dynasty of Henry IV the hostilities of the Hundred Years War flared up again.

---

31. See Delaruelle et al., *L'Eglise*, 1:78, and Morrall, *Gerson and the Great Schism*, chap. 2.3.
32. See Kaminsky, "The Politics of France's Subtraction of Obedience."
33. When the siege was over, Benedict presented Louis of Anjou, his first visitor, with the beard he had grown during his imprisonment (Delaruelle et al., *L'Eglise*, 1:107).
34. Gerson at one point believed that if the houses of Orléans and Burgundy could only reconcile their differences the Schism could be solved. See Morrall, *Gerson and the Great Schism*, p. 59.
35. Indeed, Palmer claims that the first initiative to end the Schism came from England (in a letter from Richard II to the king of Navarre in 1388). See "England and the Great Western Schism," pp. 516–17.

Even though the withdrawal of obedience had been a failure in that Benedict XIII still refused to abdicate, "it changed the climate of opinion even in the obdurate Roman papacy." There was now a "new unionist sentiment" that "could [no longer] be ignored."[36] Boniface IX's successors Innocent VII (1404–6) and Gregory XII (1406–15), who as Angelo Correr had been the first Venetian ever elected to the papacy, both agreed to negotiations should the other side be willing. In addition, following some earlier ideas, there was agreement that "no formal recantation of error [was necessary] on either side" and consequently there would be no further discussions on the legitimacy of either pope.[37] But these new conciliatory efforts encountered numerous obstacles, especially in the shape of Pope Benedict XIII.

In 1404 and 1405, exploiting a perceived weakness of Innocent VII, the Avignon pope moved farther south—all the way to Genoa, which was now in French hands, with the famous Boucicaut as governor. The French government as well as the clerics began to complain again about Benedict's fiscal policies and other transgressions and decided that the restitution of obedience had been a mistake; the obedience was again withdrawn in 1406, and in 1408 France declared itself neutral in the papal conflict. Now the pressure was on both popes finally to come to an agreement.

An intense period of negotiations over the place and terms of a meeting began. Savona, a town on the Mediterranean coast west of Genoa, was chosen as an appropriate location, and now all that was needed was to get the two popes there at the same time. But it was not to be. Excuses, delays, and enigmatic, incoherent, and contradictory pronouncements that made Gregory seem like a sphinx obstructed any progress. The chronicler Dietrich of Niem shows the exasperation of all those involved when he calls the obstreperous popes Benefictus and Errorius,[38] apparently living in a world of fantasy and error.

Finally the cardinals took matters into their own hands and assembled the Council of Pisa from March to August 1409. But the two papal opponents refused to appear: Benedict convened his own council in Perpignan, while Gregory did likewise in Cividale. In a decree read by Simon de Cramaud, who had also been instrumental in the withdrawal of French obedience, the two popes were deposed and accused as "schismatics, fosterers of schism, notorious heretics deviating from the faith, ensnared in notorious crimes of perjury

---

36. Kaminsky, "The Great Schism," p. 692.
37. Morrall, *Gerson and the Great Schism*, p. 62. For Gerson all these questions are in any case in the realm of *dubia* because there are no doctrinal differences between the two papacies.
38. Delaruelle et al., *L'Eglise*, pp. 132–33.

and violation of their oaths, and notorious scandalisers of the church: . . . they have been notoriously incorrigible, contumacious and stubborn in these respects."[39]

As serious as this deposition sounds, it had little effect on the two popes. In their view, they remained popes, despite the council's election of the Greek Pietro Philargi, a Roman cardinal, as Pope Alexander V. He was soon succeeded by Baldassare Cossa as John XXIII. Instead of two popes Europe now had three. Both Benedict and Gregory still hung on to reduced obediences, but large parts of Europe, including France, England, Portugal, most of the Empire, and the Scandinavian countries, now adhered to the Pisan pope (Map 2).[40]

Benedict, now more than eighty years old, moved to Spain, where he eventually took up residence on the rock of Peñiscola on the Spanish coast (1411), claiming to be the legitimate pope until his death in 1423. Gregory, rejected by his hometown of Venice, finally settled in Rimini after a series of dangerous peregrinations. John XXIII, now recognized by a number of important nations, established good relations with the newly elected emperor Sigismund but encountered growing difficulties with France and especially Naples, whose troops sacked Rome in June 1413 and chased the pope to Florence. The combined weaknesses of the three popes made another move toward union possible. It was the emperor Sigismund who took the initiative and announced in a "universal edict" on October 30, 1413, that a General Council would be held the following year in Constance. Everyone was invited, but not everyone came. For now, we leave our protagonists in the year 1413; the Council of Constance and its results will make a brief appearance in the Conclusion to this book.

Some Methodological Reflections and a Preview of This Book

Two distinct insistent voices first alerted me to what were for me new aspects of the Great Schism: one of them mysterious and mediated, the other forceful and direct. The first belonged to Constance de Rabastens, whose visions, recorded by her confessor Raimond de Sabanac, included dramatic images of the schismatic popes; the second belonged to Christine de Pizan, whose allegorical and political writings repeatedly lament the divided church. Until I

---

39. Kaminsky, "The Great Schism," p. 695. On Simon de Cramaud, see Kaminsky, *Simon de Cramaud and the Great Schism.*

40. Again we can find divisions on the microlevel. See Bornstein's *Sister Bartolomeo Riccoboni: Life and Death in a Venetian Convent,* showing how the nuns in this one convent were divided between two of the three post-Pisa popes.

encountered Constance, the Great Schism had been a background problem for me—certainly something one must know about, but at the same time something that had been studied at extraordinary lengths and had therefore been "dealt with." But in the vast scholarly literature on the Great Schism, although Constance was mentioned a few times, no one wondered why an ordinary woman from southern France in the 1380s would have visions about the divided papacy. Was the Schism a concern that transcended the boundaries of the political, university, and ecclesiastical milieus and that spilled out into the lives of the ordinary faithful, be they widows from Languedoc or an Italian-French woman writer active in early fifteenth-century Paris? Slowly bits and pieces of my other areas of interest began to form a picture: Catherine of Siena's letters, which I had studied in other contexts; political allegories by Philippe de Mézières and Honoré Bovet, texts that I had taught many times without zeroing in on the Schism; strange prophecies and images that I had encountered in various manuscripts—all these fragments coalesced into what I would call the *imaginaire* (more about this term below) of the Great Schism. Poets, saintly visionaries, and prophets—these were the groups that spoke most forcefully and most imaginatively about the Schism outside the "official" literature associated with this crisis, and it was these groups that I chose to make the focal points of this book.

This emotional entry into the subject matter helps explain what this book is not. It is not a history of the Great Schism; rather, I use the Great Schism as a problem to illuminate medieval thought processes. In other words, I analyze how a variety of people responded to one of the greatest crises the medieval church had ever experienced.[41] How did they express their anguish and frustration? By which means did they try to intervene in the politics of their time? What kinds of solutions did they offer? For the most part I stay away from the numerous polemical tracts, treatises on conciliar theory, and mutually insulting invectives sent by one or the other pope and their supporters, which make up a great part of the literature on the Schism. These texts, most of them in Latin, do hover in the background, and I do cite some of them occasionally, but they are not my principal sources. Since I want to investigate the *imaginaire* or

41. An intriguing ancestor of our texts is Rupert of Deutz's 1095 *Carmina de Sancto Laurentio*, a despairing lament on the schism of the church in Liège caused by the simoniac heresy. It features the allegorical figure of Ecclesia bemoaning the attacks on her integrity, and it is full of Boethian echoes and apocalyptic imagery. But this text also highlights the differences with the literary production of the Great Schism: it was more localized, and there was no widespread production of poetic or visionary texts for this schism. For a detailed reading of the *Carmina*, see Arduini, *Non fabula sed res*. (I would like to thank Barbara Newman for directing me toward Rupert and this study.) See also Van Engen, *Rupert of Deutz*, pp. 30–35.

Vorstellungswelt—neither term has a good English translation—of different groups and classes of people during the Schism, I look outside the strictly clerical tradition.

The *imaginaire* is related to the concept of mentality but is not its synonym. František Graus's definition of the term "mentality" is "the common tenor of longer-lasting forms of behavior and opinions of individuals inside of groups."[42] The French term *mentalité* also usually designates the ways a group thinks with an emphasis on collectivity.[43] While I certainly seek to reconstruct the mentality of Christians reacting to the division of the church, my target is not so much a collectivity as a series of individuals whose responses to the Schism show a rather wide variety. There are no specific sources for the history of mentalities, but only different questions that can be asked of existing sources.[44] What Georges Duby, after Lucien Febvre, called the *outillage mental* (mental tools) of medieval women and men is the subject of this history:[45] emotions and behaviors, as they are expressed in written or visual sources; iconography; language, including poetry and its metaphors; visions and prophecies.

Especially useful in this context is the notion of the *imaginaire* or *Vorstellungswelt*, which means more than the realm of the imaginary or the world of the imagination: It refers to the ideas, conceptions, and even prejudices that informed the creation of texts and images in a given period. Some of the questions I hope to answer with the help of this material are: How did people conceptualize a problem like the Great Schism? Did they see it as a man-made political problem or as a divine punishment announcing the coming of the Antichrist? As an attack on the church from the outside or as a deep-rooted inner malady? As we shall see, all these ideas appeared at one time or another. How did people hope to intervene in this crisis? Why did they speak out? Did they think their voices would be heard, some of their proposed solutions accepted? What we look for, then, is not necessarily "objective" history but the "self-interpretation of an epoch."[46] That is, although we try to pin down the facts of a given event, the way the event was processed and represented by contemporaries is equally important. I do not want to make a distinction between

---

42. See Graus, "Mentalität," 9 n. 4. "Der gemeinsame Tonus längerfristiger Verhaltensweisen und Meinungen von Individuen innerhalb von Gruppen" (p. 17).
43. See Le Goff, "Mentalités."
44. Graus, "Mentalität," p. 47.
45. Duby, "Histoire des mentalités," pp. 952, 963–65.
46. Goetz, "Vorstellungsgeschichte." See that article for the theoretical underpinnings of this approach.

"objective documents" and the literary reflections of events.[47] Each text, whatever its genre, has an agenda. Thus, the object of inquiry here is the subjectivity of the people affected by the Great Schism as it manifests itself in texts and images, the only traces that remain of their thoughts. Partisanship rather than objectivity necessarily characterizes the sources of this long-term conflict.

But the texts and images at the center of this book are not merely reflections of and reactions to the developments of the time; they themselves are part of the historical reality. Bernard Guenée has recently explored the idea that our period first saw the formation of "public opinion."[48] He adduces numerous instances where in the extensive *Chronique du religieux de Saint-Denys* the chronicler Michel Pintoin makes reference to what the common people thought and talked about in public places. Pintoin emphasizes the increasing anxiety and dismay that overtakes Christendom as the Schism wears on for more than a generation. The many texts that circulated at the time expressing anger and despair constitute the reality of the Schism years just as much as do the many royal documents and papal bulls that make up the official records of these years. And they are as much part of the historical reality as the military offensives, intrigues, and murders that punctuated the Schism years. Our allegories and visionary texts speak of what has happened, but they themselves may have a trigger function and make new things happen. Thus, they can play a pivotal role in moving negotiations forward or pushing rulers to the brink, motivating them to seek new solutions.

The Great Schism affected all of Europe, but not all countries were equally involved in the creation of texts and images commenting on the Schism. In those countries that—like England, for example—chose an obedience early on and stuck to it, larger groups of people, and especially laypeople, were not as involved in Schism polemics as they were in France and the Italian territories. Margaret Harvey has demonstrated that the Schism did not seem to be a pressing problem for English churchmen, who seemed more concerned with Lollardy and anticlericalism. Nor was there much evidence of the Schism in English chronicles before 1408, when Henry IV's government became involved in efforts to end the Schism during a brief truce in the Hundred Years War.[49] In

---

47. Rathmann discusses this set of problems for the Council of Constance, where previous scholarship has usually made this not always useful distinction. See *Geschehen und Geschichten,* esp. chap. 5 on Ulrich of Richental.
48. See *L'opinion publique à la fin du Moyen Age.*
49. See Harvey, *Solutions to the Schism,* p. 130. After Urban VI's death, though, the English hesitated for a while before recognizing Boniface IX. In most instances efforts to end the Schism were linked to peace efforts with the French (see, e.g., Harvey, *Solutions,* p. 50, for such efforts in 1391). See Chapter 5 for Honoré Bovet's depiction of English efforts to end the Schism after the death of Clement VII in 1394.

any case, the Schism was not a subject for English vernacular writers; the poets were mostly silent on this crisis. As for the Empire, few voices outside the official university and ecclesiastical circles can still be heard.[50]

My study is therefore primarily concerned with France and Italy (as seats of the rival popes), but it also considers some examples in Spain and Germany. For each area, I selected a number of specific individuals from different backgrounds and social classes who illustrate especially well the different problematics at the center of this book. Thus, I do not intend to present a survey of all possible reactions to the Great Schism, but rather a selective look at some of the principal currents evident mostly in visionary, allegorical, and prophetic texts as well as in letters and images.

My division into chapters on saints and visionaries, poets, and prophets should not be interpreted as if these were watertight categories.[51] A number of individuals could have appeared in several chapters. The distinction between visionaries, visionary poets, and prophets can and should not always be made clearly; indeed, this is for me one of the intriguing aspects of this study. As Barbara Newman observes, "If visions could inspire a devout soul to write, the desire to write could also inspire a poet to construct visions; and the outcomes of these two procedures might not be so dissimilar as scholars tend to assume." According to Newman, visions can be epiphanies, but at the same time they can be heuristic devices.[52] Often there is a political aspect to dreams and to the texts reporting them, as certainly holds true for the visionaries of all stripes that appear in the pages of this book.[53] Furthermore, on a less theoretical level, many of the people appearing in my pages knew one another and undoubtedly

50. In any case before the Council of Constance, when there were many songs, popular chronicles, and more getting engaged in this event.

51. In an early thirteenth-century manuscript of Hildegard of Bingen's *Scivias,* for example, the colophon states in regard to Hildegard's status: "What now is called a prophet (*propheta*), once was called seer (*uidens*)," thus confirming the fluidity of these categories already at that time. See Kerby-Fulton, "Hildegard and the Male Reader," p. 8.

52. Newman, *God and the Goddesses,* pp. 299, 300. Thus, the distinction between "literary/fictional" visions and "experiential" or "authentic" visions that has caused so much discussion, especially in Germany, is not very useful. (Dinzelbacher is a proponent of this distinction; see his *Vision und Visionsliteratur.*) On the many forms visions can take, see Benz, *Die Vision.* Kerby-Fulton also explores "what the writings of a 'professional' or 'real' visionary like Hildegard [can] teach us about dream-vision allegory" (*Reformist Apocalypticism,* p. 63).

53. Although not all are explicitly cited later on, the following works influenced my thinking on dream visions and politics: Miller, *Dreams in Late Antiquity;* Moreira, *Dreams, Visions, and Spiritual Authority in Merovingian Gaul;* Dutton, *The Politics of Dreaming in the Carolingian Empire;* Kagan, *Lucrecia's Dreams: Politics and Prophecy in Sixteenth-Century Spain;* Niccoli, *Prophecy and People in Renaissance Italy;* Cupples, "*Ames d'élite:* Visionaries and Politics in France from the Holy Catholic League to Louis XIV"; and Mack, *Visionary Women: Ecstatic Prophecy in Seventeenth-Century England.*

influenced each other in various ways. I try to illuminate these connections whenever possible.

Why do I include "A Twelfth-Century Prelude" as a first chapter? It seems to me that the emotional responses and the appeal to revelations and visions on the part of John of Salisbury, Hildegard of Bingen, and Elisabeth of Schö-nau during the schism of 1159 in many ways prefigure the situation of the Great Schism and have not so far been explored as an ensemble. At the same time the twelfth-century historical conditions and the contemporaries' reactions are sufficiently different that they highlight the unique nature of the Great Schism, where many more visionaries spoke out much more explicitly and did not fear to take sides. In addition, it is here that we find for the first time a political engagement of visionary women that is related to a schism in the church. Thus, this twelfth-century backdrop helps put the special nature of the Great Schism and the poetic and visionary activities surrounding it into a better perspective.

My second and third chapters focus on saints and visionaries from Saint Birgitta of Sweden (1303–73) to Saint Colette (1381–1447). Here some of the great figures of the fourteenth and fifteenth centuries appear, along with some lesser known ones. We shall first investigate the pressure some saintly person-ages like Saint Birgitta of Sweden, fr. Pedro of Aragon (1305–81), and Saint Catherine of Siena (1347–80) exerted on popes Urban V (1362–70) and Gre-gory XI (1370–78) to return the papacy to Rome. I shall then turn to the vision-aries who tried to intervene in the Schism, which many saw in fact as the result of the return to Rome. Some of them were on the Roman side, others on the side of the Avignon pope. Some found papal approval, others ended their lives as outcasts. It is certain that visionary activity increased during the time of the Great Schism as a distinct response to this grave crisis.[54] In addition to saintly visionaries we find ordinary laypeople, mostly women, who normally would not have had the ear of rulers and prelates, trying to intervene in the politics of their time through their visions and revelations. They suffered because of the Schism, both mentally and physically, and hoped—mostly in vain—to per-suade the popes and secular rulers to end the Schism,

The same goal informed many of the political allegories and dream visions I consider in my third and fourth chapters. There I am concentrating on France (neither in England nor in Italy was the Schism a major theme for allegorical visions) and on partisans of the French position: Philippe de Mézières (1327–1405), Eustache Deschamps (ca. 1340–ca. 1404), Honoré Bovet (ca. 1350–after 1409), and Christine de Pizan (ca. 1364–ca. 1430) will be at the center of

---

54. See Vauchez, "La sainteté mystique en Occident au temps des papes d'Avignon et du Grand Schisme."

these chapters. These prolific authors wrote on a wide variety of topics, and while only Bovet wrote separate works dealing with the Schism, for all of them it was a troubling issue that appeared in many guises in their allegories, prose texts, and ballades. The use of French in most of their works made their texts accessible to a nonclerical audience, thus widening the target for these polemical poems and enabling a nonlearned though still literate segment of the population to think about the Schism along these authors' lines. Bemoaning the disastrous consequences of the Schism, these poets at the same time provided shrewd political analyses and offered solutions, such as the convocation of a General Council, that were adopted later, whether because of their efforts or not is impossible to say, however.

My last chapter is devoted to prophets and prophecy. The first text to be treated was one of the most popular and opaque works in medieval Europe: the *Vaticinia de summis pontificibus* (Prophecies of the last popes), a kind of emblem book with intriguing text-image combinations.[55] Dating from a somewhat earlier period, the texts, but especially the images, were reconceived after the Great Schism and applied to the popes engaged in this conflict. Other parts of this chapter deal with prophets like Jean de Roquetaillade (d. ca. 1365) who anticipated the Schism in sometimes eerie detail, and Telesphorus of Cosenza (active 1380s), who wrote directly, if almost incomprehensibly, about the Schism. A bearded prophet with a political mission who mysteriously appeared in Genoa in 1386 will also make an appearance. Heinrich of Langenstein and Pierre d'Ailly will close this chapter; they were connected not only by their conciliar writings but also by their interest in the prophecies of Hildegard of Bingen. But only Pierre was destined to become one of the most active participants at the Council of Constance and see the end of the Schism. These events will be considered in the Conclusion.

For each chapter, I also study some illustrations in the manuscripts and occasionally printed editions whenever they can give us clues about the conceptualization of the Schism. The striking images in many of these manuscripts and books often serve as commentaries or supply additional ideas that sometimes support and sometimes contradict the texts they accompany. These illustrations are not meant to constitute a separate or comprehensive iconographical study of Schism images but should be seen as an organic part of the *imaginaire*—and, I hope, as a respite from too many pages of printed text and as a stimulus for further reflection.

---

55. As do most modern critics, I refer to this anonymous text as the Pope Prophecies, though the titles of manuscripts and editions vary.

One

A TWELFTH-CENTURY PRELUDE:
HILDEGARD OF BINGEN, ELISABETH OF SCHÖNAU,
JOHN OF SALISBURY, AND THE SCHISM OF 1159

In order to understand the Great Schism of the later Middle Ages in all its political and emotional complexity it is useful to take a look at one of the earlier schisms, that of 1159–77. Here we shall consider two female visionaries, Saint Hildegard of Bingen (1098–1179) and the blessed Elisabeth of Schönau (1129–65), the only two women who commented publicly on the division of the papacy brought about through emperor Frederick Barbarossa's power politics. From among the many male and mostly clerical writers and politicians who in a large array of works expressed their opinions on this schism, I chose John of Salisbury (1115/20–1180), a prominent churchman, diplomat, writer, and supporter of Thomas Becket, because he, more than his contemporaries, was at one point intensely interested in Hildegard's opinions on the 1159 schism. This trio will introduce some of the ideas and problems we shall encounter in the rest of this book.

Both Hildegard and Elisabeth were aware of and consulted on the ecclesiastical crisis of their time They thus serve as early examples of medieval visionary women's potential political roles, offering other voices complementary to those in the male-dominated clerical debates. John, for his part, provided one of the most dramatic and emotionally charged accounts of the double election of 1159. The attitudes and responses of these twelfth-century witnesses both adumbrate and are in many ways different from those of the later prophets and clerics embroiled in the Great Schism. Through them we can bring the special features of the Great Schism into sharper focus.

John of Salisbury

John of Salisbury was much involved in the church politics of his time. Between 1148 and 1154, a period chronicled in the *Historia pontificalis* (Papal history), he was a papal functionary. Subsequently he became a counselor to Theobald, archbishop of Canterbury, and later to Thomas Becket, representing the see of Canterbury at Henry II's court and on the continent. His stormy relationship with King Henry II caused him to leave England in 1164, but he returned in 1170, the year his friend Becket was murdered. The last four years of his life, John was bishop of Chartres. John is thus a privileged witness to the events of his time.

John of Salisbury's letter to his friend Ralph of Sarre of mid-1160 contains a dramatic account of the problematic papal election of 1159. While reporting on the Council of Pavia (1160)—which tried to sort out the claims of the rival popes but was really a one-sided endorsement of the antipope Victor IV— John backtracks and lays out a version of the events of 1159, based on letters and various treatises authored by the cardinals of the rival popes.[1] The facts may never be completely clear, but it is generally agreed that John's letter provides one of the best, if not the most balanced, reports. What is remarkable is the extremely emotional opening of the letter: "I do not doubt, dear friend, that you share our anguish. . . . We have been smitten by the javelins of cruel Fortune at close range, and matter for endless toil, grief, and mourning is ever at hand and before our eyes. Our bitter lot allows neither time nor place for happiness or repose" (*Letter 124*, 1:205).[2] The accumulation of such terms as *angustia, dolor, maeror,* and *amara sors* highlights the emotional repercussions of political events. The very first sentences, then, set the tone for this long letter, which masterfully combines a sarcastic account of the papal election, a shrewd evaluation of its consequences, and a scathing indictment of the emperor Frederick Barbarossa.

1. John of Salisbury, *Letters*, 1:204 n. 1.
2. "Angustarium nostrarum, dilecte mi, te non ambigo esse participem. . . . Nos e uicino iacula fortunae saeuientis excipimus, et in manibus nostris est, et oculis iugiter subest continui materia laboris, doloris et maeroris. Non locum, non tempus indulget amara sors laetitiae aut quieti."

Frederick Barbarossa's power politics, generally referred to as the "Grand Design," had indeed contributed greatly to this particular schism. By creating a kind of axis of three great river basins, that of the Rhine, the Rhone, and the Ticino, Frederick had hoped to unify the administration of Swabia, Burgundy, and Lombardy with a "bold [but] not fantastic" design that would have changed the face of Europe.[3] John describes this design in terms that are not found elsewhere and that make clear the role the pope was to play in his scheme:

> For I was at Rome under the rule of the blessed Eugenius [in 1152], when at the outset of Frederick's reign his first embassy arrived and by their rash utterances and insufferable pride revealed the shamelessness of his vast and audacious scheme. He promised that he would reshape the governance of the whole globe and would make the world subject to the City, saying that he would subdue all things with ease, if the favour of the Pope alone was on his side. He designed that as soon as any man was denounced as an enemy, the emperor should wield the temporal sword against him, while the Roman church should use the spiritual. (*Letter 124*, 1:207)

Thus, the pope's support for the Grand Design was deemed essential. Frederick's stake in the next papal election was immense and makes comprehensible his attitude toward the double papal election of September 5, 1159, which pitted Cardinal Roland against Cardinal Octavian, the leader of the imperial party among the cardinals.[4] Frederick's hostility toward Cardinal Roland had many causes; one of the most obvious was that the cardinal had claimed at the Diet of Besançon (1157) that "the imperial dignity was a papal *beneficium*."[5] On this occasion Roland barely escaped with his life. After the death of Pope Adrian IV, whose territorial ambitions had clashed many times with those of Barbarossa, a riotous and contested papal election took place.[6] Roland was elected as Alexander III by about two-thirds of the college of cardinals, and Octavian as Victor IV by a minority. Through the intervention of a mob, Victor was enmantled first (albeit with such haste that his mantle was upside down[7]) but not crowned until October, while Alexander was crowned in

3. See Munz, *Frederick Barbarossa*, p. 103.
4. Munz, *Frederick Barbarossa*, p. 199.
5. John of Salisbury, *Letter 124*, 1:206 n. 5.
6. On other instances of the threat—and outbreak—of violence at papal elections, see Stroll, *The Jewish Pope*, p. xiv (in reference to the schism of 1130), and below for the Great Schism.
7. Munz, *Frederick Barbarossa*, p. 211.

September. Subsequently Frederick Barbarossa supported Victor, while the rest of Europe adhered to Alexander. Frederick's support of a series of anti-popes following on Victor continued to isolate him and certainly did not further his ambitious "Grand Design."

For John, the ceremony of Victor's immantation was nothing but a theatrical performance,[8] and he strongly condemned Frederick Barbarossa and the Germans. "Who has appointed the Germans to be judges of the nations? Who has given authority to brutal and headstrong men that they should set up a prince of their own choosing over the heads of sons of men?" he asks sarcastically (*Letter 124*, 1:206). In the past, he continues, these men have received their comeuppance, and it is here that John evokes the (now lost) paintings he had seen in the Lateran palace, showing the legitimate popes using the antipopes as footstools, an iconographic motif recalling the subjugation of the barbarians.[9] It is interesting that John claims that even laypeople will be able to read here the fate of the antipopes,[10] which seems to imply that even the laity had a stake in this schismatic election. This is a rare reference to the possible interests of the nonclerical and perhaps nonaristocratic segment of society. In the later Great Schism the stakes of laypeople will come into better focus, and some of the anxieties of the laity will find a clearer and more dramatic expression, often in the form of revelations.

John himself knows that some prophesying related to the schism has been going on in Germany. In a letter to Thomas Becket in the late summer of 1165 he writes: "And to give you the whole story, they say that some German prophetesses have been prophesying; and the result is greater ardour to the fury of the Teutons and new life to the schismatics" (*Letter 152*, 2:55).[11] It is believed that John refers to Hildegard and Elisabeth here, and we shall see shortly what kind of prophecies he may have had in mind. However, let us first look at another letter, which shows a dramatic change in tone and attitude and which again allows for a glimpse of John's anxiety regarding the schism. Writing in mid-October 1166 to his good friend Gerard Pucelle, who seems to possess an enviable collection of books, John states wistfully:

> If you do not come on anything else not available to our folk, at least
> the visions and prophecies of the blessed and most famous Hildegarde

8. "Scenae theatralis" (*Letter 124*, 1:212).
9. See Ladner, *Die Papstbildnisse*, 1:197 n. 1. See also Walter, "Papal Political Imagery," part 2, p. 109.
10. "Ubi hoc in uisibilibus picturis et laici legunt" (*Letter 124*, 1:208).
11. The translation reads "German Sibyls," but John actually wrote "prophetissas Teutonicas" (*Letter 152*, 2:54).

are available to you. I hold her in commendation and reverence since Pope Eugenius cherished her with an intimate bond of affection. Look carefully too and let me know whether anything was revealed to her as to the end of this schism. She foretold in Pope Eugenius' time that he would not have peace and favour in Rome save in his last days. (*Letter 185*, 2:225)

Clearly, some new information must have caused John's change of heart with regard to Hildegard's prophecies. Perhaps her bond to Pope Eugene III had not been known to him before but now endorses this formidable Sibyl in his eyes.[12] In any case, the two times he mentions her, he does so in the context of the schism, suggesting that she played a major role in prophesying about and perhaps trying to resolve this conflict. We know from the opening of *Letter 124* that the 1159 schism caused John to be overcome by anguish and anger; he saw this event as yet another example of the nefarious consequences of Barbarossa's imperial politics. Given the political stalemate, does John's only hope now lie with this German prophetess? But did Hildegard actually address herself to this problem, and if so, how?

Hildegard of Bingen

Hildegard of Bingen is to this day venerated as a seer, an author of a wide range of works, from musical compositions to medical texts and allegorical visions. She also wrote almost four hundred letters to popes, kings, emperors, abbots, and laypeople. After spending her youth with the recluse Jutta of Sponheim at Disibodenberg, she left to found her own convent in Bingen, at the Rupertsberg. This move, not exactly welcomed or facilitated by the monks of Disibodenberg, was the direct result of her empowering visions. Unlike any other religious woman of her time, Hildegard preached publicly, traveling mostly along the Rhine valley. Despite her contemplative activity, she was aware of the political and ecclesiastical problems of her time, commenting on them in her visionary works, where she advocated—in terms not always hidden under the veil of allegory—radical church reform.[13]

---

12. See Schrader and Führkötter, *Die Echtheit* (pp. 7–8), on this issue. Hildegard had also written to Pope Adrian IV (1154–59), an Englishman close to the archbishop of Canterbury, whose secretary was John of Salisbury. Generally, on the reception of Hildegard's writings in England, see Kerby-Fulton, "Hildegard of Bingen and the Male Reader."
13. See Kerby-Fulton, *Reformist Apocalypticism,* chap. 2, and "Prophet and Reformer."

There are few instances when Hildegard speaks directly about the contemporary schism in her letters, but there is no doubt that the schism influenced her attitude toward Frederick Barbarossa and may have changed her vision of history. In her visionary works, however, there is only one vague reference to a schism. We shall look at each topic in turn.

Sometime between 1164 and 1169 Hildegard wrote to the abbot of St. Nabor: "It does not please God that I should pronounce myself on the schism of the church."[14] This evasiveness is striking, given her eloquence and forcefulness regarding other contemporary matters.[15] Clearly, there were people who expected her to be an arbiter. An urgent letter sent to her by another troubled, unnamed, abbot also appealed to her for a judgment in the schism.[16] As the church labors under the schism, its leadership is divided, and everything seems to perish, this abbot wants to know from Hildegard when and how God will put an end to this trouble. He begs her to write to him, since she is inspired by the Holy Spirit. In anything she says, he will obey. Her response is longer than that to the abbot of St. Nabor, but not any more explicit or detailed. She agrees that the church is in terrible shape and that the sun of justice wavers. But she does not spell out who is the pope and who the antipope, as the abbot had requested. Instead, she proposes a prayer that the abbot could address to God that He may enlighten those rulers who are deaf to their creator and fail to end the schism.[17] She ends the letter on a personal note, comforting the abbot by saying that she sees a bright splendor in him that is darkened by the schism and other problems.[18] These are rather slim pickings, considering that the abbess wrote almost four hundred letters.

Hildegard's attitude toward Frederick Barbarossa was initially very positive.[19] In a letter early in Frederick's reign (1152 or 1153) Hildegard congratulates his subjects that they have such a *dulcem personam* (sweet or mild person) as

---

14. "De schismate Ecclesiae non iubet me Dominus loqui" ("Hildegardis ad abbatem [St. Nabor]"; *Epistolarium* 197, 2:449). See Schrader and Führkötter, *Die Echtheit,* p. 95.

15. See Newman, *Sister of Wisdom,* and Widmer, *Heilsordnung und Zeitgeschehen.* Widmer finds it "remarkable" that Hildegard should not be more explicit here (p. 259). On Hildegard as letter-writer, see Ahlgren, "Visions and Rhetorical Strategy in the Letters of Hildegard of Bingen," and Ferrante, "Correspondent: 'Blessed Is the Speech of Your Mouth.'"

16. *Epistolarium* 265, 3:14. On this letter, see Czarski, "The Prophecies of St. Hildegard of Bingen," pp. 112–13.

17. *Epistolarium* 265R, 3:15–16.

18. "Ego autem auroram sicut splendorem in te uideo . . . turbinem quoque propter *has* et alias uicissitudines in te discurrentem, qui aliquando splendorem in te obnubilat" (*Epistolarium* 3:16; my emphasis). I take *has* (= these) as a reference to the vicissitudes of the schism.

19. See the section on "Kaiserbriefe" in Schrader and Führkötter, *Die Echtheit,* pp. 124–31. See also Czarski, "The Prophecies," pp. 110–12.

him as king.[20] She then gives him advice on how to rule. After this auspicious beginning, the relationship between these two forceful personages changes for the worse. In fact, Hildegard's growing hostility toward the emperor can be directly linked to his attitude in the schism, that is, his continued support of the antipapal line even after the death of Victor IV in 1164. In the second preserved letter to Frederick she reports that she saw him in a mystical vision *velut parvulum, velut insane viventem* (as a small child, living insanely) who has the power to reign righteously but is blinded to the truth.[21] Her last letter to Frederick, following his support of the third antipope, Calixtus III, in 1168 is brief and to the point. It consists of three lines of divine threats, ending "Hoc audi, rex, si uiuere uis; alioquin gladius meus percutiet te" (Hear this, King, if you want to live; otherwise my sword will strike you).[22] Throughout these tense years of the schism Hildegard supports Pope Alexander III, whom she praises in lyrical terms in a letter of 1173. Though the bulk of the letter is a complaint against her former community of Saint Disibodenberg, the opening gives us a radiant image of Alexander III: "O lofty and glorious one, first appointed through the Word of God . . . be the Morning Star which precedes the sun, a guide to the church, which for far too long has been lacking in the light of God's justice because of the dense cloud of the schism."[23]

This image of the cloud of the schism, evoking the darkening of Christendom through the warring papal factions, also appears in her great visionary work, the *Liber divinorum operum* (Book of divine works), composed between 1163 and 1173. In the third part, dramatically prophesying the end of time, the allegorical figure of Iustitia (Justice) complains in a lugubrious voice: "My crown is darkened through the schism of the spirits led astray, since everyone constitutes his own law according to his will."[24] Hildegard does not name the schism of 1159 explicitly here; in fact, it is difficult to decide whether she has a specific schism in mind or whether this is a more general diatribe against those

---

20. Edited in Schrader and Führkötter, *Die Echtheit,* pp. 126–27, here p. 126.

21. *Die Echtheit,* p. 128.

22. *Epistolarium* 315 (3:75). This sentence is identical in the different manuscripts of this letter edited by Pitra (where it is letter 227) in *Analecta Sanctae Hildegardis,* p. 561, and Schrader and Führkötter, *Die Echtheit,* p. 129.

23. *Epistolarium* 10, 1:23–24; *Letters* 10, 1:45–46. Here p. 45.

24. "Nam ego iusticia Dei lugubri uoce dico: 'Corona mea scismate errantium mentium obnubilata est, quoniam quisque secundum uoluntatem suam legem sibi constituit.'" *Liber divinorum operum* 3.5.10–11, p. 427. A more dramatic image, one we shall find again in the polemics of the Great Schism, appears in a poem by Gautier de Châtillon (composed before 1163) in which the personified Church complains of having been "ravished" or "raped" (quo me rapit) by the schism. See Gautier de Châtillon's poem on the schism in *Moralisch-Satirische Gedichte,* pp. 89–96, stanza 8.

who disturb the spiritual and political order.[25] In view of the image of the cloud of the schism in her letter to Alexander III and the fact that the composition of the *Liber divinorum operum* falls in the period of the election of further antipopes and her threatening letters to Frederick, one cannot exclude that this apocalyptic vision targets the actual schism tearing apart the twelfth-century church. Further, the word *obnubilare* (to darken through a cloud) also appeared in her letter to the unnamed abbot, here in reference to his own *splendor* that is darkened by the cloud of schism. Hildegard's apocalypticism was mostly reformist in nature—that is, in her view only a radical change in the behavior of the clergy could avert the imminent arrival of the Antichrist.[26] But that does not mean that historical events cannot enter into the allegory, albeit in a veiled manner. As Bernhard Töpfer suggests, the tensions between "ecclesiastical and secular powers brought on by the papal schism of 1159, which set the church against the state," are at the very heart of the kind of prophecy of the end of times as laid out by Hildegard in the *Liber divinorum operum.*[27] Indeed, it seems that the 1159 schism was a "major cause of a shift from her early view, in the *Scivias,* that the present spiritual condition of the church was basically a continuation of the positive spiritual condition that had existed since the apostles to a more apocalyptic outlook."[28] But unlike the fourteenth- and fifteenth-century chroniclers and theologians she does not present this particular schism as a man-made outrage whose creators will receive divine punishment. On the specifics Hildegard remains silent.

Hildegard addressed the problem of the schism in a variety of contexts, but on the whole more implicitly than explicitly. She never reproached Frederick Barbarossa directly with his support of the antipopes, nor did she make any pronouncement of who was the legitimate pope in the letters to the two abbots. But as a theme of divisiveness, of a darkening of the bright light of the church, the schism was present in her works. Her reticence, or rather lack of specific reprimands related to the schism, makes her different from the prophets we shall encounter at the time of the Great Schism. Nonetheless, in her afterlife Hildegard was seen as one of the major prophets of the Great Schism.[29] Her linking of schism, apocalypse, and church reform also foreshadows later prophecies, as we shall see in Chapter 6.

25. On this possibility, see Widmer, *Heilsordnung,* pp. 244–45. Widmer refers to Augustine's more general definition of schismatics in Sermon 71 (*Patrologiae latinae,* 38, col. 466).

26. See Kerby-Fulton, *Reformist Apocalypticism,* chap. 2.

27. Kerby-Fulton, *Reformist Apocalypticism,* p. 37, citing Töpfer's *Das kommende Reich des Friedens,* p. 35. See also McGinn, "To the Scandal of Men, Women Are Prophesying," esp. pp. 59–69.

28. Czarski, "The Prophecies," p. 114.

29. See the end of Chapter 6 for Heinrich of Langenstein's and Pierre d'Ailly's interest in Hildegard's supposed predictions of the Great Schism.

Elisabeth of Schönau

Elisabeth of Schönau, the visionary woman who was during her lifetime much more explicitly concerned with the schism of 1159 and who spoke out on this crisis much more directly, did not enjoy a posthumous reputation as a schism expert. Elisabeth was like Hildegard a Benedictine nun, but she did not play as forceful and public a role as did the famous abbess. The two women knew and corresponded with each other. As Anne L. Clark has shown, her visionary texts, composed in Latin by her brother Ekbert, were more widely read and distributed than those of several celebrated mystical visionaries (including Hildegard) combined.[30] In her visionary experience we can observe a trajectory not unlike that of such later visionaries as Constance de Rabastens (active ca. 1384–86)[31]: her perspective widens from personal and internalized issues to more universal ones. About two years after her first visions Elisabeth considers herself "divinely commissioned to announce her visions."[32] One of the first texts in this vein, the *Liber viarum Dei* (Book of the ways of God), known also as the *Ständepredigt* or sermon on the different estates in society, describes the ways in which different groups, such as active people or contemplatives, rulers or hermits, can find the path to God. It is at the end of this work that Ekbert, after Elisabeth's death, appended a letter written by her on June 29, 1157, to the archbishops of Trier, Mainz, and Cologne. Here she adopts a public, chastising voice, ordering these three eminent men, who through their office were also *Kurfürsten* (dukes) of the empire, to disseminate her visions throughout the church and to all people. For good measure she adds: "Correct yourselves and turn from your errors."[33] This is a forceful but vague exhortation. Yet, in her visions it becomes clear that clerical corruption and avarice preoccupied her most intensely for the impact they had on the faithful. In particular, as Clark points out, she located clerical failures in the Roman papacy.[34] The schism exacerbated everything that was wrong with the supreme pontiffs.

Thus, two years later, after the schismatic papal election, we find Elisabeth taking a more explicit political stance. As for the visionaries of the later Great Schism, we can surmise that this event had a kind of trigger function, encouraging her to speak out even more forcefully and take sides in a contested political

---

30. Clark, ed., *Elisabeth of Schönau: The Complete Works*, p. xi (henceforth Clark, *Works*).
31. See Blumenfeld-Kosinski, "Constance de Rabastens: Politics and Visionary Experience," and Chapter 3.
32. See Clark, *Works*, p. 3. See also Clark, *Elisabeth of Schönau*, pp. 90–93 (henceforth Clark, *Elisabeth*); Beyer, *Die andere Offenbarung*, p. 92; Ruh, *Geschichte der abendländischen Mystik*, 2:72–73.
33. Clark, *Works*, p. 207. Elisabeth of Schönau, *Visionen*, ed. Roth, p. 122.
34. See Clark, *Elisabeth*, p. 120.

situation. Given the fact that Elisabeth was an enclosed nun, we have to ask how she became aware of the crisis of the schism. Undoubtedly, she was informed through her brother, so in this context we need to explore briefly what function her brother's connection to Rainard of Dassel, one of the most powerful players in the drama of schism, may have had in her partisanship.

It is not surprising that Rainald of Dassel, archbishop of Cologne from 1159 to 1167 and chancellor of the empire, appears in a negative light in John of Salisbury's letter to Ralph of Sarre. According to John, Rainald's election as archbishop of Cologne "was condemned by the blessed Adrian, pontiff of Rome" (*Letter 124*, 1:212). He was probably the one "largely responsible for Frederick's violent and politically disastrous proceedings at Pavia" and was apparently "obsessed by . . . hostility to the papacy."[35] Indeed, numerous contemporary witnesses blame him for the papal schism.[36] He was also a friend of Ekbert of Schönau. Might there be an intersection of the family's political connections and Elisabeth's visionary activities? Despite his association with Rainald, Ekbert does not take sides in the schism but rather seems to condemn both popes.[37] In a letter congratulating Rainald on his election as archbishop of Cologne, the very election John of Salisbury contests in such harsh terms in his letter to Ralph of Sarre, Ekbert bemoans the recent schism: "Behold, strife has been poured out over the princes of the chief church, which is mother of all, and they have sundered the unity of the high priesthood, broken the bond of ecclesiastical peace, in such a way that they devour each other, destroy each other, anathematize each other. Still, it is uncertain which of the two sides strikes with the sword of Peter, because it cannot be divided into parts, nor, undivided, can it be turned against itself."[38] He goes on to describe the bitterness, even madness, of these events that make the fathers of the church, who should love each other, hate one another and cruelly persecute their adversaries. Like later critics of the Great Schism, Ekbert highlights the unnaturalness of a divided church that should figure the union of the faithful in Christ and not the strife of schism.

Elisabeth, though guided in most things by her brother, takes a different stance in this conflict. In a letter to Hillin, archbishop of Trier,[39] she adopts the

---

35. John of Salisbury, *Letters* 1:212 n. 23. Munz, *Frederick Barbarossa*, p. 125.
36. For a list of contemporary chroniclers in addition to John of Salisbury, see Munz, *Frederick Barbarossa*, 213 n. 2.
37. On this question, see Munz, *Frederick Barbarossa*, p. 289, and Clark, *Elisabeth*, pp. 121–22.
38. Translated in Clark, *Elisabeth*, 121. Roth, *Visionen*, ed. Roth, p. 315.
39. Hillin supported the antipope Victor IV but then after his death switched his allegiance to Pope Alexander III. Clark, *Elisabeth*, 185 n. 86. This letter is translated in Clark, *Works*, pp. 236–37. *Visionen*, ed. Roth, 140.

humble persona of a "vermicul[us] ho[mo]" (worm person) animated by a spark "sent from the seat of great majesty." She admonishes him to tend to his flock in humility and to shun pride and avarice. She threatens him with the judgment of God and adds that in reference to the schism God wants her to reveal to him his choice: "And you should know that the one who has been chosen by Caesar is more acceptable to Me." Clark suggests that the statement "electus est a Cesare" "betrays a certain ignorance of the events that led to the enmantling of Victor IV in 1159."[40] But could this view simply reflect her knowledge that Victor was Barbarossa's candidate—or in any case the candidate elected in opposition to Cardinal Roland, who was detested by the emperor? Be that as it may, Elisabeth, unlike Hildegard, makes her support for the antipope clear, though we cannot know whether it was Elisabeth's exhortation that led to Hillin's support of Victor IV. It is important to see that within Elisabeth's general reformist revelations one specific political problem stands out as clearly defined and judged: the schism of 1159. More than other events of Elisabeth's time, however traumatic they may have been, it was this one that incited the divine voice to become partisan and to pronounce itself explicitly on a contemporary problem.

Conclusion

None of our three twelfth-century witnesses to the schism was a layperson. It was only in the thirteenth century that new opportunities for lay religious activity were created, such as the Beguine movement or the Third Orders of the mendicants. Visionary activity could thus extend more easily past the walls of the cloister. The institutional support so necessary for the recognition of saints and visionaries later included confessors who might take on the cause of a female lay visionary for their mutual benefit.[41] The visionaries and prophets at the time of the Great Schism also show a much wider social spectrum. From saintly aristocrats like fr. Pedro of Aragon (1305–81) to women coming from the simplest of circumstances, like Ermine de Reims (d. 1396) or Marie Robine (d. 1399), we find a whole gamut of people engaged in and speaking out about the Schism. This change also reflects the much wider-ranging consequences of the Great Schism. The schism of 1159–77, while it caused much anguish and bloodshed, did not lead to the vast production of polemical, allegorical, and mystical-visionary texts we find in the late fourteenth and fifteenth centuries.

40. Clark, *Elisabeth*, p. 122.
41. On what makes and unmakes a potential saint, see Kleinberg, *Prophets in Their Own Country*.

The division of Europe did not go as deep as it did during the Great Schism, for outside the empire the antipope Victor IV and his successors had basically no supporters.

In the late fourteenth and early fifteenth centuries, by contrast, we saw that every part of Europe had to choose an allegiance. The rifts between papal factions had repercussions in individual dioceses, where people may have had to choose between rival bishops, as well as in convents, where the nuns could be divided in their support for a given pope.[42] Our twelfth-century witnesses gave the most forceful expression to their feelings and predictions about the schism in letters, not in their philosophical, allegorical, or visionary works. While letters remain one of the preferred forms of attempted political intervention, new forms appear in the later centuries and are put to use in the polemics of the Great Schism: narratives of mystical visions with a political content and, especially in France, political allegory, mostly in the shape of dream visions. The activities of our twelfth-century precursors thus adumbrate those of the activists of the Great Schism. The differences we highlighted allow us to see the later clerics and visionaries in a clearer light and to appreciate the particular features of one of the deepest crises the Western church has ever experienced.

---

42. See the Introduction for examples. In addition, for the divisions within the diocese of Cambrai, for example, see Guenée, *Between Church and State*, pp. 181–89.

Two

SAINTS AND VISIONARIES I:
FROM THE 1360S TO THE BEGINNINGS OF THE SCHISM

The popes' move to Avignon in the aftermath of the conflicts between the French king Philippe le Bel and Pope Boniface VIII at the beginning of the fourteenth century had shifted the papal power balance: the popes now were French and in the sphere of influence of the French monarchy.[1] While the popes were comfortable and secure in their impressive fortress in Avignon, the feeling outside France was quite different. The stay in Avignon was seen by many as exile, or in Petrarch's words a "Babylonian captivity" that deprived Rome to its claim as the center of Christendom.[2] The church was sometimes represented as a widow or as a mourning wife abandoned by her husband, as in the striking image from the fourteenth-century Pope Prophecies (fig. 1), frequently interpreted as Pope Clement V's departure for Avignon. The caption reads: "See here the spouse of the Babylonian woman who flees from the wife abominable to him, leaving her in the state of a widow."[3] According to this interpretation, the church was left behind in Rome—having been abandoned

---

1. On this period, see esp. Mollat, *Les papes d'Avignon*.
2. See Petrarca, *Book Without a Name*, where he calls Avignon the "Babylon on the Rhone, the foulest of cities" and "the whore with whom the kings of the earth have committed fornication (Apoc. 17, 1–2; 18, 3)" (pp. 108, 111).
3. The Pope Prophecies will be treated in detail in Chapter 6.

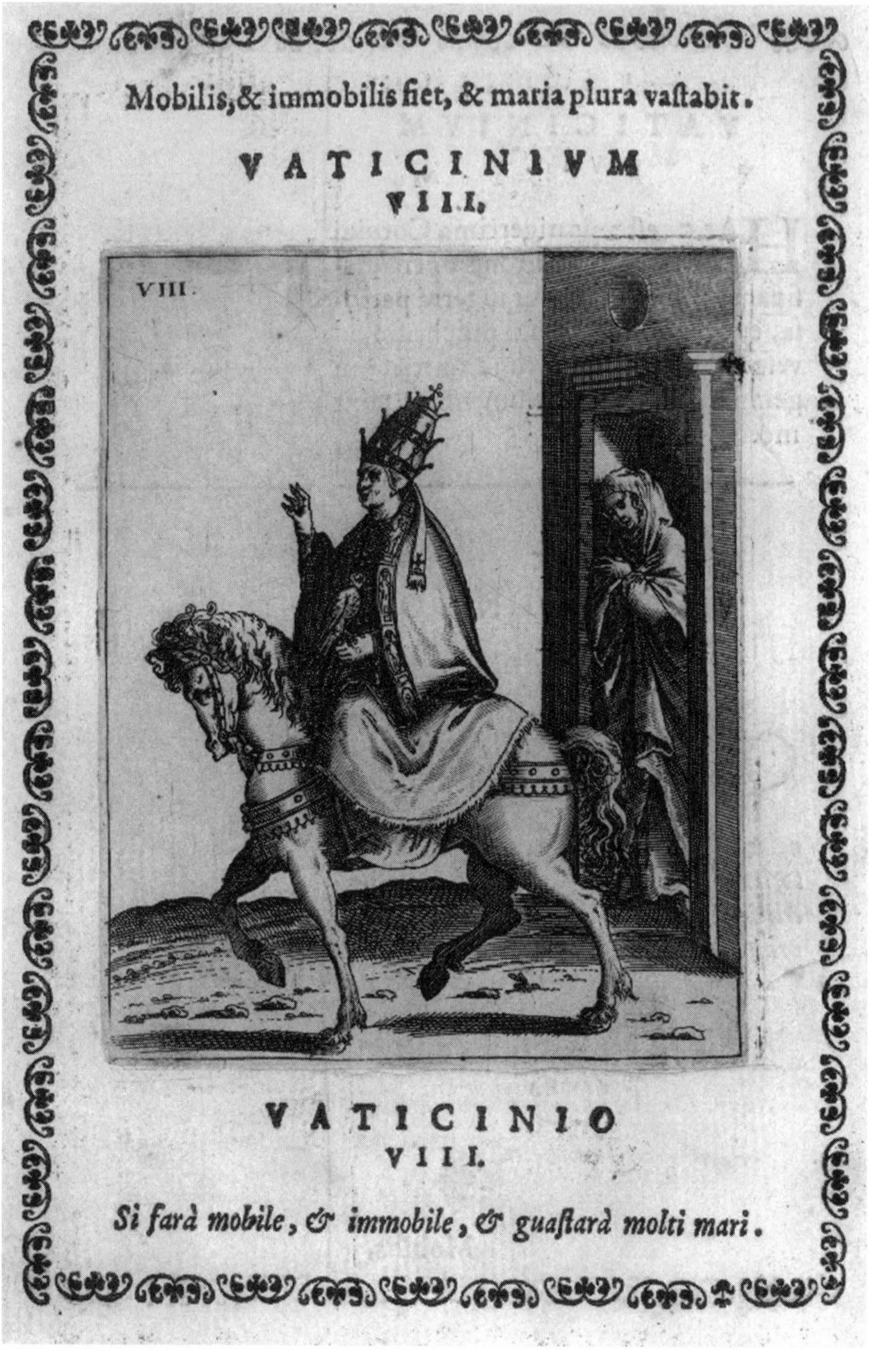
Mobilis, & immobilis fiet, & maria plura vaſtabit.

VATICINIVM

VIII.

VIII.

VATICINIO

VIII.

Si farà mobile, & immobile, & guaſtarà molti mari.

FIG. 1 The pope leaves behind the Babylonian woman (the Roman church) and departs for Avignon. Plate VIII from the Pope Prophecies, ed. Pasquilino. Venice: H. Porrus, 1589.

by her spouse, the pope—and efforts needed to be made to bring the errant husband back into the matrimonial fold.

The desire that the popes should reside again in Rome was shared by a large variety of individuals. From Saint Birgitta of Sweden (1303–73) to Petrarch (1304–74), from Saint Catherine of Siena (1347–80) to the saintly Franciscan nobleman fr. Pedro of Aragon (1305–81), people joined forces in the campaign to persuade the popes to return to Rome. Petrarch even argued to Pope Urban V (1362–70) that his very name indicated that he should return to the original *urbs* (city), which can be no other than Rome.[4] But Rome at the time was "little more than a large village, ruled by petty local tyrants, organised by a corrupt city administration, and affected by dissent, neglect, and turmoil." Indeed, "grass grew on the steps of Saint Peter's Basilica where goats also grazed."[5] No wonder, then, that the pope, and especially the cardinals, favored the "fleshpots of Avignon" over the problematic Roman environment.[6]

The advocates of the pope's return to Rome used revelations as the preferred means of communicating with the various popes. Revelations are inspired speech, a privileged discourse that allows ordinary people to gain extraordinary authority when addressing the prelates and secular rulers of their time. But revelations, with their mixture of autobiographical elements, political agendas, and religious mandates, can also tell us much about medieval anxieties, hopes, and expectations.[7] They are in fact a privileged site for an exploration of the medieval *imaginaire.* The focus of Chapters 2 and 3 will thus be on visionaries of all stripes who reacted to and/or attempted to intervene in the crisis of the Great Schism. The confusion and disorder occasioned by the division of the church are well illustrated by the fact that both sides, the Clementists as well as the Urbanists, could boast major saints in their camps,[8] such as Saint Vincent Ferrer (1350–1419), until late in life a supporter of the Avignon papacy, and Saint Catherine of Siena, Pope Urban's champion. Both

---

4. See *Senili* 7:1, cited in Dupré Theseider, *I papi di Avignone,* p. 122.

5. Morris, *Saint Birgitta,* p. 95, and Ullmann, *A Short History,* p. 292.

6. These are the words of Alfonso of Jaén in his *Informaciones* of 1379 ("Quia magis volebant stare in Egipto super ollas carnium . . . et ad ollas carnium in Egiptum, id est Avinionem"). See the *Informaciones* by *Alfonso of Jaén,* ed. Jönsson, pp. 190–91. For more on the *Informaciones,* see below. For pro-Avignon arguments as they are summarized in the 1378 *Songe du vergier,* see the first section of Chapter 4.

7. See Dinzelbacher, "Revelationes," p. 75.

8. See Seidlmayer's remarks on this issue: "In order to illustrate the utter confusion into which the church fell in 1378, historians have often pointed to the fact that in both camps we find saints who use the weight of their spiritual authority to tip the balance for one or the other pope." *Die Anfänge,* p. 164.

have equal claims to sainthood, although for Vincent even modern biographers see his support of Benedict XIII as an aberration or sin for which he atoned through his later preaching activities.[9] The Schism is thus far from over in modern historiography.

In the pre-Schism period the visionaries who advocated the pope's return to Rome could not foresee that this much-desired move would lead to the Great Schism. Guided by hindsight, the great French theologian Jean Gerson (1363–1429) could accuse some of these visionaries of having contributed to the Schism by their insistent exhortations to Urban V and then Gregory XI finally to leave Avignon for Rome. In a famous passage of his *De examinatione doctrinarum* (On the examination of doctrines), composed in 1423, Gerson recreates the deathbed scene of Pope Gregory XI (1370–78), who regrets his ill-fated move to Rome (he died the year after his arrival) and sees himself as a victim of the bad advice with which certain visionaries had "seduced" him.[10] Though he does not name them, it seems clear that Gerson means visionaries like Saint Birgitta, fr. Pedro of Aragon, and Saint Catherine of Siena.[11] But the move to Rome did not put an end to visionary activity related to the papacy. The outbreak of the Schism in fact contributed to an unprecedented visionary activity, a phenomenon one could call mystical activism. Thus, Constance de Rabastens (active 1384–86), for example, took the side of the Roman pope in a series of dramatic visions, however ill-advised this kind of activity was for her time and region, the Clementist Languedoc. These visionaries, then, supplemented by some who appeared on the scene later, will take center stage for the Roman side in this and the next chapter.

9. See the preface to his *Vita*. See also Salembier's partisan views: "In the opposite camp we find persons as saintly as they were eminent who continue [to be] attached to the pontiff of Avignon. There is no doubt that they were in good faith, but it is impossible to regard this as a presumption against the lawfulness of the popes of Rome." *The Great Schism*, p. 78.

10. "Experti pluries loquimur, et Gregorius XI papa testis fuit idoneus, sed tardus nimis. Hic positus in extremis, habens in manibus sacrum Christi corpus, protestatus est coram omnibus ut caverent ab hominibus, tam viris quam mulieribus, sub specie religionis visiones loquentibus sui capitis; quia per tales seductus esset, dimisso suorum rationabili consilio, ut se et Ecclesiam ad discrimen schismatis tunc imminentis traxerit, nisi misericors provideret sponsus Ecclesiae Jesus; quod horrendus usque adhuc nimis heu patefecit eventus." Gerson, *Oeuvres*, 9:469–70.

11. Though this passage has often been used to prove Gerson's distrust of female visionaries, which was certainly strong, this passage clearly indicts men (tam viris quam mulieribus) as well. On Gerson's texts dealing with the discernment of spirits, see Boland, *Concept of "discretio spirituum"*; Voaden, *God's Words, Women's Voices*, chap. 2; Roth, *Discretio spirituum*; Elliott, "Seeing Double"; and Caciola, *Discerning Spirits*, chap. 6. For a brief overview of Birgitta and Catherine's political activities, see Dinzelbacher, *Mittelalterliche Frauenmystik*, chap. 10 ("Das politische Wirken der Mystikerinnen in Kirche und Staat: Hildegard, Birgitta, Katharina").

The opposing side, supporting the Avignon popes,[12] also features a fascinating cast of characters. Our focus here is on Marie Robine (d. 1399), a visionary who was enlisted as a spokeswoman by Clement VII (1378–94) and then by Benedict XIII (1394–1423), and Saint Vincent Ferrer, whose life's work of supporting the Avignon pope Benedict XIII—that is, his compatriot Pedro de Luna—in the end came to nothing and was seen even by himself as a huge mistake. The saintly boy cardinal Pierre de Luxembourg (1369–87) will also make a brief appearance, as will a strangely charismatic papal official turned hermit named Jean de Varennes (1340/45–1396?) and Ermine de Reims (d. 1396), much interested in this hermit, a simple woman beset by horrifying visionary experiences for the last ten months of her life.

All these people were engaged by the traumatic events of the Schism. The dual election of 1378 had created a situation that affected not only the prelates and rulers of the time,[13] as had been the case for most previous schisms, but also created great anxiety among the ordinary faithful, who felt betrayed by the very institution that was meant to ensure their salvation. The activists and visionaries of this chapter, then, in part tried to speak for ordinary Christians and they attempted to intervene in the political situation of their time by a variety of means.

For some, like Catherine of Siena, letters—whose arguments were supported by her visionary experiences—were the preferred medium of expression. Others, like Constance de Rabastens, gave accounts of their visions that were then transcribed by their confessors. Sermons, visits, accounts of healing miracles, and other public testimonies were also part of the propaganda supporting one or the other pope. Furthermore, none of these visionaries existed in a vacuum, and we shall therefore also look at their support systems: who aided them and who profited from their activities. Questions of gender will also be considered. The structure of these two chapters is essentially chronological, beginning with the years preceding the Schism when the pope's return to Rome was on the agenda of a variety of mystical activists.

To Rome

The most influential voices of visionaries that urged the pope's return to Rome belonged to three people who came from totally different backgrounds but

---

12. I shall avoid the term *antipope* here, for, contrary to what some modern encyclopedias claim, the Council of Constance did not call the Avignon line antipopes but rather maintained a neutral position toward the two papal lines. See Valois, *La France*, 4:502–3, and my Conclusion.

13. See Introduction.

who had in common visionary experiences focusing on the necessity of this return. Here we shall examine the major themes and strategies of these visionaries' exhortations, the images they used, and the threats they may have uttered.

Pedro of Aragon was the fourth son of King Jaime II of Aragon and the uncle of King Pedro IV of "El ceremonioso," who played an important role in defining the attitude of the Spanish kingdoms toward the two-headed papacy. Pedro had been married to Jeanne of Foix and had four children with her, but after his wife's death in 1358 he became a Franciscan friar in response to a vision.[14] He received a series of revelations dealing with a variety of issues, such as the pope's return to Rome, the imminence of the last days, and the Great Schism. He was Vicar General of the Franciscans and died en route to Rome in November 1381.[15]

Birgitta of Sweden, daughter and wife of Swedish lawmakers and mother of eight children, moved to Rome in 1349 after having spent five years as a widow in the Cistercian abbey of Alvastra. She also undertook numerous pilgrimages, including one to Jerusalem in 1372. A constant flow of revelations allowed her to gain authority and to formulate a political agenda centered on the papacy's return to Rome and the pursuit of a particular kind of monastic life based on the *regula salvatoris,* a rule that had been revealed to her by Christ.[16] Late in life her principal confessor, confidant, and editor was the Spanish hermit Alfonso Pecha (1329/30–1389), former bishop of Jaén, who compiled and edited her approximately seven hundred *Revelaciones* (Revelations) after her death and submitted them to Gregory XI in the move toward her canonization. She died in Rome in 1373 and was canonized no fewer than three times, due to the vagaries of the Schism.[17]

Catherine of Siena came from quite a different milieu. The twenty-third child of the Sienese dyer Giacomo Benincasa, she acquired her preeminent role as a political adviser to several popes and the Italian city-states through her extreme piety, her ascetic life, and the support of a group of faithful followers, the Bella Brigata and of her confessor Raymond of Capua, who, in 1380, became master general of the Dominican Order.[18] The mystical marriage with

14. I shall refer to him as "fr. Pedro" to distinguish him from his nephew.
15. See Pou y Martí, *Visionarios,* pp. 308–96.
16. Generally on Birgitta, see Morris, *Saint Birgitta,* and Sahlin, and *Birgitta of Sweden.* The literature on her is vast. See the bibliographies listed by Nyberg in Strayer, ed., *Dictionary of the Middle Ages,* 2:247.
17. In 1391 by the Roman pope Boniface IX; in 1415 by the Pisan "antipope"; and finally in 1419 by Martin V, the only pope who emerged from the Council of Constance.
18. On the interaction between Catherine and Raymond, see Coakley, "Friars as Confidants." On the function of "pressure groups" behind saintly women, see Kleinberg, *Prophets in Their Own Country,* and Dinzelbacher, *Heilige oder Hexen.*

Christ in 1367, and the stigmata she received in 1375, gave her authority an additional boost.[19] Her principal concerns were the pope's return to Rome, peace (especially between the pope and the hostile Italian city-states), church reform, the mounting of a crusade against the infidels as a means to unify Christendom,[20] and eventually the abolishment of the Schism. She died at the canonical age of thirty-three, worn out by multiple illnesses and her efforts at ending the division of the church. She was canonized in 1461 and, in 1970, became a doctor of the church.

At the papal court in Avignon serious apprehensions about a possible move to Italy persisted; the climate in Rome was much worse (malaria was a constant danger), the papal states were unsafe, hostilities with the city-states could erupt at any moment, and the food and drink were reputed to be inferior to the supplies at Avignon.[21] The brief return to Rome of Urban V had done nothing to allay the cardinals' fears of this hostile place.

Urban V's provisional return in 1367 had been partly motivated by the strong urging of fr. Pedro of Aragon and Birgitta of Sweden. In the prophetic tradition that evolved from Jean de Roquetaillade (d. after 1365), of the South of France, fr. Pedro stood out for his "new political topicality."[22] The order he received from the Lord in an early vision was clear: go to Avignon to urge Pope Urban V to reform the church and move to Rome. In case he refused, fr. Pedro predicted the pope's imminent death and most important, as Alfonso Pecha tells us in his eyewitness account, the *Infomarciones* of 1379 (in which he makes the case for Urban VI's legitimacy), the pope's failure to accomplish these two tasks would give rise to a painful schism in which thousands and thousands of innocent people will perish ("daret locum doloroso scismati in proximo venturo, in quo milia et milia innocencium debebant deperire"; p. 186).[23] When Alfonso composed this text in 1379 (it is significant that it was at the moment when Pope Clement VII was forced to leave Rome for Avignon) the full extent

19. On Catherine's political role, see esp. Seckendorff, *Das politische Wirken;* Denis-Boulet, *La carrière politique;* and Luongo, "The Politics of Marginality." See also Scott, "Saint Catherine of Siena, 'Apostola.'" Luongo and Scott both insist on the inseparability of her mystical experiences and her political activism. The former, in fact, made the latter possible.

20. On this topic, see Rousset, "Sainte Catherine de Sienne et le problème de la croisade," and Cardini, "L'idea di crociata in Santa Catarina da Siena."

21. All these points are elaborated in the polemic of Petrarch and Jean de Hesdin. See Dupré Theseider, *I papi,* chap. 3. The reality was more complex, of course. It seems, in fact, that Gregory XI had envisioned his return to Rome already in 1372. See Denis-Boulet, *La carrière politique,* pp. 125–43.

22. See Chapter 6 for more details on Jean de Roquetaillade and the Schism. The quotation is from Lee et al., *Western Mediterranean Prophecy,* p. 81.

23. Alfonso of Pecha gives his account of fr. Pedro's activities in *Informaciones,* pars. 13–19, pp. 186–87.

of the effects of the Schism were not yet known. But in emphasizing fr. Pedro's prophecy—made years before the Great Schism in the 1360s—of the destruction to come, Alfonso himself sounds a warning note; so far, everything fr. Pedro had predicted has come true, so end the Schism now before these thousands of innocents die. By incorporating his account of fr. Pedro's prophetic activities, Alfonso reinforces his own text's political message, which acquires a new significance in the troubled period of the Great Schism.[24]

As for the characteristics of fr. Pedro's visionary experiences, they are of an auditory nature in the form of rather straightforward command visions,[25] dispensing with complicated imagery and hence interpretation. As for the visions' orthodoxy, the questioning by the inquisitor Nicholas Eymerich yielded nothing objectionable.[26] This is an important point, because his later visions were judged quite differently: in 1365 the political content of the vision was noncontroversial for Aragon because there was only one pope every country adhered to; the same cannot be said of the visions of 1379, which had a direct bearing on the Schism, as we shall see below. As did other visionaries, fr. Pedro linked the return to Rome to church reform. Urban V followed fr. Pedro's advice and, certainly to the pleasure of the Holy Roman Emperor Charles IV, traveled to Rome in 1367, only to return to Avignon in 1370. Fr. Pedro's intervention is an early example of the use of visionary authority in this particular political context.

Saint Birgitta's persuasive strategy addressed to Urban V and his successor Gregory XI in some ways resembled that of fr. Pedro but was even more insistent because it was not crowned with success, at least not permanently in her lifetime. Indeed, her prophetic pronouncements are characterized by an increased "tone of aggressive frustration."[27] When Urban V returned to Avignon, Birgitta was sixty-seven years old; time was running out for her to see the fulfillment of her most ardent desires. In the Life of Saint Birgitta, composed by her confessors for Gregory XI, her futile attempt to keep Urban V from returning to the more pleasant environs of Avignon is recounted as follows: "Moreover, when the lord pope, Urban V, wanted to return from Italy to Avignon,

24. For more details on Alfonso's propaganda for Urban VI, see Colledge, "*Epistola solitarii ad reges*: Alphonse of Pecha." See also Gilkaer, *The Political Ideas of St. Birgitta and Her Spanish Confessor.*

25. On the distinction between visionary (*visio*) and auditory (*vox*) revelations, see Obermeier and Kennison, "The Privileging of *Visio* over *Vox*." On audition, see also Benz, *Die Vision*, pp. 413–17.

26. See Ulibarrena's introduction to the new 1991 edition of Pou y Martí, p. lxiv. All these materials, together with countless other documents related to the Schism, were later collected by the cardinal Martin de Zalba and are still at the Vatican Archives, Armarium LIV. On Zalba's life and activities, see Millet, "Le cardinal Martin de Zalba."

27. See Birgitta of Sweden, *Saint Bridget's Revelations to the Popes*, p. 65.

the Virgin Mary appeared to the said Lady Birgitta and said to her some words in a vision, saying that this same lord pope should not return from Rome, nor from Italy, to Avignon; otherwise, the outcome would be to his loss in a brief time."[28] And indeed, Urban died a relatively short time after returning to Avignon. Cardinal Beaufort, the future Pope Gregory XI, was present at the occasion when Birgitta presented this vision to Urban V in Montefiascone. In fact, he himself had been asked to hand over this particular vision to the pope but had not dared to do so.[29] On this occasion he thus received a foretaste of what awaited him at the hands of this forceful visionary. Obviously, no pope relished Birgitta's predictions; indeed, as the great Birgitta scholar Arne Jönsson puts it, "the successive popes to whom she sent her divine messages had in the main been lukewarm or outright suspicious."[30]

Birgitta believed that she was called to "serve as God's mouthpiece," and it is interesting to note (as we shall for Constance de Rabastens) that there was a progression from "ecstatic visions and auditions . . . imparted to her primarily for her own edification" to more public and political messages.[31]

Gregory XI was the recipient of a number of Birgitta's visions, in particular *Revelaciones* 4.139–43, also published separately as part of Alfonso's *Tractatus de summis pontificibus*. With these visions buttressing her political advisory role, "Birgitta pushed the limits of women's normative behavior," as Claire Sahlin observes.[32] Yet, despite her divinely inspired speech she used male intermediaries to convey its message. The contrast with fr. Pedro of Aragon is worth noting here, for no one ever suggested that this highly placed male aristocrat *needed* visions—though, of course, he had plenty of them—as a pretext for offering his advice to popes or kings or that he should not speak for himself. In fact, he was constantly engaged in various diplomatic missions, mostly on behalf of his nephew.[33] For practical purposes fr. Pedro's visions are, at least in 1365, merely icing on the cake. Yet, fr. Pedro's visions are part of a pattern of attempts at political intervention based on visionary experiences that begins to form around this time.

Was Gregory XI particularly susceptible to other people's influence? The deathbed scene evoked above certainly suggests a certain remorse on the pope's part for having been "seduced" by visionaries. Georges Mollat has reevaluated

---

28. Morris, *Saint Birgitta*, p. 95.
29. See Alfonso's *Informaciones*, pars. 24–25: "Sed idem tunc Cardinalis Bellefortis dominus meus familiarissimus non fuit ausus hoc facere" (p. 187).
30. Jönnson, *Alfonso of Jaén*, p. 29.
31. Sahlin, "Preaching and Prophesying," p. 73.
32. Sahlin, "Preaching and Prophesying," p. 83. See the edition of book 4 by Aili.
33. On his diplomatic activities, see Pou y Martì, *Visionarios*, pp. 316–25, 352–54.

this judgment and sees a good part of confabulation in Gregory's supposed lack of resolution.[34] For any pope, Rome must have exerted a kind of mythic attraction that was not consistent with its current status as an embattled and hostile place. Persuading the pope in great part entailed opposing the cardinals, the majority of whom were also French or at least from the Limousin.

Gregory was barely elected pope when Birgitta had an account of a vision sent to him via Latino Orsini that described how, rapt in prayer and "her spirit consoled by divine strength" (diuino robore confortabatur spiritus eius), she had heard the voice of the Virgin, who, after reminding her of the prophecy sent to Urban V, was now sending a message to the new pope.[35] Just like a mother who lifts up and warms a naked and hungry child, the Virgin will treat Gregory, provided he returns to Rome with the intention of staying there and reforms, with due humility and charity, the abuses of the church. Should he decide against this move, or plan to return to Avignon once in Rome—the Virgin has not forgotten Urban V's change of heart—his life will be cruelly abbreviated. This terrible threat induced the pope to quickly seek confirmation from Birgitta.

The next revelation (4.140), also dictated as a letter to Alfonso of Jaén, confirms the first. Gregory now learns that the devil retains him at Avignon, specifically because of the carnal love and consolation he and those dear to him experience in that city.[36] This reference to the good life in Avignon certainly highlights one of the reasons the pope and his cardinals desired to stay there. Birgitta confirms that it is God's will that by April 1371 he should be in Rome. She adds that France must repent for its many transgressions against God. The Virgin commands that Alfonso should seal the letter, but show a copy to the papal nuncio and the count of Nola before destroying it, thus enlisting witnesses to the supernatural commands. Finally, a very concrete threat is added: if the pope does not return to Rome the papal lands will be dispersed among his enemies.

In January 1373 Birgitta receives another revelation (4.141), which shows Gregory as a paralytic (similes paralitico; p. 394) who can move neither hands nor feet. And because the illness of paralysis derives from corrupted and cold blood and humor, Christ concludes that Gregory displays the same tepid or even cold attitude toward God. Birgitta is aware that many people, the queen

---

34. See Mollat, "Grégoire XI et sa légende."

35. *Revelaciones* 4.139, ed. Aili, pp. 388–90; quotation on p. 388. See also Dupré Theseider, *I papi*, pp. 194–95. For a brief evaluation of Birgitta's influence on Gregory, see also Rusconi, *L'attesa della fine*, pp. 23–25.

36. "Dyabolus vero et alii consiliarii eiusdem pape consuluerunt ei tardare et in illis ubi nunc est partibus demorari et hoc propter carnalem amorem et eciam propter parentum et amicorum carnalium mundanam delectacionem et consolacionem" (*Revelaciones* 4.140; p. 392).

of Naples, the French king, the cardinals, and others, want to retain him in Avignon (and even marshal supposedly divine visions [diuinas reuelaciones et visiones; p. 394] to this effect!), but quoting Jeremiah, Birgitta assures Gregory that God will lead him to Rome.

Two further revelations urge Gregory's move to Rome.[37] One, received in February 1373, shows the pope on his knees at a distance before the enthroned Christ (4.142). This vision contained such a forceful indictment of the pope's familiars that Alfonso had to deliver it to the pope in secret, for he was certain he would be killed were the message discovered.[38] Christ wonders if Gregory hates him, because he has spurned the divine order to go to Rome and instead despoils heaven by enriching his temporal friends. In his papal court, greed, simony, and pride reign; in fact, Gregory is on the way to hell. He should shun the advice of his earthly friends and follow only that of the Lord. Finally, in June 1373 Birgitta answers what must have been a request for "three signs" from the pope—just like the Pharisees who always need signs, Birgitta scornfully remarks (4.143; p. 398). Nonetheless, the three signs are listed: first, the eternal consolation Gregory will experience once he has returned the church to its pristine state; second, the loss of all temporal and spiritual goods and endless tribulations that await him if he does not go to Rome; and third, the revelations and conversations Birgitta has had with Christ. As for the pope's troubles with Bernabo Visconti, Gregory should seek peace at all costs. This last point reveals that Birgitta is aware of Gregory's very specific worries. She sees him as a kind of marionette who is torn in two different directions: the multitudes who want him to stay in Avignon and, on the other side, only one force—but that force is God. The word *patibolo* (p. 399), a kind of forked piece of wood on which strings are attached, also suggests a gibbet,[39] perhaps meant as another threat to the procrastinating pope.

The strategies of persuasion revealed to Birgitta were quite varied. In some ways she used the carrot-and-stick approach. Being nestled against the Virgin's bosom and experiencing great consolations is balanced against the threat of endless tribulations, of death, and of hell. One image stands out: that of the paralytic, richly suggestive of the spiritual cost of Gregory's dithering. But for the most part, understanding the revelations requires no particular interpretive skills. As Claire Sahlin defines it: "Birgitta's writings belong to the broad genre of religious literature known as revelations—texts that claim to impart

---

37. Pp. 395–400. See also Dupré Theseider, *I papi*, pp. 197–99.
38. Jönnson, *Alfonso of Jaén*, p. 53. See *Informaciones*, pars. 43–46, pp. 189–90.
39. On Birgitta's imagery, see the brief remarks by Sahlin, *Birgitta of Sweden*, pp. 23–24, and esp. n. 36, for references to indexes of Birgitta's images and vocabulary.

direct messages from God."[40] The commands and the consequences of disobedience are presented in a clear and straightforward manner. The mysterious imagery of many mystical experiences, or even visions, related to the reform of the church is absent in this context. As an example we can look at *Revelaciones* 4.49, where Birgitta sees the corrupted clergy in the figure of a ruined church building. Right after the vision is concluded the voice "from the left" asks the "voice from the right" to explain the vision: "'Interpret spiritually,' it said, what you have said in corporeal terms" ('Expone,' inquit, 'spiritualiter, que dixisti corporaliter'; p. 165). Indeed, just as for fr. Pedro of Aragon, the didactic message in the revelations regarding the return to Rome is received relatively undisguised. The seer's subjectivity, her feelings, and her experiences recede before the content of the vision, which defines her mission.[41]

Gregory, close to a decision, may have needed just one more push, but this push could not be Birgitta's since she died shortly after this last revelation. A new saintly adviser was therefore needed, and Gregory contacted Catherine of Siena. He found the perfect messenger in Alfonso Pecha. As Catherine wrote to two Dominican friars in 1374, the pope sent "one of his vicars; he was the one who had been the spiritual father of that countess who died in Rome; and he is the one who renounced his bishopric for love of virtue" (uno suo vicario; ciò fue il padre spirituale di quella contessa che morí a Roma; e è colui che renunziò al vescovo per amore della virtù).[42] At the time, Catherine was already a well-known figure. As Francis Thomas Luongo observes, Catherine emerged "into the public eye in 1374" not as "a solitary figure" but at "the instigation of high church leaders with an already established network of politically aware and active clerical supporters and promoters."[43] Her political activities were manifold and initially dominated by the tensions between the pope and the Tuscan city-states. For our present purposes I want to highlight only her efforts to persuade the pope to return to Rome and, in the next section, her forceful interventions in the Great Schism. The two events are unhappily linked, for as Claudio Leonardi rightly states, Catherine was instrumental in Gregory XI's decision to return to Rome but what she could not foresee was Gregory's quick death and the fragmentation of the church. Tragically, "Catherine thus saw coming true the exact opposite of what she had desired."[44]

---

40. *Voice of Prophecy*, p. 19. See pp. 6–12 for a concise presentation of the tradition of women's prophecies.

41. See Newman, "What Did It Mean to Say 'I Saw'"?; for Birgitta, esp. pp. 37–41.

42. Jönnson, *Alfonso of Jaén*, p. 54. Letter T 127, DT 20. See note 46 for details on the editions used.

43. Luongo, "Politics of Marginality," p. 114.

44. "Caterina vedeva così realizzarsi l'essatto contrario di quello que aveva desiderato." See Leonardi, "Caterina la mistica," pp. 187–88. For Catherine's supposed prophecy of the Great Schism in 1375, see below.

Catherine uses various strategies in her persuasive efforts directed at Gregory XI.[45] She tries to give him strength in the face of the strong opposition of the cardinals and other counselors, and she marshals historical precedent for the return to Rome. The language of the letters is invariably forceful; the tone ranges from maternal to exasperated. The scheme is often the same: an initial formula, spiritual or mystical lessons, concrete references to the situation at hand, followed by what Catherine wants the pope to do, and the closing formula, usually containing the phrase "Altro no vi dico" (I shall not say anything else to you).[46]

The first extant letter to Gregory XI in Avignon (T 185, DT 54) dates from January 1376. As Eugenio Dupré Theseider observes, it shows Catherine's rare psychological intuition—that is, true insight into Gregory's character.[47] It combines dramatic imagery with political acuity, and features the themes that will dominate her correspondence with Gregory: church reform, the mounting of a crusade against the infidels, and the return of the papacy to Rome. The initial image is that of a tree that must bear fruit ("the sweet fruit of blazing charity"; N 1:245). Self-centeredness will dry up the tree's roots, and virtue will be dead, just like the stillborn baby of an unfortunate woman.[48] Follows a long development of a metaphor popular in late medieval political treatises, that of the shepherd and the physician: the pope must not be too indulgent ("keep using so much ointment on his sheep") but "rescue his little sheep from the clutches of the wolf" (N 1:246). After reminding the pope that his "delaying [his return to Rome] has already been the cause of a lot of trouble"—that is, unrest in the city-states—she utters the impatient command "Up father! No more irresponsibility! Raise the standard of the most holy cross" (N 1:249). After this general exhortation to a crusade, Catherine asks the pope for something more concrete: to prevent Pisa and Lucca from joining the antipapal league (Lucca

---

45. For brief remarks on some of the major differences in Birgitta's and Catherine's different types of visions and the resulting persuasive strategies, see Dupré Theseider, *I papi*, p. 206, and Rusconi, *L'attesa della fine*, pp. 28–29. On Catherine's charismatic and rhetorical powers, see also McLaughlin, "Women, Power, and the Pursuit of Holiness," esp. pp. 115–22.

46. On this structure, see Fawtier, *Sainte Catherine de Sienne*, 2:128, and Scott, "Ecclesiastical Politics," esp. p. 100. I shall use the following numbering of Catherine's letters (references are to the editions and translation listed in the bibliography): T = Tommaseo (cited after the selections); DT = Dupré Theseider (this edition breaks off after eighty-eight letters, ending in January 1377); N = Noffke's two-volume translation, which ends with letter T 119 in December 1377. I shall cite Noffke's translation up to December 1377; translations of the letters after that date are my own.

47. For a close reading of this letter, see Dupré Theseider, *I papi*, pp. 203–6. This letter also recognizes that Pope Gregory had already started thinking about and planning his return to Rome: "Pursue and finish with true holy zeal what you have begun by holy intent" (N 1:248).

48. See Noffke's note 6 to this passage on other instances of this image in Catherine's writings.

joined on March 12, 1376). The letter closes with remarks on who will be (and should be) promoted in the Dominican order. This letter, then, is a kind of template for many more to come, but as time goes on one can observe an increase in the urgency of Catherine's tone.

In March 1376, writing just after the revolt of Bologna, Catherine refers to "evil pastors and administrators" as "stinking weeds, full of impurity and avarice" whom Gregory must uproot (T 206, DT 63, N 2:61). Again she insists that church reform, the crusade, and the return to Rome should be his three major tasks even if the devil tries to prevent them. Several times she exclaims "Come!" and adds that he should be courageous for her sake and not be a coward. These are strong words, although Catherine does not prophesy harsh judgments or even the pope's death should he resist, as did Birgitta.

In early April 1376 Catherine writes to her confessor Raymond of Capua of a magnificent vision in which she, together with Christians and unbelievers as well as Saints Dominic and John, entered the side of the crucified Christ (T 219, DT 65, N 2:92). God discloses secrets to her relating to the persecution of the church that is permitted only because it will be followed by exaltation. Indeed, God is "using suffering and persecution to free [those bloated with pride] from their shameful disordered way of living" (N 2:92). But for this great future glory to arrive the church must be without scandal and back in Rome. Undoubtedly this vision motivated Catherine to try even harder to overcome the pope's fears and hesitations. More letters follow, and finally Catherine herself goes to Avignon in June 1376. In mid-August of that year, in her seventh letter to the pontiff (T 233, DT 76), Catherine takes on the evil counselors who are preventing Gregory's departure. She compares them to Saint Peter, who wanted to prevent Christ "from going to his passion" (N 2:213). Because Catherine also mentions that Gregory's counselors speak of the threat of death awaiting the pope in Rome, this example, however exalted the comparison was, it still was not the best means to assuage Gregory's fears.

One of the most powerful letters on the return to Rome seems to be a response to a note the pope sent Catherine.[49] She now exhorts him to be as firm as a rock even though he is being harassed by his enemies. The devil's ministry and satanic furies seem to be united against the pope's departure. She now marshals historical precedent by refuting the cardinals' point that Gregory should listen to their counsel as did Clement IV (1265–68) to that of his cardinals; rather, she says, the pope should think of Urban V (1362–70), who eventually decided to act against his cardinals' advice. Gregory would be more susceptible to this example because he knew Urban V well. Skillfully, Catherine

---

49. This is stated in a rubric in manuscript B, as Noffke points out (N 2:215).

omits any reference to Urban's return to Avignon, followed by his speedy death, predicted, as we saw earlier, by Saint Birgitta. Catherine even counsels Gregory to use a "holy trick" (uno santo inganno) in order to accomplish his departure: he should pretend to delay yet further but in reality depart quickly. "Go quickly to your bride," she concludes the letter, "who is all pale, and is waiting for you to bring back her color. And the moment you arrive she will be more beautiful than any other" (N 2:217).

One more dramatic obstacle to the pope's departure emerges in early September 1376 and must be dealt with: a letter from a "holy and just man" indicating that plans are afoot in Rome to poison Gregory on his arrival. In his edition of Catherine's letters Niccolò Tommaseo believed that the author could be fr. Pedro of Aragon, whose visions, as we saw above, had been instrumental in Urban V's temporary return to Rome.[50] This is certainly an intriguing if unprovable hypothesis. In any case, the rubrics in manuscripts B and P2 indicate that Gregory had forwarded this letter to Catherine for her evaluation.[51] Catherine now faces the dilemma that a letter-writer with a saintly reputation advises the pope to do the opposite of what he should do. She uses inversion to deal with this matter; though he may appear holy, this writer is in fact "the devil incarnate . . . , a forger . . . who knows less than a toddler!" (N 2:244). This dangerous letter-writer appeals to Gregory's love of life and suggests that the pope should send other people ahead to test the waters. For Catherine and those who await Gregory's arrival in Rome this "would be the cause of scandal and revolt" (N 2:245). Masterfully spinning out the metaphor of poison, Catherine returns to the idea of the crusade and closes the letter by exhorting Gregory to be not "a timid child but a courageous man" (N 2:247). She compares the letter-writer to a breastfeeding mother who uses bitter herbs on her breasts to wean her child. But Gregory must persist; he must make his way through the bitterness to arrive at the sweet milk that is Rome.

This letter is part of the final push that convinces Gregory to depart, which he does on September 13, 1376. In October Catherine meets up with him in Genoa, where he is tempted to turn back. Catherine, back in Siena, thus has to reinforce his decision once more (T 252, DT 88). In late 1376 or early 1377 she urges him to "confront these dangerous winds like a brave man. . . . Never turn

---

50. Note 3 to T 239; see also note 3 to DT 81. Denis-Boulet, after reconstructing the prophecies of this letter, concludes: "J'obtiens un texte qui est parfaitement attribuable à ce bon franciscain [that is, fr. Pedro of Aragon] ou à quelque autre 'serviteur de Dieu,' et pas nécessairement du parti adverse" (La carrière politique, p. 138).

51. "Al soprascritto santo padre, perché aveva avuto una lettara da uno, mostrando d'essere uno grande servo di Dio, lo quale voleva impedire l'avenimento del papa in Italia, la quale lettara el papa la mandò a Caterina, e Caterina fece questa risposta." DT 81 (p. 327).

back because . . . of slavish fear, but persevere, and rejoice in the storms and struggles" (N 2:271). Taking up one of her most frequent images, Catherine urges him to be a "tree of love" with "perseverance" nested within him. Finally, in January 1377 Catherine can address a letter to Gregory in Rome (T 285), and her interests are now centered on peace with and within the city-states. In her final letter to Gregory on April 16, 1377 (T 270) all the important themes reappear, supplemented by Catherine's desire to go to Rome herself. She depicts the pope as a nursing mother who dispenses both fire and blood, "since the blood was shed with blazing love" (N 2:343). In this letter she also recognizes that the pope's return to Rome has not solved any of the problems she cared about—indeed, she presents these problems as the result of her own sins. Corruption has not vanished (the church's ministers are still "stinking weeds" that need to be replaced by fragrant flowers, N 2:345), pride is rampant, and peace is more elusive than ever. Before any of Catherine's aims can be achieved, Gregory dies in March 1378—thus setting the stage for the Great Schism.

Birgitta and Catherine were equally passionate about the papacy's return to Rome, but they used different strategies of persuasion.[52] Birgitta's auditions and visions, directly transcribed for the pope, are full of threats and prophecies of disasters to come should the pope not comply. They fit in part into the genre of apocalyptic visions. Catherine, by contrast, appeals to the pope's political reason and sense of obligation (for example, his absence fosters sedition among the city-states). She tries to speed along the decisions of a born procrastinator, yet in her letters to Gregory she does not directly evoke any visions that would have buttressed her exhortations. This apparent disconnect between her mystical life and the letters addressed to prelates and rulers is remarkable. She certainly drew her authority from her intense visionary experiences but felt no need to insist on them in the overtly polemical epistles we cited.

The Schism Begins: Catherine of Siena and Fr. Pedro of Aragon

Of Catherine's manifold political activities not much is reflected in Raymond of Capua's Vita, but one element is highlighted: Catherine's supposed prophecy

---

52. Adriana Valerio summarizes these differences succinctly: "Brigida e Caterina costituiscono le due anime dell'impatto profetico verso il mondo esterno: visionario-apocalittico l'una, razionale-parenetico l'altra. Entrambe sono impegnate a far tornare il papa a Roma: l'una con i modi del cupo profetismo escatologico che minaccia sciagure e punizione, l'altra attraverso le riflessioni del cuore et della ragione sugli accadimenti storici." *Donna, potere e profezia*, p. 145.

of the Schism.[53] In 1375, when Catherine is in Pisa, the city of Perugia revolts. Raymond, much upset by these news, is comforted by the saint with the prediction "You will have plenty to cry about later. Today's news is milk and honey compared to what is going to happen in time to come." When Raymond asks her incredulously whether she is intimating that "the very clergy will rebel against the Roman pontiff," she prophesies "a universal scandal . . . not exactly a heresy, but something like a heresy which will mean a cleavage in the Church and throughout Christendom. So now get ready to suffer for you will live to see these things."[54] Raymond refrains from asking for more details and only years later realizes what Catherine was talking about: "Later . . . when I witnessed the beginnings of the present schism in the church, my eyes were opened and I realized that what Catherine had foretold was now being verified." When he reminds Catherine of her prophecy she foretells even more dire events.[55] All this is of course filtered through hindsight, since Raymond composed the Vita between 1385 and 1395, when the Schism had become entrenched and its destructive consequences were obvious.

Raymond does tell in some detail how Catherine was summoned by Urban VI to Rome in November 1378 and how the pope used her to instill courage in his intimidated cardinals. "This weak woman puts us all to shame," Urban told his cardinals. "It is we who play the coward, while she stands undaunted."[56] And while we do learn that Catherine suffered intensely for the Schism ("Tears became her food day and night. She saw the Church of God, for love of which she was on fire, plunged in a sea of troubles by that abominable

53. Cavallini ("Le *Dialogue* de Sainte Catherine de Sienne et le Grand Schisme") believes that Catherine's feeling of an imminent disaster may have contributed to her creation of the *Dialogue* (p. 360). A curious parallel can be found in the life of the German mystic Elsbeth Achler von Reute (1396–1420), whose Life was modeled on that of Catherine of Siena (see Williams-Krapp, "Fifteenth-Century German Religious Literature," p. 118). The most important prophecy attributed to her was that of the end of the Schism at the Council of Constance (ed. Bihlmeyer, p. 107).

54. Raymond of Capua, *The Life of Catherine of Siena*, trans. Kearns, pp. 264–65. *Acta sanctorum*, April III, p. 933, par. 285. It is interesting that, though the term *heresy* was often used in the treatises of the time to describe the Schism, Catherine here, according to Raymond, clarifies that this "scandal" will not be a heresy but *divisio Ecclesiae ac totius Christianitatis*. But in her letter to cardinal Pedro de Luna written just before the second papal election (T 293), for example, she does use the word *heresy*. More on this letter below. Birgitta of Sweden was also believed by some to have prophesied the Schism. See Sahlin, *Birgitta of Sweden*, p. 43.

55. *Life*, p. 265. The *Legenda minor* also insists on Catherine's gift of prophecy. See Rusconi, *L'attesa della fine*, p. 34. Catherine's discourse before the pope as well as this prophecy may very well be fiction. In any case, there is no other evidence for them. See Fawtier, *Sainte Catherine de Sienne*, 1:205–6.

56. *Life*, p. 311.

schism"; *Life*, p. 319) and was chosen by the pope for a mission to Naples,[57] we get no sense from Raymond about the nature of the many powerful letters she dictated in the context of the Great Schism, an event that clearly galvanized her political will.[58] Of these letters, I shall highlight only some of the more dramatic ones.

Because the second papal election of Robert of Geneva as Clement VII was not proclaimed until September 20, 1378, there was a period in which Catherine still hoped that the cardinals' growing opposition to Urban VI could be defused. Two letters stand out in this context: one to Pedro de Luna (the future Pope Benedict XIII) and one to Onorati Caetani, count of Fondi, an ally of the rebellious cardinals.

The Spanish cardinal Pedro de Luna (ca. 1328–1423) was one of the towering figures of the whole period of the Schism. After an initial adherence to Urban he became a supporter of Robert of Geneva (Clement VII), and after Robert's death in 1394 the most tenacious pope in history, who, even after multiple depositions, hung on to his office until his death, when he was in his nineties. Pedro was the recipient of a strong plea from Catherine in late June or early July 1378 (T 293). Catherine wants Pedro to be a "strong column (colonna ferma) . . . in the garden of the Holy Church" lest self-love that "incapacitates any reasonable creature" take over (p. 371). Roberto Rusconi underlines the letter's insistence on reason (ragione), which marks a rejection of prophecy and apocalypticism—that is, unlike the prophets we shall encounter in Chapter 6, Catherine makes no effort to link a possible schism to the end of time.[59] Instead she both appeals to reason (the disaster to come is "demonstrated [by Raymond] by means of reason" [mostrato col mezzo della ragione]; p. 373) and emphasizes her personal suffering, which is caused by the current discord and her fear of heresy (eresia, meaning "schism" here) due to her own sins, she believes (della quale cosa dubito forte che per le mei peccati ella non venga; p. 373). In a dramatic hierarchization of conflicts,[60] Catherine exclaims that compared with the current conflict "anything else, that is, war, dishonor, and other tribulations, would seem less important than a bit of straw or a shadow" (che tutte altre cose, cioè guerra, disonore, e altre tribolazioni, ci parrebbero

---

57. She was to go with Catherine of Sweden, who refused, so the mission never happened.
58. Whether these letters were actually sent and received is a question that cannot be answered for many letters. Ols, in "Sainte Catherine et les débuts du Grand Schisme," states: "Il est probable en effet que beaucoup de ces lettres ne parvinrent jamais à leur destinataire et celles qui arrivèrent à bon port ne semblent pas avoir eu une grande influence" (p. 340).
59. Rusconi, *L'attesa della fine*, pp. 31–32.
60. This same ranking of conflicts can be found in Honoré Bovet's *Arbre des batailles*. See Chapter 5.

meno che una paglia o un'ombra, per rispetto di questo; p. 373). Indeed, to Raymond it seemed that his heart, his very life, left his body because of the pain caused by the discord in the church; he would like to sweat blood instead of water, even to faint with pain. As if suddenly aware of the utter drama of these statements Catherine adds: "Believe me, dearest father, that I'd rather be quiet than speak of these matters" (Credo, carissimo padre, che meglio mi sia tacere che a parlare di questa materia; p. 374). But may Pedro pray that the church be reformed and "questo scandalo" (p. 374) removed! May God sweep away the darkness and stink of his spouse and bring back the light. These are strong words, evidencing one view prevalent during the Schism—namely, that the church herself is infected and darkened. Other views see the church as the innocent and presumably clean spouse who is being raped by bad pastors: she remains pristine while those around her are the criminals.

When Catherine writes a "vehement and eloquent" letter to the count of Fondi (T 313) she targets one of the principal facilitators of the Schism.[61] Enraged against Urban, he allied himself with the cardinals who came to stay in his territory, a place where, according to Urban, "demons held their council."[62] The governing metaphor of this epistle is that of the vineyard of the soul, which in the count is completely "insalvatichita" (wild or overgrown with weeds; pp. 398, 401). This vineyard is infested with the thorns of pride and avarice, with the brambles of anger, impatience, and disobedience; it is full of poisonous weeds (p. 398). Should the count deny that Urban is the rightful pope he would be a heretic, a faithless Catholic, a renegade, a reprobate before God (p. 400). In what will become a prototypical approach to the events of April 1378, Catherine accuses the cardinals of fabricating the idea that they had no free will in the election. Surely God has given you enough light, Catherine argues, that you can see the truth—unless, of course, you let it be obscured by your wrath and disdain toward Urban (p. 400). Whoever causes such a schism in the church is worthy of a thousand deaths (p. 401). In a long and involved development Catherine discusses the question of free will, the tree of charity, and in a return to the image of the vineyard, that of the knife of penitence, with which the count should cut away his vices. This is a powerful, long letter, but, alas, its effect was

---

61. See Denis-Boulet, *La carrière politique,* pp. 162–64 (quotation from p. 163): Urban VI turned the count into an enemy when he refused to pay a debt of 20,000 florins incurred by Gregory XI and also removed Caetani from the government of Anagni, giving it to one of his enemies, all the time insulting him. See also Valois, *La France,* 1:77–78. Catherine's psychological insights into his situation must be understood in this context. This letter dates from between July and mid-September 1378.

62. This in a bull of March 1379 and in reference to Saint Gregory's *Dialogi* 3:7 (see Valois, *La France,* 1:77, nn. 4, 5).

nil. Catherine sees the coming schism with all its disastrous consequences. She musters the most profound arguments against a man who is engaged in a political wrangle that has nothing to do with the salvation of his soul. In this letter, Catherine's *imaginaire* of the schism places it in a scheme of heresy, perdition, and salvation, while her argumentation is both spiritual and practical—that is, based on the evidence of the election.[63] But the count's interests lay elsewhere.

In the fall of 1378 Catherine addresses herself to the three Italian cardinals (Corsini, Borzano, and Orsini) who had voted first for Urban, then for Clement (T 310).[64] According to two historians of Catherine's political career, this "terrible piece of eloquence" is the "harshest and most cutting letter Catherine ever wrote."[65] While discussing old debates on the authenticity of the letters, Noële Denis-Boulet asks: "Which hagiographer would have dared put into the mouth of his hero, with ambitions to sainthood, such invectives?" (p. 168). Indeed, the language of these letters is that of a militant, aggressive fighter for the unity of the church, not that of a humble woman deferring to the cardinals' wisdom.[66]

The initial address "dearest brothers and fathers" (carissimi fratelli e padri; p. 417) belies the tone of the rest of this very long letter; in fact, only if they leave behind the darkness and blindness afflicting them will they truly be her brothers and fathers. Together with the theme of light, these two concepts structure the letter, which is also rich in other metaphors: the cardinals were meant to feed at the breasts of Holy Church; they should be flowers in the church's garden; they were to emit a virtuous odor; they were supposed to be the beams fortifying the ship of the church, and the candles in the candelabrum dispensing light to the faithful (p. 419). All these images form part of a single sentence. After calling them bad, heretical knights, Catherine skillfully reprises these images *in negativo*, demonstrating that the cardinals are the contrary of everything they should be, indeed, that they are demons in the service of the Antichrist instead of angels.

Working with the opposition of truth and lies Catherine revisits the first papal election and proves that the cardinals' claim of having voted in fear is nothing short of ridiculous (p. 420), for if they voted under duress then, they

63. As Denis-Boulet puts it, when Catherine speaks of the truth of Urban's election in this letter, "les raisons manifestant cette vérité sont si claires qu'un idiot les comprendrait" (*La carrière politique*, p. 163).
64. The fourth had died by then.
65. Denis-Boulet, *La carrière*, p. 169, and Helbling, *Katharina von Siena*, who observes: "Die Strafpredigt, die sie den abtrünnigen Kardinälen Corsini, Borzano und Orsini hält (310), ist wohl das Schärfste und Härteste, das sie geschrieben hat" (p. 27).
66. The debates on the fate of letters like these persists, though. Were they ever sent? In how many copies (one to each of the three cardinals)? Was there any reaction? One does not know. See Helbling, *Katharina von Siena*, pp. 139–40.

also lied then when they proclaimed Urban the rightful pope. "Oh, foolish men, worthy of a thousand deaths!" (Ahi stolti, degni di mille morti; p. 421), you are liars and idolaters. The cardinals changed their minds because they could not accept Urban's reforms; he began to "bite" them, and that is when they turned against him. Pursuing the theme of blindness and lies to the end, Catherine adds new variations, such as the accusation that the cardinals are robbers and wolves devouring their little lambs (pp. 424–25).

One of the most interesting and controversial passages deals with the cardinals' lack of "passion for the fatherland, as the French [from beyond the Alps] have" (passione della patria, come gli ultramontane; p. 424). Did Catherine blame the French for their "patriotism," which resulted in French popes residing in Avignon? According to Robert Fawtier, "the feeling of an Italian nationality was as completely foreign to Catherine as it was to her contemporaries, maybe even more so."[67] However, she does address the cardinals as "Italiani" and calls the pope "Cristo in terra italiano" (the Italian Christ on earth; p. 424). Fawtier believes that these terms refer only to the fact that the pope would reside in Rome instead of Avignon. It is true that Italy was not a country then, while at the time France was a more unified nation. Yet, I believe that the term "Italiani" is a clear indication that Catherine saw the Schism as a proto-nationalistic conflict in which ecclesiastical loyalties were bound up with national ones. This is supported by a letter that the Florentine chancellor Coluccio Salutati wrote in January 1376, in which he stressed the "Italian nature" of Gregory XI's return to Rome, a symbolic move against the "French tyrants."[68] Thus, this seasoned politician portrayed the pope's return to Rome in 1377 as a conflict between two "nations," the same two nations that would end up supplying the rival popes for the Schism.

In October 1378 Catherine fired off a similar letter to Queen Joan of Naples (T 312), who after brief initial support of Urban consisting of three hundred armed men as well as cash and foodstuffs, went over to Clement. Most likely, Urban had alienated her, just as he had alienated the cardinals. Rumors circulated that the Roman pope wanted to depose Joan in favor of Louis of Hungary and banish her to a convent.[69] The main theme is again that of light (the word

67. Fawtier, La double expérience, pp. 212–13.

68. Trexler, "Rome on the Eve of the Great Schism," p. 490. Later, Salutati would describe the Schism as the most painful event of his life. See the letter of August 1397 paraphrased by Delaruelle et al., L'Eglise, 1:91.

69. See Valois, La France, 1:77–78. She probably would have been better off there, for later she was assassinated in prison on the orders of her nephew Charles Durazzo. For a reassessment of Joan's role in the early Schism years, see Voci, "Giovanna I d'Angiò e l'inizio del Grande Scisma d'Occidente."

is repeated countless times in this letter) and darkness. Catherine proves in terms very similar to those used in the letter to the cardinals that the claim of the forced initial vote is a sham, but she does add one more withering argu-ment based on Joan's gender: initially, in supporting Urban, Joan had shown herself to be enlightened (dimostrerete d'aver lume; p. 415) and to have lost "the condition of being a woman and was made a virile man"[70] (la condizione della femmina, e esser fatta uomo virile; p. 415), but then she chose another road—adherence to Clement—and demonstrated that she was "a woman with little steadfastness" (voi dimostrerete d'essere femmina con poca stabilità; p. 415). Catherine herself sounds frustrated with her feminine condition at the end of the letter, when she says that she would rather attack those who have sown so much heresy in the mystical body of the church and of all Christianity with deeds than with words (farei più tosto di fatti che di parole; p. 416).

Catherine's despair comes through in another letter to the queen (T 317), written a few months later. She again uses the light-darkness metaphor cou-pled with Joan's gender: Joan is one of those who "walk in darkness, with a woman's nature without any firmness or steadfastness" (vanno in tenebra, colla natura femminile senza alcuna fermezza o stabilità; p. 442). She also calls Joan a faithless daughter, having abandoned not only her legitimate father, the pope, but also her mother, the Church. Instead she has given herself over to "demons incarnate" (dimonii incarnati; p. 443)—that is, the cardinals, who are sowing heresy and schism, feeding the queen lies about Urban's election. But they will betray themselves by their darkness and stink (pp. 443–44). Only the truth will liberate Joan, otherwise she will be lost (p. 447).

Catherine's last letter to Joan, on May 6, 1379, predates the queen's brief change of heart in Urban's favor; it is dominated by the theme of the tears that Catherine sheds in face of Joan's weakness. These letters fit into the forceful campaign Catherine waged in favor of Urban VI throughout Italy, and even France and Hungary. Though they each show slight variations, adapted to the recipients, the major themes remain the same.

Also on May 6, 1379, Catherine dictated a letter to the French king Charles V (T 350), to whom she had written once before in October 1376 (T 235, DT 78).[71] As Paul Ourliac observes, this letter is "at the same time a mystical exhortation and

70. On the early development of this topos, see Vogt, "'Becoming Male'"; see also Newman, *From Virile Woman to WomanChrist,* for an exploration of this topos throughout medieval culture.

71. Fawtier believes that the more logical date for this letter would be November 1378 because Catherine states that the king is beginning to let himself be influenced by the University of Paris. In May 1379 the recognition of Clement VII was already a fait accompli (*Sainte Cather-ine de Sienne,* 2:232–33).

a program,"[72] begging the king to serve divine justice and work for peace. He should start a crusade against the infidels instead of waging war against his Christian brothers. He should stop being "the agent of so much evil" (operatore di tanto male; p. 228; N 2:222) and sleeping away the precious time remaining to him. Anyone familiar with the achievements of Charles V's reign will be surprised at the harshness of this letter, though the historian Roland Delachenal believes that Catherine's letter may have played a role in Charles's peace efforts even if a crusade never became reality.[73] Once the Schism begins, Catherine's tone becomes more urgent.[74] This letter, which some scholars consider a masterpiece, can also be seen as "a striking example of the total ignorance of the adversary that characterized the beginnings of the Schism and that reflected the growing estrangement between two worlds: the French and the Italian."[75] Catherine's passion in addressing Charles gives voice to one conception of the church—that of "the church of the children of light and inspired by God"—while Charles's political realism reveals another conception, that of "an institutionalized church, monarchical and reasonable."[76] To tell a ruler like Charles V that he "lets himself be led like a child" (si lassi guidare come fanciullo; p. 555) may betray ignorance of the process by which the French monarch arrived at the recognition of Clement. But it betrays even more this conception of the church not as an earthly institution subject to political vagaries but as the mystical body of Christ where only truth exists. The one who deviates from this truth is subject to all insults.

Catherine's spirituality always included a big dose of pragmatism. Her numerous letters to Urban VI show her skill in propping up an irascible but perhaps also doubtful or even fearful pontiff.[77] These letters mingle spiritual exaltation with practical advice in a remarkable way. Early on, in April 1376, Pedro de Luna and other cardinals, as well as Raymond of Capua, had been apprised of a vision Catherine had had that "exalted our archbishop," the future Urban VI.[78] Her faith in him thus dated back a long time and was validated by her own visionary experience. Her certainty of his legitimacy shines through in every one of her letters to him.

72. Ourliac, "Les lettres à Charles V," p. 173.
73. See Ourliac, "Les lettres," 175 n. 3. Catherine saw Charles's brother, the duke of Anjou, as the most ardent supporter of a crusade. See, for example, her letter to him in early September 1376 (T 237, DT 79).
74. On the process that led to Charles V's recognition of Clement, see Swanson, *Universities, Academics, and the Great Schism*, chap. 2.
75. Both opinions come from Denis-Boulet, *La carrière politique*, p. 174.
76. Ourliac, "Les lettres," p. 180.
77. On the early support of Catherine's circle for Urban, the former archbishop of Bari, see Ourliac, "Les lettres," pp. 176–77, and Valois, *La France*, 1:34–36.
78. See Fawtier, *Sainte Catherine de Sienne*, 2:195–96.

Toward the end of June 1378, before the second papal election, Catherine sends Urban a rather general letter on his privileges and duties (church reform) using the image of a garden that needs cultivating (T 291) and underlining the necessity of a group of good cardinals who should be his support. Undoubtedly Catherine saw the writing on the wall when, in a letter dating from perhaps early September 1378 (in any case, before Urban named his new cardinals on September 18), she warns Urban that he will have to bear the attacks of those "who with the cudgel of heresy want to pierce your saintliness" (che col bastone della eresia vogliono percuotere la Santità vostra; p. 407). The cardinals' plotting against Urban was clearly common knowledge in Catherine's circles. In late 1378, after her arrival in Rome, she exhorts Urban in forceful letters to stay the course on reform, to show his virile heart in stamping out vice (T 364). She wants to stimulate him "with prayers, and in my own voice, or in writing" (di stimolarvi coll'orazione, e con la voce viva o con scrivere; p. 496). She is in Rome, ready to support her pontiff any way she can. Her last letters to Urban are dominated by despair and hopelessness. In a letter dictated between January and March 1380 (T 371), when her strength is failing, Catherine reports that God had told her directly of his bitterness and pain at seeing the church dominated by temporal concerns and the lack of the fire of love. When Catherine asks what she herself can do, God answers that she should offer up her own life. And in one of the most moving passages in Catherine's writings, she gives up her heart so that it may adorn the Holy Spouse. God thus takes her heart, not too suddenly, so as not to break up her body completely, and presses it down (premevalo) "in the Holy Church" (nella santa Chiesa; p. 610), an act that makes the devil scream with intolerable pain. Catherine, close to death, thus becomes a martyr for the sake of the unified church. There can be no greater sacrifice.

Although, as we saw earlier, in many of her letters Catherine appeals to the recipients' reason, and although she is certainly aware of the political stakes involved in the beginning of the Schism, her final reaction is spiritual, expressed as intense physical suffering.[79] The many sides of Catherine's genius come together here; for a woman whose main ambition was to bring about peace, a crusade, and a unified reformed church, the events between 1378 and her death on April 29, 1380, could only be crushing. She offers herself as the final sacrifice, in vain.

79. Catherine's contemporary William Fleet reported in a letter that Catherine, while praying in front of Giotto's *Navicella* during Lent of 1380, felt the crushing weight of the Ship of the Church depicted by Giotto on her shoulders, so that "she collapsed on the floor" and the lower part of her body remained paralyzed until her death shortly thereafter (Meiss, *Painting in Florence and Siena*, p. 107).

Fr. Pedro of Aragon, whom we encountered earlier as a strong supporter of the papacy's return to Rome, also became a propagandist for Urban VI. Unlike France, the Spanish kingdoms engaged in a long period of "indiferencia,"[80] a period of wavering but also of examining the facts of the double papal election. After the great inquiry at Medina del Campo from November 1380 to April 1381 (among the witnesses were Raymond of Capua and Catherine of Sweden as the only woman),[81] the kingdom of Castille declared for Clement VII on May 19, 1381. In Aragon things moved more slowly, and it was not until just after Pedro IV's death that the Aragonese declared for Clement on February 24, 1387. During this time King Pedro IV forbade any of the monastic orders to agitate for one or the other pope, though he did appoint his uncle Vicar General of the Franciscans in 1380, expecting him to support the Aragonese policy of neutrality.[82] It was during this period that fr. Pedro moved heaven and earth to win the Spanish kingdoms (and France as well, though it was too late for that) over to Urban VI, though he apparently fulfilled his administrative responsibilities impartially.

His many activities in favor of Urban included travel (also to Medina del Campo), letters, and personal reports of his visions and divine commands. Through his inspired visionary experiences in particular he turned himself into what Friedrich Bliemetzrieder so aptly calls "living theological proof of Urban's legitimacy."[83] As we shall see, the contemporary evaluation of fr. Pedro's visionary experiences and their messages was influenced by the evaluators' political leanings, so that this aged Franciscan could be seen as either an inspired seer or a deluded old man.[84]

Alfonso of Pecha, who had engaged in Urbanist propaganda after the outbreak of the Schism,[85] speaks of fr. Pedro in the context of his anxious inquiries into Urban's claim to the papacy after the cardinals' "invidious conspiracy" against the pope in Anagni.[86] All the people he consults affirm that Urban is the

---

80. For a detailed account of this period, see Ivars, "La 'indiferencia' de Pedro IV de Aragón," and Seidlmayer, *Die Anfänge,* chaps. 2 and 3.

81. The protocol of this involved procedure can be found in BnF lat. 11745. Raymond of Capua's testimony has been edited along with that of others in Seidlmayer, *Die Anfänge,* pp. 258–61.

82. The king actually claimed that fr. Pedro had been vicar general already under Gregory XI in 1372—that is, pre-Schism—but this seems doubtful. See Ivars, "'La indiferencia,'" p. 59, and Pou y Martì, *Visionarios,* p. 357.

83. Bliemetzrieder, "Die zwei Minoriten," p. 441.

84. The documents related to his vision and the inquiry were assembled by Martin de Zalba, who was then a young bishop in Pamplona. After his death in 1403 the *Libri de schismate* became the property of Benedict XIII. See Seidlmayer, "Die spanischen 'Libri de Schismate,'" for the inventory of Armarium LIV at the Vatican archives, and Millet, "Le cardinal Martin de Zalba," esp. p. 283.

85. See Colledge, "*Epistola solitarii ad reges:* Alphonse of Pecha."

86. *Informaciones,* pars. 64–72, pp. 192–93.

true pope by God's will and that the Schism has come about as punishment for humanity's sins (pars. 67–68). Alfonso also listened to the account of various revelations, "among them those that Pedro of Aragon, a friar minor and the uncle of the king of Aragon, had on this subject. They were special revelations expressly made by Christ for the kings of Castille and France and other people" (par. 70), and they certified that Urban was the truest of popes (verissimum papam). We see again that this type of revelation requires no interpretive skills; the message and even for whom it is meant is built right in.

But let us also listen to fr. Pedro's own words in this context. As an example, we can look at a letter he wrote in April 1379 to the French king Charles V.[87] In it he speaks of a revelation he had two days earlier in which God spoke to him directly, showing him how out of persecutions and even crimes permitted by God (like the Jews screaming "Let us crucify him!") salvation can come. Similarly, Pedro states, the Roman population's demand "We want either a Roman or an Italian" outside the conclave of 1378 may not have been "good" in itself, but it resulted in the papacy's "translation" from the circles of the ambitious Limousin cardinals to Italy. "And why," Pedro asks God, "do you reveal these things to the small, the miserable, the poor, and the ignorant, and abandon the great to their blindness?"[88] God responds that he chose Pedro so that he can convey to the French king that he must recognize Urban as the true pope or incur God's wrath. The words "revealed" or "revelation" are repeated so many times in this letter that there can be no doubt about fr. Pedro's belief in his divine inspiration. But there is more: God's words to the humble Franciscan are specifically meant for the French king; they are a direct communication through the mouth of a privileged seer, the same configuration we shall encounter with Marie Robine below.

In the second half of 1379, fr. Pedro writes to Bertrand Atgarius, one of the cardinals who had first elected Urban and then Clement.[89] Atgarius had written to fr. Pedro to win him over to the Clementist side. Fr. Pedro's response in some ways resembles Catherine's letters on the same subject. He revisits the papal election and asserts that Urban was elected not as the consequence of a riot but in a peaceful multiday conclave. The cardinals, far from doubting the legitimacy of this election, immediately began to curry favor with the new pope, asking for a plenary absolution of their sins, benefices for their friends, and so on. Repeatedly asking "Who forced you?" (Quis coegit vos?), Pedro

87. Du Boulay, *Historia*, 4:581.
88. "Et quid est hoc tu revelas ista parvulis, miseris, pauperibus & Idiotis, & magnos in sua caecitate dimittis?" (Du Boulay, *Historia*, 4:581).
89. Edited by Bliemetzrieder in "Die zwei Minoriten," pp. 443–46.

answers his own question: no one forced the cardinals to do any of this (p. 444). After a long paragraph on the dire consequences of lying, fr. Pedro informs Bertrand that Jesus Christ himself called the cardinals liars and "your nest" (nidum vestrum), the city of Avignon, Samaria. He recounts that the present Schism was foretold to him about fourteen years earlier and that about ten years earlier the figure of Saint Paul appeared to him (cuius effigiem manifeste vidi; p. 445) and told him to go to Rome. But the most important revelation was that of Saint Augustine, who revealed to him that Christ approved of Urban's election and that he should write to that effect to the kings of France and Castille and to the duke of Verunda. He did so despite a great fight (magnum conflictum; p. 446) with the devil, who tried to prevent him from following Christ's orders. But God's spirit prevailed. The Lord also told him one evening when he was about to go to sleep: "Pedro, now is no time to go to sleep, for you must enter the city of Barcelona and there fight for me and my vicar Urban and for the Holy Church of God" (Petre, non est tempus dormiendi, qui te introeunte civitatem Barch[ino]nensem habes bellare ibi pro me et vicario meo Urbano et pro ecclesia sancta Dei; p. 446). In order to ensure the authenticity of these revelations, fr. Pedro is willing to submit them to examination by the French king and the Roman emperor. And may I burn in hell, he adds, if these visions turn out to be false and sent by the devil. But if they are true, all of you cardinals will be branded as liars. You and the adherents of your perverse opinions will be damned before the court of the Last Judgment unless you repent and remove the error you have introduced into this world. These are strong words from a well-connected, aristocratic visionary but, like Catherine's exhortations, they fell on deaf ears.

The famous inquisitor Nicholas Eymerich, an eyewitness to the April 1378 conclave, authored one of the first tracts against Urban VI, in which he asks, How can we know who is pope? Through trial by fire, or a duel, or should we listen to people that are considered holy (sancti viri nomine et devoti)? No, he concludes, Christ himself rejected these kinds of visionaries.[90] Historians agree that one of the targets of Eymerich's sarcastic remarks was fr. Pedro of Aragon, whose visions certainly did not fit into Eymerich's anti-Urbanist agenda.

Two years after Eymerich's condemnation of such visionaries as fr. Pedro, the inquiry envisioned by fr. Pedro in his letter to Bertrand Atgarius did take place, though in a different framework than the one envisioned in this letter. The commission consisted of six experts, one of whom, fr. Pedro de Ribes, only submitted written comments and was not actually present at the questioning.

---

90. Written before the second election in September 1378. See Finke, "Drei spanische Publizisten," pp. 183–87. Quotation, p. 185. See also Seidlmayer, Die Anfänge, p. 163.

The inquiry followed the procedure of the discernment of spirits,[91] focusing on the orthodoxy of the visionary and on the nature and purpose of the visions. Though the idea of discernment has a long history, it was brought into sharper focus by the Great Schism because of the crisis of authority due to the divided church. Pedro's questioners perfectly exemplify the political dimension of this procedure. Fr. Pedro's 1365 visions regarding the papacy's move to Rome were vetted back then and, in excruciating detail, again in 1380 and found to be mostly unproblematically orthodox. But one point was controversial: did Urban V's return to Avignon in 1370 invalidate fr. Pedro's prophetic powers? The opposing parties on the panel could not resolve this point, just as they could not arrive at a common opinion on the more-recent revelations under review. Fr. Pedro's visions on the legitimacy of Pope Urban could not be accepted by the Clementist contingent of the panel, and though they did concede fr. Pedro's holy life (even if inferior to that of the Evangelists; p. 381), they rejected his visions. In the words of Pedro de Ribes, "these visions work against and fulminate against the holiest lord, Pope Clement, who truly presides over all of God's church" (iste visiones moliantur et fulminantur contra sanctissimum dominum papam Clementem [qui vere presidet toti ecclesie Dei]) and therefore the panel could not believe in such visions.[92] It is interesting that Pedro de Ribes added that the Infante Pedro himself seemed to doubt his visions, perhaps a reference to the end of the letter to Atgarius, and that hence the panel must doubt them all the more.

Fr. Pedro's supporter, the Franciscan Bernardus Broll, went to great lengths to prove that Urban VI is universally supported, that in regard to Urban V, fr. Pedro correctly predicted his death, and that fr. Pedro did fulfill all the requirements for a recognition of the truth of his revelations (p. 394). But no, countered fr. Ultzina, a Clementist, these visions are nothing but "dreams or violent cogitations" (sompnia vel vehementes cogitationes; p. 395), an opinion seconded in a letter in February 1380 from his great-nephew, Pedro IV's son, Juan de Gerona, who coldly rejected any advice fr. Pedro wanted to offer him, calling his visions worthless foolishness (pegueses).[93] In the end, two of the panelists rejected his revelations, three accepted them, and one abstained in "impenetrable reserve."[94] Needless to say, the votes were cast along Urbanist-Clementist party lines.

---

91. See Boland, The Concept of "discretio spirituum"; Elliott, "Seeing Double," Roth, Discretio Spirituum; Caciola, Discerning Spirits; and for Pedro, see esp. Anderson, "Free Spirits, Presumptuous Women, and False Prophets," pp. 196–208.
92. Pou y Martì, Visionarios, p. 383.
93. Seidlmayer, Die Anfänge, p. 97.
94. Pou y Martì, Visionarios, p. 376.

Fr. Pedro's case is instructive because it shows us a powerful, well-connected saintly aristocrat, who acquired a reputation as a visionary over several decades, being subjected to the scorn of his relatives and masters of theology, not for any personal failings or lack of holiness but simply because his revelations did not conform to the political agenda of Aragon. The divisions caused by the Schism are reflected in the divided opinions of the discernment panel, whose members differ not on points of doctrine but on their allegiance to Rome or Avignon. Pedro IV's efforts at neutrality, in which he imposed his will on his people in forceful ways, could not endorse the kind of prophetic and visionary propaganda his uncle engaged in.

Fr. Pedro's life ended well before a decision was finally made in Aragon. After Castille's declaration for Clement VII, fr. Pedro received a divine order, transmitted by the apostle Saint Peter, to go to Rome, and aged as he was (and being afraid of Clement's armed galleys, and despite the efforts of his nephew to dissuade him), he set out for Rome, but died en route on November 4, 1381, in Pisa. During a conversation with Saint Peter, voicing his fears about this voyage, fr. Pedro had received the prediction of his death on his arrival in Rome. Like Catherine of Siena he was willing to give his life for the rightful pope, and like the Sienese saint, he did. But neither his nor Catherine's sacrificial deaths had any effect on the development of the Schism. It not only persisted but became more and more entrenched.

Three

By the mid-1380s the two papal obediences had become established, and the European powers had declared themselves for one or the other pope. But this situation did not lead to general acquiescence. On the contrary, it was around this time that a new group of visionaries, laywomen for the most part, added their voices to those of clerical and saintly figures denouncing or supporting one of the popes; calling for an end of the Schism; or even engaging in shuttle diplomacy between the two papacies. Representatives of each of these groups will be at the center of this chapter.

Constance de Rabastens, a Lay Visionary as Supporter of the Roman Pope

The three visionaries considered in Chapter 2 had a number of things in common. Both Birgitta and Pedro were aristocrats with good connections, though fr. Pedro had considerably more influence through the important political role he played in the kingdom of Aragon. Catherine early on acquired supporters in the shape of her "famiglia" and Raymond of Capua, and was even officially summoned to popes to serve as a consultant. Their revelations, at least as far as they related to specific political events and agendas, were relatively straightforward command visions and auditions that authorized their attempts at intervention in the events of their time. Thus, however forceful and urgent their revelations were, there were no dramatic apocalyptic visions of the "wrong" pope as there were for Constance de Rabastens.

Constance de Rabastens provides an extremely interesting counterpoint to our more famous visionaries. Nothing is known about her lineage or family; all we know is that this woman from Rabastens, a small town about halfway between Toulouse and Albi, had dramatic visions between 1384 and 1386. Like her illustrious predecessors encountered in the previous chapter, she attempted to influence the politics of her era by supporting, through her revelations, the Roman pope—although her region was Clementist. But it is worth remembering that the count of Foix, whom she idolized, officially pursued a policy of neutrality similar to that of the Spanish kingdoms, though there is some evidence of arrangements with the Avignon papacy.[1] We can conjecture that perhaps Constance's focus on Gaston Fébus took into account the fact that he had declared for neither of the two rival popes and that Constance may have hoped to sway him in favor of Pope Urban VI. Her actions thus resemble those of fr. Pedro of Aragon and Catherine of Siena, but unlike these two or the humbler Marie Robine (d. 1399), about whom we shall hear more below, Constance was denied any official recognition; in fact, at one point she extracted herself from an inquisitorial interrogation only with great difficulty. Because she provides the unusual example of a simple layperson engaged in visionary activity with the end of intervening in the Schism, we shall devote considerable space to her. In the section that follows we shall explore the nature and progression of her visions (involving both *visio* and *vox*); her ideas on the Schism; her public role; her relationship to her confessor (including his preoccupation with the discernment of spirits); and finally the reasons for her failure.

"Una fembra peccadora"—a sinful woman. That is what Jesus Christ calls Constance de Rabastens in one of the later chapters (2.63) of her visions.[2] But despite this sinfulness, she receives divine visions and interprets the Scriptures for learned men, although she never learned to read them; she is called on to proclaim that the archbishop of Toulouse backs the wrong pope in the Schism and will go to hell for his wrong choice; she sees Gaston Fébus, the count of Foix, as the savior of France, and she brands the count of Armagnac another

1. See Tucoo-Chala, *Gaston Fébus,* pp. 328–30.
2. References are to section and chapter in Constance de Rabastens, *Les Révélations,* ed. Pagès and Valois. Parenthetical page references are also to this edition. Translations are my own.

Pilate. How did Constance de Rabastens arrive at this authoritative stance? What were the risks she ran? Who supported her in her daring ventures?

Constance began to have visions in 1384 when her husband was near death. In fact, her first vision was of a crowd of dead people, accompanied by the Voice—one of the most frequent manifestations of divine power in the *Révélations*—who predicts a great mortality. Shortly afterward her husband died. As in the case of Birgitta, the onset of her visions coincided with widowhood and her early forties. All the information about Constance's life emerges from the *Révélations*. Unlike Marie Robine, she left no traces in the works of other authors, nor are there any other documents mentioning her. The few facts we learn are that she had a daughter (2.15) and a son who was a Benedictine monk in Toulouse (2.20), that she lost her husband (2.1 and 2.2), and that at one point she was in prison.[3] Furthermore, her interactions with her confessor, some lords of the region, and the authorities in Toulouse can be pieced together from various passages in the *Révélations*.

This collection of visions, put together by her confessor and preserved only in a Catalan translation in Bibliothèque nationale de France (BnF), MS lat. 5055, is the only vernacular text in a manuscript containing a large variety of Latin pieces.[4] We do not know whether the language of the original was Latin or Provençal; the writing indicates the fourteenth century and the area of Rousillon (then part of Aragon), according to one of the editors (p. 242). We can speculate that perhaps a Catalan translation was made of the text so that it could circulate in the eastern part of Aragon (still engaged in the famous "indiferencia" toward both popes), where just a few years earlier fr. Pedro had been a great propagandist for Pope Urban.

The dossier consists of a preface; a long series of visions as recounted by Constance to her confessor, Raimond de Sabanac (probably a law professor from Toulouse); another series of visions transmitted to Raimond by Constance's son; and finally six letters from Constance to the inquisitor in Toulouse, probably written for her by that same son.[5]

3. This fact is mentioned not in the text of her revelations but in a heading to part 3 in the manuscript, which indicates that the revelations following were transmitted by Constance's son to her confessor "quant ella fo encarcerada" (when she was incarcerated). *Révélations*, p. 273.

4. This manuscript is interesting because it is extremely messy and even torn in several places—except for the folios that contain Constance's revelations (fols. 35r to 58r), which are beautifully written and clean. The fifteen texts in this manuscript include treatises by Flavius Josephus, Anselm, Seneca, and Augustine as well as an anatomical treatise and a poem in hexameters on games.

5. *Révélations*, pp. 242–43. I have not been able to find any evidence that Raymond was employed by the count of Foix, as suggested by Tanz, *Spätmittelalterliche Laienmentalitäten*, p. 187. Tanz deals with Constance on pp. 179–91.

The *Révélations* begins with an extensive preface in which Raimond shows his awareness of the contemporary concern with the discernment of spirits.[6] He places Constance squarely within orthodoxy by insisting that her virtues of obedience and humility clearly put her into the safe area of those who receive authorized visions. He assures his readers that his examination of Constance covered all the elements of the discernment procedure in order to avoid "perilous error" (perillosa error; p. 250). This procedure involves not only an examination of the person's virtues but also consideration of a person's visions in view of the Augustinian distinction between corporeal, imaginative, spiritual, and intellectual visions. Furthermore, one must determine whether a vision is in accord with the Scriptures or "whether it shows some monstrous thing or something excessive and unheard of in nature" (si demostra alcuna cosa mostruosa o superflua en natura e novella; p. 250). True visions must also induce good moral behavior. Clearly, for Raimond, Constance's revelations meet all these criteria.

Seen as a whole, Constance's visions cover a most interesting trajectory from a personal experience of Christ, focusing on her sinfulness and need for penance as well as on her intimate identification with Christ's pain, to a rather well defined and urgent political mission. Constance's visions begin on a personal note, and nothing in her early revelatory experiences prepares us for the strong political stance she will adopt later on. Her earliest visions are tailored to her situation just before and after her husband's death. Thus, the Voice reassures her: "Do not fall into doubt, but know that you will raise your children well and that you will abandon the world" (No duptes, car sapies que a tos infans daras bon recapte, e tu lo mon lexaras; p. 251). One time she feels a great illness coming on, but it disappears when the Voice pronounces her healed (2.4). Then Christ appears to her as a man dressed in satin and assures her that He is in her heart, "for your body was in pain and did penance" (car lo cors esta en dolor e fa penitencia; p. 252).

The next few visions show her to be the opposite of the whited sepulcher: a young man shows her an old, rotten traveling trunk and tells her that this is her body from the outside but that penance has made the interior beautiful (2.9). The sexual temptations she had endured for thirteen months—her presence had reduced a novice Franciscan to virtual hysterics—finally come to an end when six paupers appear to her and identify themselves as angels, assuring her that the sexual temptations are now over. And indeed, she no longer feels anything; it is "as if [she] were dead" (com si fos morta; p. 253).

---

6. I translate and comment on this preface in my forthcoming "The Discernment of Spirits." For a detailed study of this procedure, see Elliott, *Proving Woman,* esp. part 3, and for a history and study, see Caciola, *Discerning Spirits.*

At this point the scope of her visions widens. She sees the Last Judgment (2.13–14), the heavens open with a huge fruit tree in the middle, and twenty-four aged men sitting on clouds being serenaded by a children's choir (2.16). The Voice then presents the Book of Revelation to her, a book of which she had never heard before. When she asks her confessor about it, he shows it to her and makes her look at it closely, and she is "most amazed and frightened" (molt maravellade e spaventada; p. 256). Paradoxically, it is after this bookish vision, giving a scriptural base to and thus authorization of what is to come, that Constance begins to be particularly troubled: she wonders again and again whether the visions are truly from God (2.19) and finally decides to go to Toulouse in order to ask Raimond to consult the inquisitor (2.20). A strict interdict against writing down or revealing her visions follows in a letter by Guillaume de Luc, a master of the archbishop's entourage, on January 31, 1384. And indeed, Raimond, for a time at least, refuses to transcribe any further visions.

This trip to Toulouse is clearly a turning point for Constance. By leaving the limited area of Rabastens, she makes herself known to the ecclesiastical authorities who now become aware of her visionary activities. And although the most explicit political visions appear only later in the collection, she seems to be considered a threat.[7] Despite Guillaume's prohibition, Raimond eventually resumes his recording of Constance's revelations after having been struck by an illness that the Voice identifies as a sign from God (2.21–22). The Voice now urges an increasingly public role on Constance and begins to define her political mission by issuing an unambiguous order to write: "Write the things I reveal to you, for it is necessary to the people that you should write . . . for in no time was there as much evil as there will be presently" (Scriu les coses que jot revel, car necessari es al poble que scrives . . . e null temps no foren tants de mals com are seran; p. 257). The Voice then commands her to send a letter to the King's Council in Toulouse denouncing the support of the pope at Avignon and the activities of the count of Armagnac vis-à-vis the English as treachery (2.23–24).

Let us look in some detail at the terms and images she uses in these denunciations. The French cardinals who elected Clement VII are compared to false prophets (p. 261) who "know well that the election of the pope of Avignon was done against my will and is false" (saben be que eleccio de Papa de Vinyo es feta avolment e falsa; p. 265). To counteract them "the red beast, that is, the pope of Rome, will rise, of whom John had spoken in his book of Revelation, and the color red signifies the fire of justice with which he will destroy them" (levarsa la bestia roja, ço es la Papa de Roma del qual John havia parlat en lo

---

7. The manuscript was put together by a later compiler, and we cannot be completely sure of the order of the visions. Only some indicate dates, as do the letters.

libre de revelacions, e la rojor significa foch de justicia ab la qual los destrohiria; p. 265). It is disconcerting that Constance equates her beloved Roman pope with Saint John's red beast of Revelation 12:3, since a few verses later John explicitly identifies the red dragon as "Devil and Satan" (Rev. 12:9).[8] Here we have to ask how well Constance knew the biblical text. Perhaps she was fixated on the color red as the color of justice and simply omitted any reference to Revelation 12:9 in order to make her point. We shall see below that she repeats the equation between the Roman pope and the red beast—she is clearly not bothered by the inconsistency of designating Pope Urban as a beast representing Satan.

Continuing her anti-Clementine polemic in 3.2 she designates the Avignon cardinals as "anticardonals" (anticardinals) who surround their "antipapa" (p. 273). Constance presents this pope in a variety of unpleasant contexts: "I saw a temple full of smoke and darkness, and the pope of Avignon was inside" (veya un temple tot ple de fum et de scuredat, e lo Papa de Vinyo era dedins; 2.48, p. 267). Smoke as an image for the corrupted papacy also appears in other contemporary texts, notably in Honoré Bovet's prologue to his *Arbre des batailles* (Tree of battles; see my Chapter 5), an exegesis of the biblical Book of Revelation in the context of the history of schisms and particularly the Great Schism. Here the smoke rising from the apocalyptic abyss envelops Pope Urban VI, who is thus designated as the illegitimate pope. Each visionary, whether of a poetic or a more mystical persuasion, thus uses identical imagery for each of the opposing popes.

Somewhat later Constance sees three ships, of which two signify the world and one the church. A limping man enters the ship of the church and instantly makes it sink to the bottom of the sea: "This limping man who has entered it represents the pope of Avignon . . . and he will be thrown into hell" (aquell ranch qui es entrat significa lo Papa de Vinyo . . . ell sera cabuçat en infern; p. 269).[9] Constance, though apparently unlearned, here inscribes her visions into the long tradition of representing the church as a ship. A similar image is used by Nicolas de Clamanges (ca. 1363–1437), a famous humanist and papal official in Avignon who exhorted the newly elected Benedict XIII in a letter of 1394 to be a better "captain" of the ship of the church than Clement VII had been. Christopher M. Bellitto observes: "He indicted Clement as a sleeping captain who did not look to the safety of his ship, blaming him and his crew for

8. The same red dragon is used as a negative image of Pope Urban in some of the *Vaticinia* manuscripts. See Chapter 6 and fig. 6.
9. Clement VII actually limped. See the description of Robert of Geneva, the future Clement VII, by Valois: "Jeune, un peu boiteux, un peu louche, doué pourtant d'une stature et d'une figure avantageuses." He was multilingual and a good writer (*La France,* 1:81).

the Church's division. Lacking a leader, the Church was tossed by a storm and threatened by deluge or shipwreck."[10] It is interesting that the imagery of endangering or even sinking the ship of the church used here comes from "opposite sides" on the papal divide: Constance's pro-Roman stance makes her see Clement VII as a nefarious personage who destroys the church, while the pro-Avignon Clamanges uses a similar image to exhort Benedict XIII to be a better leader than Clement and perhaps bring about the union of the church.

Pope Clement is further accused by Constance of wanting to dominate the whole world (2.53) and is compared to a leper who makes others perish by spreading out before them contaminated treasures (2.51); an angel holds a bloody sword above him as if he was about to kill him (4.1). We can observe here striking differences with Catherine and Pedro's argumentation against Pope Clement, which was based on accounts of the legitimate election of Urban and of the behavior of the cardinals and thus appealed to their audience's rationality. Neither of them had visions like Constance's in which the illegitimacy of Pope Clement was dramatized in a variety of horrific images and thus proven beyond any doubt.

Another target of Constance's wrath is the late bishop of Autun, Pierre de la Barrière (d. 1383), who had refused an appointment as cardinal from Pope Urban but then accepted one from Clement. In 1379 he wrote, for Charles V, a treatise in favor of Pope Clement, refuting de Legnano's pro-Urban *De fletu ecclesiae* (On the tears of the church).[11] For Constance (but not for Raimond, who is aghast at these accusations), this prelate sows perilous errors (2.23) and, when she sees him with three other cardinals in hell, he is as black as coal (4.4.). His first name (Pierre = stone) signifies the barren places where no good seeds can take hold; his last name stands for the barrier he has erected between Christ and himself (4.4). This negative depiction of the bishop of Autun stands in sharp contrast to what the *Grandes Chroniques de France* and those who knew him say about him—namely, that he was a greatly learned man, wise and prudent, someone who could not get his fill of learning.[12] In other sources there is no suggestion of a diabolical nature of this bishop. How could Constance know about this cleric and see him so negatively? We can only surmise that someone must have mentioned his anti-Urban treatise to her, and maybe even his refusal of Urban's offer of a cardinal's hat. Because Constance translates both "Pierre" and "de la Barrière" into suggestive metaphors expressing his stance of opposing everything she embraces, she may also have singled him out

---

10. Bellitto, *Nicolas de Clamanges,* p. 54.
11. See Valois, *La France,* 1:131. The treatise is printed in Du Boulay, *Historia,* 4:529–55.
12. See the introduction to Constance de Rabastens, *Révélations,* pp. 245–46.

for his evocative name. In any case, the strong and colorful images attached to the bishop of Autun leave no doubt about the nature of her political mission.

This new focus of Constance's visions thus marks the decisive transition from the private to the public sphere. Given the strong support of the French king and bishops for Clement VII of Avignon, this new development is nothing short of stunning.

Turning toward the form Constance's visions take, we see that some of them, particularly (but not only) the early ones, are primarily visual, perhaps inspired by some of the art in her local church. Thus, the Tree of Life she sees in 2.16 resembles a four-meter-high tree in a fresco in the Chapel of Saint Martin in the Church of Notre-Dame du Bourg in Rabastens; the Christ in majesty who descends from the cross in order to beat a group of women (2.61) seems to bear a strong resemblance to a fresco showing the crucified Christ surrounded by a crowd of men and women in the Saint James Chapel of that same church.[13] But while some of these visual details can be explained by visits to the Church of Notre-Dame, we would be hard-pressed to find the origin of the increasingly urgent and powerful commands of the Voice, particularly since we know nothing of Constance's education or background.

The most specifically political communications from Christ are, as they were for Birgitta and Pedro, of an auditory nature. Constance is urged to speak for Christ to the people and prelates alike. This function of speaking for the divine authority may explain why auditory experiences dominate in this context and were especially important for women: instead of interpreting a possibly complicated or even ambiguous vision, the Voices heard by these visionaries provided them with a ready-made script for their public performances. The risks involved in these performances were manifold. Janette Dillon points out: "Women who spoke with the voice of God, especially from outside the walls of a convent, challenged the authority of the clerical establishment even as they sought it. Though they needed the support of respected confessors and the orthodox church, their authority to speak, if it was established as divinely inspired, superseded the very authority that validated it."[14] In other words, with this kind of public activity comes risk, and with the revelation of God's will to the pope and the prelates comes the possibility that their view of God's will might differ considerably from that of the visionary, as is the case for Constance. In addition, she was not of the stature of Catherine of Siena, whose support group, the Bella Brigata, was numerous and persuasive (although even

---

13. For illustrations of this church and its artwork, see Hiver-Bérenguier, *Constance de Rabastens*, figs. 4–12; the Tree of Life appears in fig. 10, Christ on the cross in fig. 11.

14. Dillon, "Holy Women and Their Confessors," p. 128.

Catherine, who supported the Roman pope in Italy—a noncontroversial political stance—had her detractors). Nor was Constance as well connected as Birgitta of Sweden, whose aristocratic origins allowed her to speak to popes and
kings on a level close to that of social equality. Constance ran graver risks, and
she paid the price.

After Guillaume de Luc's intervention Constance's visions become increasingly complex and feature more and more proofs of authenticity to counteract
the growing unorthodoxy of her revelations. In 2.26 the Voice tells her that she
has been elected to transmit these important messages, not only the messages
concerning the Great Schism but also an exhortation addressed to Gaston
Fébus, the count of Foix and a great patron of Froissart, to counteract the
treacherous behavior of this second Pilate, the count of Armagnac, who refuses
to recognize not only Jesus Christ but also the "young tree," Charles VI of
France. After putting the right pope on the throne and destroying Armagnac,
Gaston Fébus will undertake a crusade to avenge the death of Jesus Christ. We
saw above that a crusade, in addition to the return of the pope to Rome and the
establishment of peace in Europe, was also part of Catherine of Siena's agenda.
Philippe de Mézières, as well, advocated, in his *Letter to King Richard II* of 1395,
a crusade as a remedy for the Great Schism because such an enterprise would
reestablish unity within the church.[15]

But there are more connections among the political allegories we treat in
Chapters 4 and 5 and Constance's visions. Indeed, although a theme of
unlearnedness runs through Constance's *Révélations,* she inscribes herself here
in a very learned tradition represented by such contemporary writers as
Eustache Deschamps and Philippe de Mézières. Reminiscent of de Mézières's
techniques is the brief allegory that presents the count of Foix as "the crane
with the crimson head . . . who will lift up the just man, that is, the Roman
pope, and will put him on his seat" (la grua ab lo cap vermell . . . qui lavera
l'ome just, ço es lo Papa de Romae metral en sa Seu; p. 258). We have to assume
that the Voice is speaking of the Languedoc region, for, to all intents and purposes, a number of countries believed that the Roman pope did already sit in
his seat. The image of Charles VI as a sapling (arbre jove; p. 258) who will be
the target of the apostate count of Armagnac could equally well come from a
text like Philippe de Mézières's somewhat later *Letter to King Richard II* or
Christine de Pizan's *Vision* of 1405. Of course, as Barbara Newman has
observed, mystics often professed unlearnedness to "emphasize that the source
of [their] revelations was divine, not human."[16] At no point does Constance

15. See Chapter 4, section on Philippe de Mézières.
16. Newman, "Sibyl of the Rhine," p. 7.

indicate that she did any particular reading; in fact, any literacy she admits to seems to be of miraculous origin, as had been claimed for Catherine of Siena.[17] Like other unlearned mystics, Constance is Christ's apprentice when it comes to understanding and even interpreting the Scriptures, though it is not clear whether she can ever read while Christ is absent.

Nonetheless, in 2.63 Christ says explicitly that she should explain the Scriptures to learned church men: "And it is a great miracle that a sinful woman such as you explains to them the Holy Scriptures, something which you have never learned" (e gran miracle es que una fembra peccadora, axi com tu est, los declares les santes scriptures, e que null temps non hajes après; p. 273). Any literacy and learnedness that Constance can lay claim to is presented in the *Révélations* as given directly by Christ or the Voice. How the learned church men would have reacted to Constance's interpretive lessons is of course another question.

Constance does indeed hesitate to transmit all these important messages, because, as she claims, she is an unworthy sinner, but the Voice insists that she should do so. A striking example is 2.23, where the Voice tells her—while she is "ravished" (en ravissement)—that the letter she must send to Toulouse concerning "the betrayal" (that is, the support of Pope Clement VII), should be written "just as you have seen" (axi com vist; p. 257). And what she saw was the election of the "just man" who is the true pope. Since Constance was probably illiterate, the technique of transcription envisaged her by the Voice is extremely interesting. She "saw" the true election and now has the power to transcribe it in the letter to the archbishop of Toulouse.

It is significant that Constance was consulted by the powerful men of her time, as had Birgitta and Catherine. Interspersed throughout Constance's visions we find numerous instances of official queries addressed to her, a proof of her growing presence in the public arena. In 2.31, for example, a baron of the Bordelais asks her about a group of Saracens who came to France looking for some sort of treasure. Constance quickly informs him that the Saracens are the disciples of the Antichrist who seek to defeat the Christians. Another instance demonstrates the strength of her political views and of her language. A clerk wants to know from her whether the death of the duke of Anjou in 1384 is advantageous for the cause of the church.[18] She consults the Voice, which tells

17. See par. 881 of the *Vita*.
18. The duke of Anjou, a brother of the French king Charles V (and also a recipient of letters by Catherine of Siena, for whom he was a kind of savior figure and future crusader) was the regent during Charles VI's (1368–1422) minority and had hoped to obtain the kingdom of Naples with the help of Clement VII. See Denis-Boulet, *La carrière politique*, pp. 121–25, for details of Catherine and the duke of Anjou in relation to the projected crusade.

her to respond as follows (using the same image of the red beast of the Apocalypse we briefly considered above):

> You will answer that he who carried the sign of the beast is dead,
> namely the duke of Anjou. As for the church, tell him that the time of
> the evil beast has arrived of which John spoke in the Book of Revela-
> tion where he (also) saw a red beast, that is, the Pope of Rome. And
> the evil beast will not be so well hidden in the close that it cannot be
> found.

> [Tu respondras que mort es aquell que portave lo senyal dela bestia,
> ço es lo duch d'Enjou; de la Esgleya, digues que temps es que la mala
> bestia de que Johan havia parlat en lo libro de revelacions que vahe
> una bestia roja, ço es lo Papa de Roma, e no sera tant amagada la mala
> bestia en la closa que no sia trobada.] (p. 266)

Here Constance interprets the Schism in terms of Revelation 12:3, likening
Pope Urban, "the just man who is the true pope" (home just qui es vertader
Papa; p. 257), to Saint John's red dragon—the rather curious equation for the
pro-Roman Constance we encountered above.

The next chapter (2.46), in an interesting twist, tells of a letter sent to her by
a great lord who wants to know who the true pope is and whether the Schism
and the Hundred Years War will last much longer. Her answer is at first star-
tling: she does not occupy herself with questions like these. But this is
explained a moment later when it turns out that the letter was a trap set for her
by the bishop of Narbonne, who may have tried to trick her into expressing
compromising or even heretical views. The Voice exhorts her to respond
obscurely to an obscure letter ("car ell t'a scrit scur, yo vull que tu li scrives
scur"; p. 267), and so she makes vague predictions (no one knows when the
Schism will end; the war will end when the "bad herbs" are torn out from
French soil . . .).

When we consider some of her specific predictions we see that the most
precise ones, described above, deal with Gaston Fébus.[19] But not one of these
noble aspirations ever comes true. In fact, there is only one prophecy that
could be seen as fulfilled, the one in which, in 1385, she seems to predict the
madness of Charles VI, which begins to manifest itself in 1392: "Write in red
letters that the world will only last another seven years and that in seven years

---

19. Tanz points out that Constance completely misconstrued the political roles of Jean of Armagnac and Gaston Fébus. See *Spätmittelalterliche Laienmentalitäten*, pp. 186–87.

in the kingdom of France there will be great disorder, that is, an overthrow, for it supports the pope of Avignon" (Scriu ab letres vermelles que lo mon ha sino .VII. e per .VII. lo realme de France vendra a gran percussio, abatiment ço es, car soste lo Papa d'Avinyo; p. 263). Thus, while she on the one hand supports Charles VI, the "young tree" of vision 2.26, she also sends out a warning— continued support of the "wrong" pope will result in great calamities—thus highlighting the centrality of the Schism in her consciousness. How great the calamities would be that would engulf France years later not even Constance could have imagined.

As Constance's voice becomes more and more public and insistent, her confessor becomes increasingly timid and for a time refuses to transcribe her visions. Even though she is being consulted as a visionary by some lords of the region, as we just saw, Raimond sees the writing on the wall in the form of Guillaume de Luc's letter forbidding further revelations and their transcription. Recent studies have shown how important and sometimes ambivalent the relationship between a saintly woman and her confessor can be.[20] Male confessors and biographers found in these women an otherness that indicated the presence of the divine and that would allow them a more direct access to God. The women, for their part, needed the confessors to legitimate their visions and to help them record and disseminate them. Thus, Raymond of Capua both supported and was dominated by Catherine of Siena; he was the one who created a "partnership" between the saint's charisma and the ecclesiastical authorities.[21] And although even women like Birgitta were not without critics and detractors, her prompt canonization validated her supporters' efforts.

Raimond de Sabanac found himself in a different position. Constance was not a religious, nor had she the support of the kind of *famiglia* or *bella brigata* surrounding Catherine of Siena. Although, on the one hand, she was consulted by various highly placed people, she was, on the other hand, also accused of being crazy: "She was told that certain estimable people had called her mad" (hom li recomta que algunes gents d'estament la havien apellada folla; pp. 265–66), and there were even people who "say that I have the devil in my body" (dien que yo he lo demoni al cors; p. 268). These accusations, testifying also to the public's knowledge of her visionary activities, may explain Raimond's ambivalence about his function as the recorder of Constance's visions. Even after a particularly powerful vision (2.32)—in which the Voice qualifies her prayers as more efficacious than those of Abraham and in which she

20. See Coakley, "Friars as Confidants"; Kleinberg, *Prophets;* and Mooney, ed., *Gendered Voices,* for numerous case studies.
21. Coakley, "Friars," p. 234.

becomes Christ-like by offering to take upon herself the suffering of this world (provided it does not last forever!)—Raimond seems to delay as long as he can before writing anything down. And somewhat later (2.56) he describes how he asked God for a sign whether he should write or not, such as taking away his eyesight. And indeed, God takes away his eyesight to such a degree "that I could only see with my glasses on!" (que no podia veura sino ab ulleres; p. 270). Constance herself is aware of Raimond's conflicts, for one day after mass she complains to the Lord: "Lord, what should I do, and who will give me faith if even my confessor doubts the things I say?" (Senyor, que fare yo ne qui deu donar fe, e mon confessor ja dupte en les coses que yo dich? pp. 270–71). The Voice then predicts that just as He, Christ, left Mary in desolation, so she will be left, but that her torments will be the proof of Christ's power. Since Raimond transcribed Constance's visions and words (including this paragraph, we must assume) he was well aware of the doubts wracking the woman in his charge.

Indeed, Raimond's reluctance to write is echoed by the many instances in which Constance articulates the problems of finding an authority for her unlearned and sinful voice. A striking example is 2.50, where the Voice commands Constance to write the things she has seen and proclaim to the archbishops and the prelates the humiliation awaiting the unhappy ones. Constance objects that no one will believe her and that, as we saw in the passage quoted above, people will claim that she is possessed by a demon. Christ now exhorts her to *imitatio:* she must endure almost everything he has endured, he tells her, and adds that people said of him as well that he was possessed by a demon. She must nevertheless proclaim the truth to prelates and priests and "who has ears will hear" (qui ha orelles o entena; p. 268). Despite this clear prophetic mission, Constance continues to be accused of error: "Know that great rumors are circulating against you through false testimonies that accuse you" (Sapies que gran brugit se leva contra tu per falsos testimonios quit acusen; p. 269). Again the Voice reassures her and predicts the sudden death and prompt dispatch to hell of Clement VII. No wonder, then, that "my confessor does not want to write them [the visions] down" (mon confessor no les vol scriure; p. 275), as she complains in a letter to the inquisitor in Toulouse.

These letters were written at the moment early on in her visionary career (1384) when Raimond would write no longer for her. In these daring letters defiance struggles with a desire for safety; the urgency in her voice is extraordinary. After the formula "I humbly commend myself to your grace" (humilment me recoman a la vostra Gracia; p. 274), Constance, already quite aware of the riskiness of her proclamations, warns the inquisitor that the Voice promised divine vengeance on the city of Toulouse for any harm done to her. She insists that this threat comes not from her but from the Voice, and she says, "I believe myself to be quite exonerated from all this" (yo creu de aço esser asats scusada; p. 274). She then adds that she will abide by his counsel (p. 275). However, this submission to the inquisitor's will does not include that she will cease to have visions and to ask to have them written down. In fact, since Raimond refuses to write for her she goes so far as to ask the inquisitor to send her some secretaries who would record and disseminate her visions, "for I am commanded to pronounce them and to proclaim them loudly and to trumpet them over the high mountains" (car a mi es menat que diga, cridant aquelles, e que trompe per alts puygs; p. 277). Furthermore, she warns the inquisitor of his impending death and insists that an accurate transcript of the trial be made: "He should see that the record of the trial actually accords with the trial itself, and that God tells him that he will have to render account to Him both of the trial and the transcript" (que vege be si la relacio concorda be ab lo proces, e que Deus diu a ell quel retra raho devant ell del proces e relacio; p. 275). No transcript of the trial was ever found.

No matter how much she wants to submit to the inquisitor, Constance insists in the letters, the visions will not cease. Based on what the Voice tells her, Constance, in her fourth letter, dramatically indicts the French cardinals, singling out the above-mentioned Pierre de la Barrière, whom she sees roasting in hell "in great torments and pains" (en grans turmens e penes; p. 276). She adds that it was this vision in particular that Raimond urged her to reject. And once again she articulates her belief in the godlike Gaston Fébus, detailing his actions on behalf of the French king, his ending of the Great Schism, and his undertaking a crusade.

Why does she not keep these visions to herself? In a crucial statement she explains: "For now I receive many revelations which concern the damnation or the salvation *of the community*" (com are me sien fetes moltes revelacions les quals guarden dampnatge *o profit de la comunitat;* p. 277, my emphasis). Had the visions remained private, concerned only with her own sins and penance, she might have been ready not to prophesy publicly any longer. However, the Voice conveys powerfully to her that the well-being of her community is at stake. For this cause, she affirms—Christlike—she is as ready to die as Catherine and Pedro had been: "And be it known to you that I am ready and prepared to die for the honor of God and the salvation of the people" (E sapiats que yo son presta e apparallada morir a honor de Deu e salvacio del poble; p. 277). Was this statement prophetic? We do not know, for after 1386 nothing more is heard of her.

Why would Constance constitute such a threat to the ecclesiastical and secular authorities? Robert Cabié speculates that the very act of telling these highly placed people how to conduct their affairs may have been enough reason to silence her. Apparently, she was never accused of doctrinal errors or heresy.[22] Unfortunately we do not know whether she ever carried out any of the many missions urged on her by the Voice. Did she ever write to the archbishop of Toulouse, Jean de Cadailhac? To the royal council or the college of cardinals? Undoubtedly, as Noël Valois indicates, she severely tried the patience of the ecclesiastical authorities.[23] Her convictions were often contradictory: she blamed the French king for his campaigns in Flanders yet supported him against the treacherous count of Armagnac; in fact, she championed Charles VI, at least for the time being, despite his support for Clement VII. As for the Schism, her revelations were clear-cut: Clement VII is a demon-like figure who brings down the Ship of the Church, and salvation can be found only in adherence to Urban VI. She does not conceptualize the Schism as a political problem or as a conflict between two ambitious individuals and their followers, but rather as an apocalyptic struggle between good and evil.

The Schism Continues: Pierre de Luxembourg, Saint Vincent Ferrer, and Marie Robine, Supporters of the Avignon Popes

If fr. Pedro of Aragon was living "theological proof of Urban's legitimacy," then Pierre de Luxembourg (1369–87) was his counterpart on the Clementist side. This young scion of the powerful house of Luxembourg was a cousin of the French king Charles VI and of Pope Clement VII. He quickly became a protégé of the latter, who hoped to profit from these connections.[24] A canon at Notre Dame before he was even nine years old, he became archbishop of Metz and a cardinal at the age of fifteen.[25] The following year he was called to Avignon, and at eighteen he was dead. He was never canonized, despite multiple efforts of his supporters, but he was finally beatified in 1524.[26]

---

22. "Une mystique?" p. 51.
23. Révélations, p. 248.
24. For a brief sketch of his life and bibliography, see Hasenohr, "Pierre de Luxembourg," and Vauchez, La sainteté, pp. 354–58. For an analysis of his life and of his ascetic practices, see Kieckhefer, Unquiet Souls, pp. 33–44. For his miracles, see Prouvost, "Les miracles de Pierre de Luxembourg."
25. Metz was a city divided by the Schism. While the clerics adhered to Clement, the bourgeois were loyal to Urban. See Fourier de Bacourt, Vie, pp. 96–98.
26. See Acta sanctorum, July 1, p. 433. Pierre d'Ailly initiated the first proceedings in 1390; in 1432 a cult is attested but no canonization; another effort failed in 1433–35 under Pope Eugene IV at the Council of Basel.

Two figures, much involved in the Schism, were his mentors: Pierre d'Ailly (1350–1420), chancellor of the University of Paris from 1389 to 1395, who later worked in vain toward his canonization, and Philippe de Mézières, whom he met when Philippe, until then a very active politician, had retired to the Celestins in Paris. Philippe mentions the young Pierre together with Marie Robine in his *Songe du Vieil Pelerin* as proof of Clement's rightful claim to the papal See.[27] How did Pierre come to stand for the legitimacy of the Avignon papacy? We have to distinguish two aspects. On the one hand, Pierre was used by people like Pierre d'Ailly and Pope Clement to buttress their arguments; on the other hand, he himself planned to go on a complex diplomatic mission, visiting the European rulers with the aim of ending the Schism.

Before looking at the details of his case, we have to consider that after the Council of Constance Pierre's role could well be seen as that of a supporter of the antipope, as someone whose saintliness has to be reconciled with his misguidedness. Thus, we find in the *Acta sanctorum* for July 2 a long commentary that precedes the *Vita prima* and the *Vita altera* as well as the (unsuccessful) canonization proceedings. Supported by the annalists Baronius and Raynaldus, the author here inculpates Pierre by adducing his youth and consequent ignorance, which made him incapable of discerning who was the right pope. Furthermore, because a number of countries and learned men also adhered to Pope Clement, this preface states, Pierre cannot be blamed. He died among pseudo-cardinals (inter pseudocardinales) with the antipope, whom he believed to be the true pope, just like Vincent Ferrer, who venerated the antipope Pedro de Luna in error (p. 447). In view of the ways that the Avignon papacy exploited this poor young man, these later judgments are extremely revealing.

Richard Kieckhefer has painted a sympathetic portrait of Pierre, describing his love of peace, his extraordinary piety, and his asceticism. Like Petrarch, Pierre was shocked by the "immorality of Avignon . . . and made efforts to escape."[28] But the temptation to flee the papal court to become a hermit was short-lived. A witness at the canonization trial stated that Pierre had already secretly procured for himself the keys to a city gate when he was dissuaded by his confessor, who told him that the "schismatics would be overjoyed and would say that he (Pierre) left because he believed that our lord Pope Clement was not the true pope."[29]

27. See below, Chapter 4, section on the *Songe du Vieil Pelerin*. See also Jorga, *Philippe de Mézières*, pp. 460–62 on their relationship.
28. Kieckhefer, *Unquiet Souls*, p. 39.
29. *Acta sanctorum*, July 1, p. 483. Parenthetical references are to this text.

As for Pierre's own attitude toward the Schism, we have no writings of his own in this context (though he did author a devotional *Livret*), but only what the contemporary author of his *Vita* tells us. It seems clear that the Schism was one of his major preoccupations, because he "wanted to inform himself about the Schism with the help of learned men" (p. 452) and was willing, like his saintly counterparts on the opposing side, to become a martyr for the peace of the church. His mission was to take the form of a journey to the emperor as well as to the kings of England and France in order to bring peace between France and England and to effect a reduction in taxes that impoverished the common people.[30] But the most important task was to bring an end to the "detestable Schism that reigns in the church" (p. 452). Though he had already determined his itinerary, he died before he could bring this project to fruition.

But even after his death Pierre was exploited for Avignonese propaganda. Michel Pintoin, the chronicler of Saint-Denis, records his death in devout and almost tender terms, stressing that Pierre's piety, chastity, and generosity made it seem as if he lived in heaven even while still living on this earth. Pintoin also mentions the many miracles that occurred at his tomb.[31] His saintly death and the subsequent miracles become the instruments in Pierre's posthumous function as the poster child for Clement VII and later for Benedict XIII. But Pierre could also be appealed to as arbiter in the Schism; in June 1395, for example, when the French dukes came to Avignon to hold Benedict to his promise to abdicate (he preferred calling a council), they also laid the foundation stone for the Celestin convent meant to be Pierre's last resting place. On that occasion, one of the Paris theologians suggested putting a writ with the two possibilities of abdication and council next to Pierre's body in the hope that a miracle on Pierre's part would endorse the first choice![32]

Pope Clement VII prayed at Pierre's deathbed that "this blessed soul will appease the wrath of God and will bring about peace in the church."[33] But this peace remained elusive, and the continuing division of the church combined

---

30. See Fourier de Bacourt, *Vie*, pp. 188–91.

31. *Chronique du religieux de Saint-Denys*, 1:478. In the *Vita* his biographer urges the Urbanists to turn to Clement because such miracles took place in Avignon and, as Valois puts it (based on Baluze, *Vitae paparum* 1, col. 515), Clement's power was much consolidated by these events (*La France*, 2:365).

32. Valois, *La France*, 3:59. The location of the convent, outside the city walls—that is, at a distance from Benedict's papal palace—underlines Pierre's posthumous alienation from the "irreverent" Benedict, who, unlike Clement VII, does not "heed France." See Rollo-Koster, "Politics of Body Parts: Contested Topographies," p. 90.

33. Fourier de Bacourt, *Vie*, p. 209. Pierre d'Ailly makes the same point in his request for Pierre's canonization. See "Collatio M. Petri de Alliaco pro Apotheosi Petri de Luxemburgo," in Du Boulay, *Historia*, 4:651–62, esp. p. 661.

with the Turkish threat distracted Clement from the petition for Pierre's canonization made by Marie de Bretagne and presented by Pierre d'Ailly. In terms
of Avignonese propaganda the most important function of the miracles at
Pierre's tomb—in addition to proof of his sanctity—was to prove the Avignon
pope's legitimacy.[34] On his own deathbed on September 16, 1394, Pope Clement
is said to have cried out for Pierre's help: "Oh, oh! Luxemburg, I pray you that
you may help me" (Ha! Ha! Luxembourg ie te prie que tu me vueille ayder).[35] It
is significant that, from among all possible saints Clement could have invoked
at this critical moment, the pope chose Pierre, from whose sanctity he had
expected so much, both for himself and for the Avignon papacy.

The intricate links between papal legitimization and sanctity are played out
to perfection in this story.[36] Even though Pierre's own ambitions were directed
at ending the Schism, he became a tool in the propaganda war between the two
papacies, legitimizing one over the other. Dead, even more than when he was
alive, he was used by the Avignon pope and his adherents to give the same kind
of saintly support to their side that Pope Urban enjoyed through such personages as fr. Pedro of Aragon and Catherine of Siena.

Another saintly personage who dedicated a good part of his life to supporting Benedict XIII was Saint Vincent Ferrer. Born in 1350 in Valencia, he
became a Dominican friar in 1368 and eventually the confessor to the Avignon
pope. He had accompanied Pedro de Luna on his mission to convince the
Spanish kings to adhere to Clement VII, thus establishing a loyalty to the Avignon papacy that was to last until three years before his death. In 1380 he wrote
a forceful treatise, *De moderno Ecclesiae schismate* (On the modern schism of
the church), making the case against Urban and for Clement. He left Avignon
in 1399, died in Brittany in 1419, and was canonized in 1455. His complex life
was dominated by itinerant preaching in various parts of Europe as well as by a
prolific literary production. Vincent deserves a new biography of his own,[37] but
here we shall look only at one brief but crucial visionary episode that caused
him to abandon the papal court and spend the next twenty years on the road as
a charismatic preacher.

34. Robert Gervais writes in his Schism tract that the miracles of Pierre de Luxembourg had the
    express purpose of confirming Clement's merits and the efficacy of his prayers. The logical
    conclusion: *Igitur adherere et obedire domino Clementi septimo non est error* (in Baluze, *Vitae
    paparum* 2, col. 835).
35. Du Boulay, *Historia*, 4:953.
36. For a later case of the exploitation of Pierre's sanctity by the Avignon cardinals against Bene-
    dict XIII in 1401, see Rollo-Koster, "Politics of Body Parts: Contested Topographies,"
    pp. 89–90.
37. Philip Daileader is currently working on a biography tentatively entitled *Saint Vincent Ferrer,
    1350–1419: Apostle of Europe.*

Vincent's 1380 treatise on the Schism was composed in a sober scholastic tone, explicitly eschewing, as Roberto Rusconi argues, a prophetic voice, most likely because of his belief that the risk of false prophets is greater in a time that could see the coming of the Antichrist.[38] Although the Antichrist theme is already present here, it is not central. It is in Vincent's later sermons that the imminent arrival of the Antichrist becomes more and more important, mostly linked to a general moral reform that could still avert the reign of the Antichrist. In 1380, then, Vincent was convinced of Clement VII's legitimacy. Ending the Schism was up to the Roman pope, whose election Vincent presented as illegitimate. But as the years progressed, Vincent's attitude changed. From an ardent supporter of Clement's successor Benedict XIII, Vincent slowly became a fighter to end the Schism.

Vincent's *Vita*,[39] written in 1455–56 by the Sicilian Dominican Pietro Ranzano and based on the far-flung canonization inquiries of the preceding years, gives a prominent place to Vincent's efforts directed at healing the church. Indeed, the very first chapter is entitled "Labores in schismate Ecclesiae" (His labors on behalf of the Schism in the church). Ranzano underlines his diplomatic forays to the kings of France and Spain and the emperor Sigismund. Here he speaks about a later period in Vincent's life, since he mentions the post-Pisan three popes and the emperor Sigismund, who came to power in 1411. According to Ranzano, Vincent's anguish about ending the Schism induced a severe illness, from which he was cured by a vision. This vision, linked by the hagiographer to the reunification of the church,[40] actually took place in October 1398 and was reported by Vincent to Benedict XIII in a letter of 1412 in which he refers to himself as *dictus* or *iste Religiosus* (this monk). However, the context was not the end of the Schism; rather, Vincent adduced this vision as proof that what Saints Dominic and Francis later told him about the coming of the Antichrist was as true as their curing him of his illness back in 1398.[41]

---

38. See Rusconi, *L'attesa della fine*, p. 228. The biblical citations about false prophets come from Matt. 24:24 and 1 Tim. 4:1–2.

39. In *Acta sanctorum*, April 1. On Ranzano's reshaping of Vincent's *Vita*, especially in relation to the miracle of the chopped-up baby, see Smoller, "Saint Vincent Ferrer and the Case of the Chopped-Up Baby." Smoller argues that the baby represents the church made whole again by Saint Vincent. Fages makes a similar point in *Histoire*, 2:55. He calls this miracle "une parabole sinistre de l'Eglise déchirée."

40. See Ranzanus, *Vita*, 1.4: "Ex hac corporis aegritudine et mentis angustia te liberabo: cito enim pax Ecclesia reddita." On the iconography of this vision and Vincent's eventual dissociation from Benedict XIII in images, see Rusconi, "Vicent Ferrer e Pedro de Luna."

41. This letter is edited in Fages, *Notes et documents*. For Brettle, the church-political crisis of the Schism had a direct negative influence on Vincent's emotional life, and the deep contradictions in Vincent's nature can be attributed to the Schism (*San Vicente Ferrer*, pp. 47, 196). On the letter, see also Rusconi, *L'attesa della fine*, pp. 228–30.

While lying on his sickbed, Vincent had seen appearing to him Christ, flanked by the two saints, who proceeded to caress his cheek and urge him to go on a preaching mission. Inspired by Saints Francis and Dominic, Vincent was to announce the imminent arrival of the Antichrist and move people to repentance. Thus, although Vincent did not explicitly renounce Benedict XIII until 1416, he left the papal court in 1399, despite the pope's efforts to retain him, rejecting (as Pierre de Luxembourg would have liked to) offers of becoming a bishop or even cardinal (*Vita*, 1.5). Instead he became a second Moses or John the Baptist, as he stated in his letter, and went off on his apostolic mission.

Though Vincent himself does not place this vision and its result in the context of the Schism, his hagiographer, as we saw, suggests that his illness was caused by anguish over the division of the church. The timing of both illness and cure is extremely significant: just three months after the French withdrawal of obedience, which undermined Benedict's authority and legitimacy. Vincent's abandonment of Avignon, motivated by the vision described in his letter, signifies his turning his back on overtly political activism linked to Benedict XIII. As Father José Garganta observes, Vincent's preaching did not explicitly concern the Schism, and thus his new apostolate marks a definite change in his attitude toward this problem. In his Schism treatise of 1380 Vincent had "indicated that one of the most serious obligations of a preacher was the proclamation of who is the true pope,"[42] a mission he now no longer subscribed to. Indeed, in the revelations underlying his preaching the Schism is not a major issue while the coming of the Antichrist is. Thus, unlike some of visionaries in this chapter, Vincent does not put his visions to the polemical use of supporting one or the other faction.[43]

Sigismund Brettle suggests that Vincent changed his mind on Benedict XIII's legitimacy in the period between 1412 and 1415. Finally, in January 1416, when Ferdinand of Aragon officially withdrew obedience from Benedict XIII, Vincent publicly denounced the pope by reading the act of subtraction before an immense crowd: Benedict, among many other things, was accused of wiliness, and it was stipulated that he should no longer be allowed to disturb the peace of the church by sowing his "dragon seed."[44]

---

42. Garganta, *San Vicente Ferrer*, p. 79.
43. On this point, see Montagnes, "Prophétisme et eschatologie." See also Delaruelle, "L'Antéchrist."
44. Brettle, *San Vicente Ferrer*, pp. 62 and 65 n. 8. Brettle disagrees here with Valois, who sees Vincent as a strong supporter of Benedict XIII until Ferdinand of Aragon's withdrawal of obedience on January 6, 1416, and presents him even then as defender of the pope's legitimacy, even though pragmatic reasons led Vincent to publicly agree with the king's position. See Brettle, *San Vicente Ferrer*, p. 62, and Valois, *La France*, 4:348.

Thus, when Vincent looks back in 1412 to the decisive moment of his life in 1398, he interprets the vision as encouraging him to make a break with his former life at the papal court. We find here the opposite mechanism that we will observe in Marie Robine's life: her first recorded vision calls her *to* political involvement, while Vincent's 1398 vision turns him away from it. And unlike Pierre de Luxembourg (whose saintliness was exploited, especially after his death), Vincent, after 1398, refused to have his prophetic and visionary powers explicitly enlisted for the support of a papacy about whose legitimacy he seems to have had growing doubts.

Marie Robine at first also had no doubts about Avignon's legitimacy. Given the propagandistic use of Pierre's posthumous miraculous powers, it is fitting that this visionary, who was to become a spokeswoman for the Avignon papacy, should have been brought to Avignon by the account of these very miracles. We know from Robert Gervais's *Myrrha electa,* a book composed before 1389 with the purpose of "dissipating the stink of the Schism,"[45] that Marie "la Gasque" (that is, from Gascogne) came from the village of Héchac, today in the département des Hautes-Pyrénées, in order to seek help in Avignon. She apparently suffered from some kind of spasms that were cured at Pierre's tomb (between 1387 and 1389) in the presence of Clement VII, whose claims to legitimacy were thus greatly enhanced. It seems that Clement instantly understood the possible usefulness of this woman's support, and he, and later his successor Benedict XIII, provided handsomely for Marie.[46] Though she mostly lived as a recluse at the cemetery Saint-Michel in Avignon, she did travel to Paris in 1398 as a spokeswoman for Benedict XIII. Her revelations, undoubtedly collected by her confessor Jean, exist only in manuscript 520 of the Bibliothèque municipale of Tours (folios 115–28). This manuscript, studied by Matthew Tobin, is a most interesting collection of prophetic texts, including revelations by Hildegard of Bingen and Birgitta of Sweden, and an assortment of standard medieval prophecies, including the *Vaticinia de summis pontificibus* (Prophecies of the last popes).[47]

Her twelve known revelations trace a fascinating trajectory from an inspired eagerness to intervene in French politics on behalf of the Avignon pope to

45. Valois, "Jeanne d'Arc et la prophétie de Marie Robine," p. 453. This article contains everything known about Marie's biography. See also Tobin, "Le 'Livre des Révélations.'"
46. The bull giving her twenty-four florins for herself, the same sum for her steward, and twelve florins for her servant is edited in Valois, "Jeanne d'Arc," pp. 464–65. This money comes from the offerings made by the faithful at Pierre's tomb, and the Celestins are threatened with serious penalties by Benedict if they do not comply! (Valois, "Jeanne d'Arc," p. 455).
47. See Tobin, "Une collection." This manuscript originated at the abbey of Marmoutier. It is likely that not all her visions were recorded there. On the *Vaticinia,* see Chapter 6.

complete disillusionment. These complex revelations, received between early 1398 and her death in November 1399, touch on a variety of topics, of which one of the most important was the problem of the Schism.

Marie arrived in Avignon almost ten years before her first recorded vision. Her first revelation coincides with an extremely critical moment in the development of the relations between the French monarchy and the Avignon pope, a crisis that may have triggered her visionary activity. After Clement's death in 1394, Pedro de Luna had accepted the papacy with the promise of quick abdication (cessio) should the Roman pope, Boniface IX, also be willing. Around Pentecost 1395 the French king sent his uncles, the dukes of Berry and Burgundy, and his brother, Louis of Orléans, to Avignon to negotiate Benedict's abdication, a move decided on at a national council in Paris in early 1395. The ins and outs of this embassy, Benedict's procrastinations, and the roadblocks he threw in the ambassadors' path are recounted in lively detail by the chronicler Michel Pintoin.[48] Suffice it to say that the illustrious visitors got nowhere with the new, stubborn Spanish pope and returned to Paris with more promises but no results. The second Council of Paris in 1396 considered what kinds of pressure France could exert on Benedict and began to discuss the possibility of subtracting obedience from the Avignon pope, an action that was finally taken in July 1398.[49] It is just before this serious decision on the part of the French king that we can locate Marie Robine's first vision, which significantly took the form of a letter addressed to King Charles VI.

Marie's visions, more precisely than those of Constance de Rabastens, reflect and parallel the political situation of her time. We find a kind of visionary transposition of attitudes prevalent in learned circles and of the endless discussions and treatises produced by the theologians at the University of Paris. The first revelation (February 22, 1398), of an auditory nature, takes the form of a dictation of a letter to the French king by a divine voice. The king is exhorted to effect union in the church, but he is also cautioned "that he should not subtract obedience from the pope—that is, Benedict XIII—or allow this to be

---

48. Pintoin, *Chronique du religieux de Saint-Denys*, vol. 2, bk. 16. See also Valois, *La France*, 3:37–67. Pintoin draws mostly on the journal of Gontier Col for this account—not always correctly, according to Valois. An excellent witness to the events in Avignon is the chronicler Martin de Alpartil, who in his *Cronica* speaks of some supernatural phenomena reminiscent of some details in Marie's visions. See Rollo-Koster, "The Politics of Body Parts: Contested Topographies," pp. 84–88.

49. The intricate negotiations leading to this decision cannot be treated here. See Kaminsky, "The Politics," and his *Simon de Cramaud*. Because Louis of Orléans always supported Benedict XIII, this moment also marks the beginning of the tensions that would ultimately lead to Louis's assassination on the orders of his cousin, the duke of Burgundy, in 1407 and to the subsequent French civil war.

done" (Et caveat ne subtractionem pape, scilicet Benedicto XIII, faciat, nec eam fieri permittat; p. 248).[50] Furthermore, Charles should pursue a program of reform of the French dioceses that would consist of founding three *maisons:* one "for paupers" (pro pauperibus); one for "poor scholars" (pauperibus scolaribus), who should then teach useful knowledge to ignorant people; and one for those who will fight against the infidels (whom she sees primarily within the church) (p. 248). Needless to say, King Charles did not respond to this promising program. However, although these points are not directly related to the Schism, they are evidence of the connection between ending the Schism and reform that we saw in Catherine of Siena and of the growing "impatience of people with the Schism."[51] Indeed, throughout the Chronicle of Saint-Denis we find, especially for the years leading up to the subtraction of obedience, numerous references to the "fatal Schism, the deadly scourge" that brings ruin to the church and, most important, destroys the faith of ordinary Christians. It is in this context that we must understand the visionary activities of simple women like Constance and Marie.

The second vision (April 26, 1398) is memorable for the image of a burning wheel equipped with thousands of swords that threatens to descend toward the earth along a metal column. Only the efforts of thirteen angels, holding on to chains attached to this wheel, prevent the wheel's descent. And although humans are seen as a "stinking cauldron," Marie is ready to sacrifice herself for humanity; she tells God, "Make it so that your whole sentence falls on me and that I alone will die and everyone else will live" (Fac ut tota sententia tua cadat super me, et moriar ego sola et vivant omnes alii; p. 250). This readiness to sacrifice herself brings her in line with the other saintly personages treated in this and the previous chapter.

And indeed in the very next vision she is dragged before Lucifer by three demons, who, surrounded by burning wheels with which he is prepared to torture her, wants her to swear that henceforth she will not talk about the union of the church (p. 251). She refuses, is tied to the wheel, but then is saved at the last minute by a divine spirit whom she invokes in a prayer. She then sees God divide "the city of humanity" into four parts with various degrees of salvation. It is important that Lucifer's attempt to silence her precedes Marie's visit to Paris in June 1398, where she gains access to the council but is rejected without being heard (intravit concilium prelatorum, sed repulsa fuit sine audentia; fourth vision, p. 252). Marie's audience can make the connection: Lucifer tried to silence her unsuccessfully, but the council of prelates silenced her effectively!

---

50. All parenthetical page references are to Tobin, "'Le Livre des Révélations.'"
51. Tobin, "'Le Livre des Révélations,'" p. 234.

This moment marks the beginning of Marie's disenchantment with her political activism.

The sixth vision, most "obscure and scary" (p. 254), takes place on November 9, 1398—that is, after France's subtraction of obedience from Benedict XIII—confirming the failure of Marie's mission. Here she sees the curious image of weeping men turning around a star whose tears are collected by angels and poured back on them so that they can weep some more. This "exercise in futility," as Tobin puts it (p. 240), represents, according to the Lord who shows her all this, the discussions of the Parisian theologians (Et hec que audisti et vidisti dic magistris in theologia universitatis Parisiensis; p. 254). It would be difficult to find a better visual representation of the endless but ultimately fruitless deliberations of the University of Paris. For although the subtraction was finally agreed on and executed (1398–1403), it did not result in Benedict's abdication.[52]

In March 1399 we find Marie back in her oratory at the cemetery in Avignon. John the Evangelist appears to her on his feast day, May 6,[53] and is very surprised that the Schism is still ongoing ("You still do not have a union?" [Et nonne habet unionem?]; p. 255). John is willing to pray for peace in the church. After a rather strange Eucharistic vision in which Christ drinks his own blood that then can be seen to "enter into his veins" (quem vidit entrare in venas suas; p. 255), Christ takes John by the hand, and the latter keeps his promise to try to intervene on behalf of the church. Christ informs John that peace and war cannot coexist and warns humans that they are responsible for their own actions; they have no excuse for the war in the church (non possunt se excusare; p. 256). But if Saint John thought the Lord would enlighten him about who is the true pope so that he could carry this message to the world, he is sadly mistaken: only a general warning to humanity is forthcoming (p. 256). This refusal on the Lord's part to take sides is highly significant. The subtraction of obedience has eroded Benedict's authority; the Roman pope is as unwilling to step down as the Avignon pope is. Neither is thus a viable candidate to be the true pope. Furthermore, the Schism has expanded into bloody conflicts between Benedict and his own cardinals, with the pope becoming a prisoner in his own palace, from which he does not escape until 1403.[54] This moment marks one of the lowest points of the Schism years.

---

52. See Swanson, *Universities, Academics, and the Great Schism*, chaps. 5 and 6.
53. Saint John's feast day is May 6, not June 6 as Tobin states (p. 241), a date that would scramble the chronological order of Marie's visions.
54. See Valois, *La France*, 3: chap. 3. See 3:194 for an example of a violent encounter resulting in the death of Pierre de Vimenet, the abbot of Issoire.

After this vision Marie's indictment of Clement VII, Benedict XIII, and his cardinals becomes more and more pronounced. In visions from May 12 and 13, the late pope Clement VII appears to her, but she does not believe anything he tells her. An angel informs her that now he speaks the truth, even though in life he lied to her (p. 257). This retrospective undermining of Clement's authority puts into question Marie's early role as an instrument for Clementist propaganda. Her distrust of the ecclesiastical establishment culminates in an extended vision of May 18 that transports her into the valley of Josaphat. There she sees Christ surrounded by all classes of society. The pope and the prelates do not recognize Christ, do not follow his orders, and are depicted as hypocrites whose cruelty provokes the cries and weeping of those betrayed by them (pp. 257–58). The most violent indictment is reserved for Pope Benedict, who "was unwilling to abdicate in case his adversary agreed to do so." Christ "condemns [him] with all his excuses" and calls him a thief and homicide (p. 259). By repeating the precise terms of Benedict's original oath at the conclave of 1394 regarding his planned abdication, Christ's words demonstrate great political astuteness. Benedict is convicted by his own words. Marie is charged to convey this lengthy vision to the church, though she knows that people will grumble "about such a long text" (de tam longa scriptura; p. 259)!

Marie's last two visions are complex, alternating between hope for a renewed church and utter pessimism for humanity's fate.[55] Although for the most part these revelations are removed from the political preoccupations that marked the earlier visions, there is a strong condemnation of Charles VI for his failure to end the Schism, coupled with a prediction that he will be deposed by his own subjects (p. 261). And finally, in the context of humans' lack of repentance and Christ's vengeance, we see the Lord brandishing a sword with the inscription "It is said that here once was Paris" (Dicetur hic fuit Parisius; p. 263). Paris—that is, the French monarchy and the University of Paris—has betrayed the Christian faithful as much as Avignon and its pope have, and the French capital is therefore obliterated. Two weeks after this vision, Marie dies.

Marie's visionary trajectory thus parallels the political developments of the last two years of her life. Her initial willingness to serve her pope is quickly transformed into disillusionment. Her dramatic revelations are an indictment of ecclesiastical and secular rulers alike, whose self-interest and inability to compromise have inaugurated an even more divisive and destructive phase of the Schism instead of solving it.

55. On her views of purgatory and the end of times, see Tobin, "Les visions et révélations de Marie Robine," esp. pp. 315–20.

Shuttle Diplomacy: Ursulina of Parma
in the Service of the Roman Papacy

In 1472 a Carthusian prior from near Treviso named Simone Zanacchi composed a Life of the blessed Ursulina of Parma (1375–1408) at the behest of the nuns in the Benedictine convent San Quintino in Parma.[56] It tells the extraordinary story of a young woman who followed a saintly path similar to that of Catherine of Siena, at one point in her life engaged in a kind of shuttle diplomacy between the Avignon and Roman popes, was imprisoned as a sorceress, and was almost poisoned by the Avignon cardinals. Only two papal bulls issued by Boniface IX in 1396 regarding her choice of confessor and her pilgrimage to the Holy Land confirm her existence.[57] The rest of her fascinating story exists only in the *Vita*, but whether true or not, it forms part of the *imaginaire* of the Schism in that it shows how a pious man several generations later could imagine a young woman's dealings with the papacy at a crucial moment of the Schism: Clement VII's last days and the brief interregnum before the election of Benedict XIII in September 1394. The story also dramatizes anxieties over supernatural powers given to women that were put to the use of political intervention.

Ursulina's visionary experiences began in childhood, but she never wanted to become a nun and, in a rather unusual move, she shunned all preachers because she wanted to protect the authenticity of her own revelations, which, she feared, would be contaminated by what she heard in church (1.8).[58] The vision that introduces her mission to the Avignon pope is indeed rather unusual (2.11): she sees Christ wandering around near a church, looking for a place to sit, and offers her knees, which he gladly accepts. Then Christ gets up, leads her into a house, and pours her some wine. Amazingly, she says, unlike some people who get inebriated and can no longer talk straight, she could think more clearly and see farther in this state. It is this intimate contact with Christ that leads up to her being charged through the Lord's voice to go with her mother to Avignon, "where the pseudo-pope Clement lives." "Don't you know that because of him there is a great Schism in universal Christianity?

---

56. See Mannocci, "Orsolina di Parma," col. 1272. Her cult was confirmed in 1786, her feast day is April 7. The *Vita* is in *Acta sanctorum*, April 1. Citations will be by chapter and section. Bruce Venarde and I are preparing a full translation and commentary of Ursulina's *Vita* for the series "The Other Voice in Early Modern Europe" (University of Chicago Press).

57. Or, as Graziano puts it poetically, "L'apparire della b. Orsolina fu veramente come una meteora presto scomparsa senza lasciar traccia" ("Tre sante," p. 179).

58. Her visions apparently were recorded and took up several volumes, all lost today. Parenthetical references are to chapter and section of the *Vita*.

There you should go" (2.12). The political parameters are immediately defined for our naïve traveler: Clement is the guilty party in the Schism, and Ursulina's job, as yet a mystery to her, will be to make him abdicate in favor of the Roman pope.

Ursulina's mother is confused, asking what they should do there, whereupon her daughter reassures her that the Lord will provide (2.13). It is certainly remarkable that a mother and daughter would set out for a journey across the Alps without a clearly defined mission or a protective entourage. Fortunately Saint John the Evangelist, who had been so surprised at the continuing Schism in Marie Robine's vision, accompanies them as their guardian. Once in Avignon, Ursulina is told to go see the antipope and convey to him the words the Lord will inspire her to say once the time comes. Immediately admitted to the papal chambers by the "pseudo-cardinal" Peter of Podio (2.16), Ursulina kneels down in front of Pope Clement, extends her hands, and pronounces "Gloria Patri et Filio et Spiritui sancto," stupefying everyone (2.16). After being left alone with Ursulina, Clement learns that a place has already been reserved for him in hell, right next to Lucifer (2.17). Clement's reaction is one of fear and trembling, yet he gets up to escort Ursulina on her way out, thus earning the scorn of his cardinals: "The pseudo-cardinals show indignation against the antipope because he gets up for a little woman and honors her so much" (Pseudo-cardinales indignati sunt contra Antipapam, quod pro una muliercula a solio suo surrexisset, & tantum honoris illi impendisset; 2.17). But he replies that he shows honor not to the little woman but to the Lord who sent her, thus defining in a nutshell a whole range of issues relating to female authority and divine inspiration. But eventually, influenced by the cardinals, Clement refuses to receive her again, and she returns to Parma (2.18). We find here the seed of an idea developed later: that Clement was willing to listen to her but was persuaded by his cardinals not to follow her divinely inspired commands.

Back in Parma she recovers from her labors and is summoned to Rome, where she tells her Avignon experiences to Pope Boniface IX, who charges her with letters to carry back to Avignon. She agrees, though "a woman and weak" (mulier et debilis; II.20). Warned by Peter of Podio that the cardinals plot her destruction, she nonetheless speaks again—inspired by divine eloquence (2.21)—to Clement about the union of the church. Her hagiographer stresses her fearlessness and the skill with which she delivers her prophetic sermons, making her a second Isaiah.[59] Just when it seems that Clement is conquered by her eloquence, which for a medieval audience undoubtedly evoked the debate

---

59. On these parallels, see Costello, "Women's Mysticism and Reform," chap. 8.

between Catherine of Alexandria and the pagan philosophers, a "monstrous" cardinal, "rapacious like a wolf" (2.27), challenges Ursulina: she should preach on the Trinity. But Ursulina refuses, since she has firsthand experience of it, while the cardinal does not, and therefore any public explanation would be useless. The "little woman's" privilege of direct access to the divinity is thus thrown into the learned cardinal's face.

The cardinals pursue her like rabid dogs (2.24), and despite her untiring efforts of preaching unity of the church she is framed as a sorceress, imprisoned, then liberated when an earthquake makes her prison crumble. She even escapes an attempt at poisoning her (2.27). But in the end all her exertions on behalf of ending the Schism by having the Roman pope prevail come to nothing because Clement dies miserably (miserabiliter vitam suam finivit; 2.28) in September 1394. The brief interregnum could provide an opening for a resolution of the Schism, but just when an embassy to Boniface is being discussed[60] (in which Ursulina would play a prominent role), the ambitious viper (ambitione ac serpentina astutia plenus; 2.28) Pedro de Luna subverts the cardinals' intentions and has himself elected pope, prompting Ursulina's return to Rome and finally to Parma.

Here the hagiographer inserts Ursulina into a well-documented episode that took place between the death of Clement and Benedict XIII's quick election, an election that the French tried hard to prevent, hoping that a diplomatic solution could be found at this point in time, when there was only one—namely, the Roman—pope.[61] No independent documentary evidence exists to place Ursulina at these crucial discussions on the future of the papacy. For her hagiographer she here represents the divinely inspired voice of reason, endorsing in effect a position—immediate negotiations with the Roman pope—that was part of the political strategy of the French monarchy and of some of the cardinals. The failure to act on this opening for peace in the church is not Ursulina's but clearly Pedro de Luna's, who is depicted as a scheming, power-hungry demon. Like Isaiah, Ursulina cannot move the truly obdurate, so her failure has an authoritative prophetic model and is not due to any lack of holiness or inspiration.[62]

In this Vita the interventions in the Schism on the part of a holy woman are given a most dramatic expression. Like a good novelist, Simone builds up the tension. Ursulina's inspired sermons are just about to move Pope Clement

60. See Valois, La France, 3:13. One of the cardinals suggested electing Boniface IX, the Roman pope, as a successor to Clement, thus immediately ending the Schism!
61. This was also the moment when Honoré Bovet wrote his Somnium. He also did not foresee the speed with which Pedro de Luna would be elected. See Chapter 5, section on Bovet.
62. See Costello, "Women's Mysticism and Reform," pp. 186–87.

when Ursulina is imprisoned; her miraculous escape exposes to her to a poison plot; and just when she is again close to persuading Clement to abdicate, the pope dies and is succeeded by one of the most astute and tenacious popes in history. Writing in the period after the Council of Constance that had resolved the Schism without assigning explicit blame to either side, the Italian hagiographer conceptualizes the Schism not as competition between two popes, between two strong-willed individuals backed by nations who sought their own advantage (a reality that had dawned on most theologians and politicians of the time), but as a clear-cut divine choice echoing Constance de Rabastens's revelations: the only true pope is the Roman one.

In the last parts of this chapter we shall take a brief look at three women who were tangentially involved or interested in the Schism, to show how this crisis touched a large variety of individuals from different classes and geographic origins.

The Strange Case of Ermine de Reims

One of the strangest visionaries from the late Middle Ages is undoubtedly Ermine de Reims (1347–96), a simple widow who in the last ten months of her life was haunted nightly by demons and frightening animals.[63] Her experiences are not really visions but occur in a waking state. As Dyan Elliott puts is succinctly: "Her turbulent inner life seems to have revolved around a series of celestial and demonic visitors—the latter never tiring to pass themselves off as the former."[64] Indeed, her uncanny ability to distinguish between apparitions sent by God and by the devil makes her "a living example of the discernment of spirits."[65]

For the most part, Ermine's experiences are personal trials in which she is being tested and mocked. One constant is the demons' attempt to wrest Ermine away from the control by her confessor Jean le Graveur, a subprior at Saint Paul du Val-des-Ecoliers in Reims, who wrote down Ermine's travails after her death. While generally removed from the historical situation of late 1395 and 1396, the time when the French were getting more and more exasperated

---

63. I investigated these animals in my paper "Saints and Animal Trouble" delivered at the International Congress for Medieval Studies, Kalamazoo, May 2003.

64. Elliott, "Seeing Double," p. 39. An account of Ermine's experiences was submitted to Gerson after her death for a test of orthodoxy. Elliott investigates his changing opinions of the revelations' authenticity. See also Caciola, *Discerning Spirits*, pp. 303–4 (Caciola mistakenly attributes authorship of the revelations to Jean Morel instead of to her confessor Jean le Graveur), and Roth, *Discretio spirituum*, pp. 203–9.

65. Vauchez, "Préface" (p. 9) to the edition of Ermine's revelations. See Arnaud-Gillet, ed., *Entre Dieu et Satan*. Parenthetical page references are to this edition.

with Benedict XIII and began discussing the subtraction of obedience, there is one striking irruption of the political reality: numerous references and queries regarding the charismatic hermit Jean de Varennes (1340/45–1396?), who had set up shop at a small sanctuary at Saint-Lié in the woods near Reims where he attracted large crowds with his preaching.[66] In the past a papal official and chaplain to Pierre de Luxembourg, Jean had left Avignon in May 1392, following a divine command to be a second Moses and preach on the reform of the church and on ending the Schism. Favorable toward the abdication of Pope Benedict XIII, he eventually broke with his former employer and preached a strong-worded sermon against him on Palm Sunday 1396. On May 30, 1396, he was arrested and probably died in prison.

As for Jean's importance for Ermine, André Vauchez believes that Jean de Varennes "is at the center of the spiritual crisis lived by this pious laywoman."[67] Like the other faithful in the diocese of Reims, Ermine was perplexed and anguished by the treatment the saintly hermit received at the hands of the authorities. Several passages in Jean le Graveur's record of Ermine's visions paint a revealing picture of the uncertainty and doubts occasioned by the Schism and manifested in people's attitudes toward Jean de Varennes. In an unusually long direct address to his audience, Jean le Graveur uses his authorial voice to introduce his account of Ermine's experiences with Jean de Varennes, stating that he struggled with himself whether to mention these experiences or simply omit them. On the one hand, people who support Jean de Varennes may discredit the whole book because they do not like the text's attitude toward the prophet; on the other hand, there are those who have been misled by Jean de Varennes and who could be aided by the truth and return to God. Therefore, in the interest of helping his fellow men, Jean le Graveur will report Ermine's experiences (pp. 115–16).

For Ermine, Jean de Varennes fits into the pattern of revelations on the part of satanic voices urging her to leave her confessor and embark on a life of begging. (Jean le Graveur's having changed his mind in regard to the prophet whom he used to support provides the argument used by the satanic voice to urge Ermine to abandon her mentor and confessor.) The voice speaks to Ermine in her chamber shortly before Ascension Day 1396—that is, after Jean de Varennes's famous 1396 Palm Sunday sermon. The "sathenas" depicts the prophet as a holy man and claims that only when he becomes pope will there

---

66. On Jean de Varennes, see Valois, *La France*, 3:28–29, 84–86. For a recent detailed study, see Vauchez, "Un réformateur religieux." The biographical information is taken from this article. Numerous letters and some devotional texts by Jean are still extant.

67. "Se trouve même au centre de la crise spirituelle vécue par cette pieuse laïque," "Un réformateur," p. 1112.

be peace in the church—that is, only then will the Schism end. All his opponents will be prey of the devil. This pronouncement leaves Ermine pensive, but
she believes it to be true (p. 116), only to change her mind the next morning at
the urging of her confessor. It is significant that the pronouncement on the
necessity of Jean de Varennes becoming pope is put into the mouth of a
demon. Thus, Jean le Graveur can report on what was undoubtedly a popular
sentiment while at the same time discrediting it. In any case, the hopes of Jean
de Varennes's simple audience were soon thwarted by the authorities.

After Jean de Varennes's imprisonment in May 1396, which Jean le Graveur
reports (p. 126), various demons discuss Ermine's confessor's views of the hermit and urge her to desert him (pp. 145, 157). Clearly, Jean de Varennes's situation has become a touchstone for Ermine's relationship to her confessor, mir-
roring undoubtedly the confusion laypeople experienced in the face of the
political wrangling between the French monarchy and the Avignon pope. Jean
de Varennes had publicly indicted Benedict XIII, but the French king still
hoped to negotiate with the pope; consequently, the subversive hermit had to
disappear. Any hopes for his reappearance, expressed by a demonic voice who
tells Ermine that Jean de Varennes has been preaching in Paris that very day
(p. 162), are dashed when Jean le Graveur informs his readers that the hermit is
still in prison. This is the last one hears of Jean de Varennes both in real life and
in Ermine's book.

Thus, the only historical personage that preoccupies Ermine (and Jean le
Graveur as the reporter of her experiences) in her otherwise timeless torments
is an important political figure who made the transition from being a strong
supporter of the Avignon papacy to one of its severest critics.[68] That a simple,
illiterate woman like Ermine should have heard of him, pondered his convictions, and agonized over his fate demonstrates that the politics of the Schism
were not confined to the upper echelons of society but left a troubling imprint
in the minds of ordinary Christians as well.

Jeanne-Marie de Maillé: A Prophet of the Schism?

The blessed Jeanne-Marie de Maillé (1331–1414) was born into a noble family in
Touraine in a milieu dominated by Franciscan spirituality. She led a life that in

---

68. Further instances that could be interpreted politically are two of Ermine's visions of the
Host, very frequent occurrences in Ermine's brief visionary life. Jean le Graveur emphasizes
(in June 1396) that Ermine saw the Host at masses celebrated by priests ordained by bishops
created by Clement VII, as well as at masses held by priests ordained by the pre-Schism Pope
Gregory XI's bishops (p. 138). Thus, Clement VII clearly was the legitimate pope.

many ways corresponded to the hagiographic paradigm of a pious childhood, a chaste marriage, exercise of charity, conversion of prostitutes, visionary experiences (like Constance de Rabastens and others she began to have visions after her husband's death), and posthumous miracles.[69] Widowed in 1362, chased from her husband's land by his family, she led a life of prayer, aiding the poor, and going on pilgrimages. Only in 1386 did she join the Franciscans in Tours, where her confessor became Martin de Boisgaultier, her future biographer. Though she had many visions and her prayers were unusually efficacious, her prophetic gifts were limited to two instances, one recounted in the *Vita*, the other, more important for our context, in the canonization inquiry of 1414–15.

Jeanne-Marie's first prophecy concerned her (correct) prediction of which gate of the city of Tours the French king Charles VI would enter for his visit there. This rather inconsequential bit of foreknowledge precedes the interesting paragraph speaking of her encounter with the king in the local castle. Introduced to Charles VI by the duke of Orléans, she has a "secret and prolix" (locuta est secreto et prolixe; 4.30) conversation with the king, to be repeated at greater length a few years later in the church of the Celestins in Paris (prolixiorem sermonem cum Rege habuit; 4.30). But what was said, alas, only God and the king knew (Rex post Deum solus novit; 4.30).

The other prophecy dates apparently from 1396.[70] A witness at the canonization inquiry testifying almost twenty years later had queried Jeanne-Marie about the following problem in the critical period before the French subtraction of obedience:

> He questioned this lady and asked her what she felt about the current Schism and the union of the church, which this witness much desired. The aforementioned lady answered him—after a long discussion of this matter—that there would be peace in the church and that the first future pope would be a Franciscan. Hence, when our lord Alexander V, of happy memory, was raised to the highest apostolate, this witness recalled the words this lady had said to him about the creation of a future pope, and he thought to himself that this lady possessed the spirit of prophecy.

69. See Vauchez, *The Laity*, chap. 17, on her life and the connections between the Franciscans and the aristocratic families of the region. There are also numerous references to Jeanne-Marie in Bynum, *Holy Feast*, and Dinzelbacher, *Mittelalterliche Frauenmystik.* Her *Vita* and canonization inquiry are in *Acta sanctorum*, March III. The efforts to canonize her in 1414–15 failed, but her cult was finally confirmed in 1871. Parenthetical references are to chapter and section of her *Vita*.

70. Vauchez, *The Laity*, p. 208.

[Interrogavit ipsam Dominam et petiit ab eadem quid sentiebat de schismate tunc currente, et de unione Ecclesiae quam multum desiderabat iste testis. Cui praedicta Domina respondit, post plura verba et colloquia habita de ista materia, quod esset pax in Ecclesia; et quod primus Summus Pontifex tunc futurus esset Ordinis Fratris Minorum. Unde quando felicis recordationis Dominus Alexander Papa V et ultimus, in apicem summi Apostolatus fuit assumptus, iste testis recordatus fuit verbi, quod dixerat ei dicta Domina de creatione Papae tunc futuri, praecogitans in semet ipso, quod ipsa Domina habet in se spiritum prophetiae.] (6.62)

Indeed, in 1409, when the Council of Pisa elected the Franciscan Alexander V (who died the following year) it seemed that the Schism might come to an end. Instead, Christianity had to put up with three popes: the indefatigable Benedict XIII, the Roman pope Gregory XII, and Alexander's successor, the Pisan pope John XXIII. But for this witness this unfortunate turn of events did not invalidate Jeanne-Marie's gift of prophecy, and he could not know that the politics of the Schism would derail her canonization.[71] It is certainly significant that the only prophecy of any consequence cited as evidence at this inquiry should have centered on the Schism, giving us yet another proof of the anxieties produced by this crisis. That Jeanne-Marie's prophecy should name a Franciscan as the savior ending the Schism is not surprising, given the strong Franciscan influence in her family and her own spiritual life.

Jeanne-Marie, like Marie Robine, was one of the visionaries who backed the person or the cause that was congruent with the dominant ideology of their areas. Ermine de Reims was much preoccupied with very local events linked to the Schism. Only Constance de Rabastens exposed herself to the wrath of her region's ecclesiastical authorities by endorsing the "wrong" pope through her divinely inspired prophetic pronouncements.

Did Saint Colette Care About the Great Schism?

An interesting final point of comparison can be provided by Saint Colette de Corbie (1381–1447), one of the great reformers of the Franciscan order. After many years of searching for a religious vocation, which took her from the Beguines to the Urbanist Clares and the Benedictines to an anchorhold in which

---

71. This is suggested by Vauchez, *The Laity*, 313 n. 4.

she lasted four years, Colette had a vision defining her reforming mission.[72] In 1406 she visited Pope Benedict XIII in Nice in order to get permission to enter the second order of Saint Francis and to reform Franciscan houses. This encounter was marked by several miraculous events: the pope fell as soon as he saw the saint; several cardinals opposing her died of the plague; and the pope himself seemed to prophesy his own unhappy end. Elisabeth Lopez suggests that Colette's biographer Pierre de Vaux "seems to want to show in filigree the pope's controversial nature; he will end his life shut in and alone at Peñiscola rather than ending the Schism by abdicating." Pierre de Vaux, Lopez contends, by emphasizing the pope's stumbling and falling down, reveals his embarrassment that Colette addressed herself to a pope who, although still legitimately recognized in France, was in large part responsible for the sorry state of the church.[73] Authorized by Benedict XIII, Colette embarked on a remarkable career. In the course of her long life she founded and/or reformed seventeen houses. But she never succeeded in establishing a Poor Clare house in her hometown of Corbie in Picardy. Despite her political astuteness, Colette seemed unable to shake the association of the reform movement with a pope who was considered one of the perpetuators of the Schism—an association that seemed undesirable in Corbie.[74]

On the whole, her biographers avoid any direct evocation of the political and religious troubles of the period, highlighting instead her spirituality: "Her mystical life does not seem to be rooted in historical, political, social, and religious reality, while her actions are directed at reform."[75] Indeed, her lifelong activism puts her into the ranks of some the visionaries we have considered in this chapter, but her goals were strictly reformist, and any political aims can only be inferred indirectly, although she did show great astuteness in getting ratification for her foundations from a changing cast of popes between the councils of Pisa and Constance.[76]

But did she get explicitly engaged in the Schism? One might think so in view of an anecdote involving the other great saint of the period, Vincent Ferrer. According to Colette's collaborator Henry de Baume, Vincent had a vision of Colette kneeling before Christ and urging Him to end the Schism and to pardon

---

72. For Ullmann, Saint Colette serves "as a typical example for the vacillating attitude that had befallen mortals" during the Schism, because she once belonged to the Urbanist Clares and later dealt with the Avignon pope Benedict XIII (*Origins of the Great Schism*, p. 97). For Colette in general, see the excellent recent study of Colette's activities and writings by Lopez, *Culture et sainteté*.

73. Lopez, *Culture et sainteté*, p. 59.

74. See Warren, "Monastic Politics," p. 208, and Lopez, *Petite Vie de Sainte Colette*, p. 36.

75. Lopez, *Culture et sainteté*, p. 56.

76. This is not to say that her saintliness was not exploited for political ends, as Warren has shown in her "Monastic Politics." See Lopez, *Culture et sainteté*, p. 266, on Colette's dealing with the various popes.

the sinners who caused it.[77] Vincent wrote to her from Saragossa that he wished to see her in Besançon in order to confer about the Schism and to deliver some sermons. He arrived in Besançon on July 4, 1417.[78] The two saints prayed and spoke together at length. It is also said that they composed a letter together to be sent to the members of the Council of Constance, urging them to persist in their mission to end the Schism and predicting that a great pope would emerge from the council.[79] No such letter survives, but nonetheless, even if a fiction, it expresses well what might be seen as a crucial endpoint of saintly activity during the Great Schism: leaving behind all the controversies related to the division of the church that may have dogged them during their lives until then, two of the great saints of the period put their heads together to write a divinely inspired missive that confirmed the end of the gravest crisis the Western church had ever known.

Conclusion

In many ways the history of the inspired activities of our saintly personages is a history of frustration. Though, as we saw at the beginning of Chapter 2, the efforts of those individuals working for the papacy's return to Rome were crowned with success, their victory proved elusive since shortly afterward the double papal election inaugurated the Schism. The many revelations, the letters replete with divinely inspired eloquence, the painful journeys, the bold interviews with the popes, and even the offers of sacrificial death that we surveyed could not in the end solve the problems of the Schism. What remains is an impression of acute anxiety, of Christians mourning the destruction of the one church. Stirred up by the idea that the Schism was a punishment of human sins, some of our saintly people preached reform on all levels or adopted apocalyptic schemes to explain the current disaster. In any case, they chose an activist role hoping to contribute to a permanent healing of the church's ills. In the next two chapters we shall see that poets as well tried to intervene in this crisis. With forceful voices and dramatic imagery, they too tried their best to make their leaders take action against the monstrous Schism and give artistic expression to the suffering of ordinary Christians.

77. Colette's other biographer, Sister Perrine, adds this detail to the *Vie* by Pierre de Vaux. See Lopez, *Culture et "sainteté,"* p. 77. See also Fages, *Histoire de Saint Vincent Ferrier*, 2:188. Fages bases his account on the late eighteenth-century *Vie de Sainte Colette* by the abbé Larceneux, based on manuscripts from Poligny, Gand, Besançon, and other places of Colette's activities.
78. They may have met earlier that year as well. See Fages, *Histoire*, 2:193–94.
79. See Fages, *Histoire*, 2:189. For a detailed study of Colette's surviving letters, see Lopez, *Culture et sainteté*, pp. 149–83. The addressees of all her letters are listed on p. 151.

Four

POETIC VISIONS OF THE GREAT SCHISM I:
PHILIPPE DE MÉZIÈRES AND EUSTACHE DESCHAMPS

"This strange practice that is the fiction of the political dream" (cette étrange pratique qu'est la fiction du "songe politique"). With those words Christiane Marchello-Nizia begins her reflections on this popular literary form, a form that seems rather peculiar to a modern sensibility.[1] Why would authors prefer the often overly elaborate framing devices of an allegorical dream vision for the expression of their political ideas when the options of, say, a polemical tract or an "open letter" were also available?[2] One reason may be the measure of protection afforded by the device of the dream. As the author of the late fourteenth-century *Echecs amoureux* (Chess game of love) argues:

> Often the dream exculpates the person who speaks of many things that would be considered wrong, if he said that this is exactly how they happened or that they were literally true. In this way, one can forgive the dreamer and always explain that this is how it seemed to him in his sleep and that one should blame the dream.

1. Marchello-Nizia, "Entre l'histoire et la poétique: Le 'Songe politique,'" p. 40.
2. "Open letters" could also draw on allegory, however, as we shall see for Philippe de Méz-
   ières's *Epistre au roy Richart II* (Letter to King Richard II). For England, see Astell, *Political Allegory in Late Medieval England.*

[Le songe excuse la personne qui parle aucuneffoiz de moult de choses qui seroient tenues pour mal dites qui les diroit ainsi estre avenues ou vrayes a la lettre, pour ce que on peut excuser le songant et respondre tousdiz que ainsi ly semblait il en son dormant et que s'en prengne au songe.][3]

Furthermore, dream allegory allows poets to "parler plus secretement et plus couvertement" (speak in a more secret and hidden manner),[4] thus giving the audience the impression that they are privy to revelations not open to everyone. Indeed, as Jon Whitman shows, the two components of the word "allegory" (*allos* [other] and the verb *agoreuein* [to speak in the assembly]) designate "guarded language" and "elite language," and therefore "the sense of secretive, guarded language had special importance for political allegory, in which the allegorist spoke, as it were, other than in the official assembly."[5] Often, this "other-speaking" took the form of giving voice to criticism through various characters within an allegorical construct. Thus, Jean de Meun, in the second part of the *Roman de la Rose* (ca. 1270), couches his attack on the mendicants and others he considers hypocrites in the words of Faux Semblant (False Seeming), himself represented as a friar.[6] Indeed, Jean de Meun can be said to be at the origin of the opening up of allegory toward the political, unlatching the gate of the closed enchanted garden of Guillaume de Lorris to contemporary concerns. It seems that political allegory lends itself particularly well to subjects that are in some way controversial and that authors strive to render accessible or more vivid; political allegory deals with "a reality that can only be expressed in a figurative mode."[7] If the real cannot be denounced overtly it must travesty itself, as Jeannine Quillet argues.[8]

Given the involved and changing nature of French policies toward the divided papacy, it should not surprise us that the writers at the center of the next two chapters frequently chose the form of political allegory for an exposition of their thoughts on the Schism. Rather than being "objectively" reported, the situations they described needed to be deciphered, interpreted; the solutions

3. Cited by Badel, *Le Roman de la Rose au XIVe siècle*, p. 343. For the dangers that can be skirted through fictive dreams, see also Kagan, *Lucrecia's Dreams*, pp. 57–58. For the problematics of dreams and visions related to questions of authority and "deniability," see Newman, *God and the Goddesses*, esp. chaps. 1 and 7.
4. Cited by Badel, *Le Roman de la Rose au XIVe siècle*, p. 344.
5. Whitman, *Allegory*, p. 263.
6. See Szittya, *Antifraternal Tradition*, pp. 186–90.
7. Quillet, "Herméneutique du discours allégorique dans 'Le Songe du Vieil Pelerin' de Philippe de Mézières," p. 1085.
8. "Herméneutique," p. 1091.

they proposed, while often congruent with those offered in the official writings of the Parisian university scholars, gained a prophetic dimension, an authorization absent from the ideas of mere mortals.

Allegory figures the eternal, and it is in the gloss that contemporary reality comes into play.[9] Several of the authors we are encountering here provided their own glosses, explaining the political and historical meaning of their own allegories. We also have to take into account that there were efforts to suppress too much public expression on the Schism. A royal edict in 1381, for example, forbade public debate of the double papal election. Nonetheless, this period saw an extremely copious production of polemical texts on the Schism.[10] Some time later, in 1395, the Prévôt of Paris issued an ordinance forbidding minstrels to sing about the pope, the king, or the princes, and especially about "that which touches on the subject of the unification of the church" (en regard de ce qui touche le fait de l'union de l'Eglise).[11] The year 1395 was a critical moment in the history of the Schism. French patience was beginning to run low with the new pope. Benedict XIII (1394–1423), who had championed the *voie de cession* (the abdication of both popes) when he was still Cardinal Pedro de Luna, continued his offers to abdicate as a newly minted pope but never followed through. As we saw in Chapter 3, in 1395 the French king began to send teams of ambassadors to Benedict XIII, trying to persuade him to make good on his promises. At the same time, the French withdrawal of obedience, as a means to pressure Benedict XIII to step down, was beginning to be discussed. Too much popular involvement in these deliberations would have destabilized the situation even further.

But aesthetic concerns also played a role in the choice of the expression of political ideas and convictions. Journeying through a political landscape populated by strange creatures and allegorical figures is far more entertaining than reading a scholastic treatise on the subject of the Schism. Anyone who has plowed through Vincent Ferrer's *Treatise on the Modern Schism* (1380) or Jean Gerson's many tracts on conciliarism and related ideas,[12] will be grateful to Philippe de Mézières's Old Pilgrim and gladly embark with him on a mad journey through Europe, witnessing the same events and discussions that are laid out dry as dust in the contemporary polemical writings. In addition, there was a venerable tradition of the allegorical journey or dialogue (presented either as

9. Quillet, "Herméneutique," p. 1088.
10. See Valois, *La France*, 1:349.
11. Cited by Boutet and Strubel, *Littérature, politique et société*, p. 168. This passage is quoted frequently as evidence of a "popular" political poetry. But as far as I have been able to ascertain, the Schism was not really a topic treated by minstrels. In fact, all the poems about the Schism I have been able to find come from a learned milieu.
12. See Garganta and Forcada, *San Vicente Ferrer*, pp. 411–62, and Huerga, "El 'Tratado del cisma moderno,'" For Gerson, see *Oeuvres complètes*, vol. 6.

a dream or as a waking vision), beginning with *The Shepherd of Hermas* (ca. 160 C.E.) and Boethius's *Consolation of Philosophy* (ca. 524), one of the most beloved books of the Middle Ages. Theodore Bogdanos has shown that the *Shepherd of Hermas* and Boethius established a prototype for medieval visionary allegory, both for "formal features and thematic intentions."[13] He describes the pattern as it was perfected in these two texts as follows:

> The dreamer-hero finds himself in a profound spiritual crisis. One or several authoritative figures appear to him in one or several visions and help the dreamer place his crisis in a new perspective of truth, thus inducing its resolution. Such truth is communicated to the visionary hero through symbolic imagery and through rational, conceptually articulate dialogue in which the authoritative figure engages the dreamer. Their encounter takes place in a visionary landscape which has an objective reality of its own . . . while at the same time functioning as an imagistic concretization of the dreamer's psychic reality. (p. 34)

This definition, which also perfectly describes Dante's *Divine Comedy*, a visionary poem (though not presented as a dream) all our writers here were familiar with, applies in just about every detail to a number of texts treated in this chapter. The profound crisis here is the Great Schism; the authoritative figures range from Ecclesia (the Church), who appears to Honoré Bovet (as she did to the shepherd Hermas), to Reine Verite (Queen Truth) and her cortège, who accompany Phillipe de Mézières's alter ego in the *Songe du Vieil Pelerin* (Dream of the old pilgrim), to the Sibyl of Cumae and Lady Philosophy (familiar from Boethius), who dispense advice to Christine de Pizan in her allegorical incarnations. The landscapes our heroes and heroines travel through are in one sense recognizable (as Rome, Avignon, or Genoa, for example), but they always have features that identify them as visionary landscapes. As for the resolution of the crisis, however ingeniously it is proposed within the allegory, it is usually deferred into the extratextual realm—where no solution to the Schism was forthcoming until the Council of Constance in 1414. Only Christine de Pizan's *Ditié de Jehanne d'Arc* of 1429 takes us into the post-Schism period, and even there its aftermath can still be felt.

Modeling their texts on Boethius's *Consolation of Philosophy* and Dante's *Divine Comedy*, authors thus felt inspired to transpose their ideas into striking

---

13. Bogdanos, "'The Shepherd of Hermas' and the Development of Medieval Visionary Allegory," p. 33.

poetic images and to create moral landscapes populated by authoritative figures that would parade ideas in concrete form before their audience. By the
late fourteenth century, then, political allegory, most often in the shape of
dream journeys or fictional debates, was a well-established genre in both the
Latin and the vernacular traditions.

One of the most important of these political dream visions was the *Songe du
vergier*. Commissioned by the French king Charles V in 1376, it was originally
composed in Latin by Evrard de Trémaugon, then translated into French in
1378.[14] This lengthy dream vision deals with the problems of the relationship
between church and state and presents an early discussion of Gallicanism.[15]
Written just before the beginning of the Great Schism, it also confronts the
question with which we began our chapters on the saintly activists of the
Schism: should the papacy return to Rome? A brief discussion of the *Songe du
vergier*'s take on this problem will provide a comparison with the arguments
used by our saints and will also set the stage for an analysis of the deployment
of political commentary on the Schism in the for the most part allegorical texts
that are the focus of Chapters 3 and 4.

The *Songe*'s framework is that of a traditional dream vision: the author falls
asleep in an orchard; two female figures representing temporal and spiritual
power appear to him; they are soon joined by a "Clerc" and a "Chevalier"—
and it is these two male figures who occupy the bulk of the text, in a seemingly
interminable disucssion. Thus, except for the intial scene, the *Songe du vergier*
is not strictly speaking an allegory, though the two debaters could be seen as
embodying the church and the state respectively.

In book 1, chapters 155–56, they argue about whether the pope should stay in
Avignon or return to Rome. The Clerc first considers in which cases wars are
justified and eventually arrives at the civil strife tearing Italy apart. He attributes these civil wars to the pope's having deserted the Holy See (pp. 318–19).
France is in much better shape, so it can certainly do without a pope at this
point; it is sinful Rome that needs the pope's help (p. 319). Furthermore, Rome
is the head of the world, the most perfect city anywhere (a seeming contradic-
tion with its just-mentioned sinful state!). The Roman church is the pope's

---

14. See Marchello-Nizia, "Entre l'histoire et la poétique"; Quillet, "Songe et songerie dans l'art
politique du XIV siècle," esp. pp. 327–40; Quaglioni, "La tipologia del 'Somnium' nel dibattito su scisma e concilio." Parenthetical page references are to Evrard de Trémaugon, *Le
Songe du vergier*, vol. 1, ed. Schnerb-Lièvre. The Latin *Somnium Viridarii* featured 552 chapters; the French translation has 468 chapters. On the sources, a large number of theoretical
texts on the relationship between the secular powers and the spiritual powers, see the introduction by Schnerb-Lièvre.

15. On the history of Gallicanism, see Martin, *Les origines du Gallicanisme*.

spiritual spouse, to whom he owes fidelity; a return to this spouse is therefore incumbent on the pope if he wants to be a faithful husband (pp. 321–22).[16]

The Chevalier could not disagree more. Although he also sees France as a relatively peaceful and harmonious place, he does not believe that this condition should induce the pope to move back to Rome. In this chapter the Chevalier in fact paints a portrait of a saintly country—far more saintly than Rome—that through its many qualities has earned its right to serve as papal abode. First, he lists the many extraordinary relics that call France home: the Holy Cross, the Crown of Thorns, and the lance, the nails, and the wooden sign hung above Christ's head at the crucifixion (pp. 325–26). France also has Saint-Denis. As for Rome, not even Christ elected to live there; he preferred Jerusalem. And as the pope is Christ's vicar on earth, the pope has the same prerogative to elect not to live in Rome but to live in a safer and more saintly place—namely, France (pp. 330–31). Echoing Petrarch's evocation of Saint Bernard's condemnation of the Romans,[17] Evrard tells us again that the Romans are untrustworthy traitors and thieves. Their brains are hardened, and they are full of ill will (p. 332). Who would not want to live in France—and especially the pope, who is aware of the long French tradition of offering protection to popes ("propre reffuge de Sainte Eglyse," p. 333)? Furthermore, French kings have always had the healing touch,[18] and Paris has always been the fountain of all science. A long list of the arts and sciences follows, all of which, according to our Chevalier, had been transported from Rome to France by Saint Charles or Charlemagne. Consequently Rome is as devoid of any intellectual allurements as it is of the security required by the papacy. Ergo, the pope's only choice is to remain in Avignon. After about another three hundred chapters the two debaters seem exhausted and the author wakes up and presents his book to the king.

In chapters 155–56 of the *Songe du vergier* we thus find a kind of summary of many of the major points that were put forward at the time for one or the other side in the debate over the pope's return to Rome. We saw in the previous chapters that the side of the Clerc proved victorious, and we also saw the results of Gregory XI's ill-fated return. Thus, the same discussions that preoccupied our saints found their way into the political dream vision. The *Songe du Vergier* is less imaginative than some of the texts we consider in this chapter and the next, presenting as it does a more or less straightforward dialogue framed by a dream. But the *actualité* of Evrard's dream vision is highlighted by

---

16. See fig. 1 for the faithless husband's abandonment of his spouse.
17. See also below for Vincent Ferrer's use of this topos.
18. On this topic, see Bloch, *Les rois thaumaturges*.

the quick translation of the Latin text into French, demonstrating a need on the part of a nonclerkly audience to be informed about the latest discussions concerning the powers of church and state. Also, the Great Schism was already on the horizon, and we shall now turn to the writers who dealt with this crisis directly.

Of the four writers considered in Chapters 4 and 5, Philippe de Mézières and Honoré Bovet wrote extensively in both Latin and French; Eustache Deschamps composed a few works in Latin, while Christine de Pizan limited herself to French. The texts at the center of our analysis are almost all in French. Bovet's *Somnium super materia scismatis* (Dream on the subject of the Schism) is written in a Latin that closely resembles French, making it accessible to a somewhat wider public. Generally these authors wrote for an audience of laypeople—upper class, to be sure, but not necessarily fluent in Latin.[19] Philippe de Mézières explains in his *Songe du Vieil Pelerin* (Dream of the old pilgrim) that he writes for "gens lays" (laypeople) who not only do not know Latin but also are ignorant of the exposition of the Scriptures and therefore need some kind of guideline as to how to interpret Philippe's own complicated allegory.[20]

Built-in interpretations are indeed a hallmark of the genre, belying to a certain extent the "exclusivity" of the intricate allegorical form. The allegorical writer wanted to compose his text in a manner that was "secret," but not so secret that the audience did not get the message. For the political message lies at the heart of these works; they are meant to draw in and move the people who were involved in the Schism, but their authors wanted to do it differently from the learned polemicists and theoreticians. The Schism was a political but also an emotional issue, creating profound anxiety in the Christian community. The writers analyzed here spoke to this twofold nature of the problem in forms that address both the intellectual and the affective capacities of the intended audience. As we shall see, the dedicatees (if they are known) of most of these works were the kings, dukes, and other noble personages who played leading roles in the drama of the Schism—that is, the same people to whom learned tracts, letters, and other official documents were addressed. This does not mean, however, that no other audiences had access to the allegorical texts. By attacking the problem from a different angle—the angle of the imagination and the emotions—our authors perhaps hoped to succeed where their learned contemporaries had failed.

19. Philippe de Mézières recommends to his pupil, Charles VI, that he read Latin texts in the original, but it is not clear whether he could actually do so (see *Le Songe du Vieil Pelerin*, 2:223).
20. *Le Songe du Vieil Pelerin*, 1:210. Philippe provides some guidance in his "Prologue." See below.

Throughout the period of the poetic activity centering on the Schism we treat here, there was also a vast production of treatises and polemical tracts, many of them focusing on conciliar ideas and most of them written in Latin.[21] Writers like Nicolas de Clamanges, Pierre d'Ailly, Jean Gerson, Simon de Cramaud, Bernard Alamant, and many others belonged to the milieu of the university, but they also knew and were in contact with the authors that are at the center of Chapters 4 and 5. The latters' works, then, in a way complement and perhaps even comment on the almost frantic production of scholarly and political texts related to the Schism. They offer a more emotional response to this grave crisis, couched in powerful poetic imagery.

Let us take a brief look at the lives of the four authors in question.

Philippe de Mézières (1327–1405) was one of the outstanding personages of his time. A pilgrimage to the Holy Land when he was twenty years old was to mark him for the rest of his life. After a stint as chancellor of Cyprus, he became a counselor of Charles V (1338–80) in 1373 and later a tutor of his son Charles VI (1368–1422). Among many other preoccupations, he worked tirelessly for recognition of the feast of the Presentation of the Virgin. He also championed the creation of a new Christian chivalric order, the *Chevalerie de la Passion*. After Charles V's death in 1380, Philippe retired to the convent of the Celestins in Paris, where he spent the rest of his life—though not in total seclusion—authoring a number of major works. When several of his projects came to naught or, like the "crusades" of 1396 and 1399, ended in disaster, he faded from the scene and died almost forgotten in 1405. The focus here will be not on his numerous spiritual compositions but on the *Songe du Vieil Pelerin* (1386–89), a vast allegorical dream journey that deals extensively (in thirty-seven chapters) with the problem of the Schism.[22]

Eustache Deschamps (ca. 1340–ca. 1404), also known as Eustache Morel, spent most of his life as a court official, first for Charles V and Charles VI and then for Louis of Orléans, the brother of the French king.[23] He wrote more than fifteen hundred ballades, a treatise on poetry, a "mirror" on marriage, and various allegories, including the *Complainte de l'Eglise* (Complaint by the church). He was a witness to the events of his era, at times playing almost the role of journalist in his poems. Many of his ballades reflect contemporary crises, and the Schism is no exception. He created a number of gripping images that reflect the monstrous nature of the division of the Western church.

21. See the Introduction for this context, and esp. Bliemetzrieder, *Literarische Polemik*, and Sieben, *Traktate und Theorien zum Konzil*. Glorieux provides a list of writings and events related to the Schism in Gerson, *Oeuvres complètes*, 6:xxxix–lx.

22. See Badel, *Le Roman de la Rose au XIV siècle* (381 n. 43) for a list of Philippe's many works.

23. For the most up-to-date account of his life, see Laurie, "Eustache Deschamps: 1340(?)–1404."

Honoré Bovet (ca. 1350–after 1409), a Benedictine monk and prior of Selonnet near Lyon, led an active political life.[24] Attached to Pope Urban V and then to Clement VII in Avignon, he became an official at the court of Charles VI in 1389, the year he completed his influential treatise on the art and rules of warfare, *L'Arbre des batailles* (The tree of battles). Of our four protagonists, he commented most consistently on the Schism. He created a number of different contexts for the Schism and devoted one entire work, his *Somnium super materia scismatis* of 1394, to this problem.[25]

Christine de Pizan (ca. 1364–ca. 1430) was as prolific as Philippe de Mézières. Unlike the men considered here, she had no official position at court and therefore no income, except what she received from the patrons of her literary production.[26] Between the 1390s and 1429 she wrote about two dozen major works (fifteen of them in the period between 1400 and 1405 alone), in many of them touching on the question of the Schism. She returns again and again to this crisis, from an early prayer to the Virgin (1403) to allegorical dream visions and more overtly polemical texts. She had various connections to our three male authors: she corresponded with Eustache Deschamps, sold some property to Philippe de Mézières, and had a touching dream vision in which Honoré Bovet appeared to her as a mentor and inspiration after his death.[27]

The four writers featured in this and the following chapter, then, can almost be considered a group of friends or colleagues; they certainly knew one another and were in contact in various ways.[28] All of them were concerned about the Schism, and this crisis appears in many of their works in a variety of guises. From ballades to allegorical dream journeys to more overt political treatises, we find the problem of the Schism treated in imaginative ways. Solutions are offered, but in a veiled manner. What did these particular authors hope for when they expressed their views on the Schism, on the respective guilt of different parties, and on the responsibility of the European rulers under poetic coverings? How do they mete out blame? Which audiences did they have in mind, given their preponderant use of the vernacular? Was the use of these

24. See Millet and Hanly, "Les batailles d'Honorat Bovet," for the most up-to-date biography.

25. Bovet may also have been the author of the *Judicium Veritatis in causa Schismatis*. This allegorical vision of the tearful *Ecclesia* in a torn cloak appearing to the author has been summarized by Valois, *La France et le Grand Schisme d'Occident*, 1:369–70. It has not been edited. Valois discusses the problem of authorship in 1:369 n. 1.

26. For her biography, see Willard, *Christine de Pizan*.

27. Her letter to Deschamps and his response in the form of a ballade are translated in my *Selected Writings of Christine de Pizan*, pp. 109–13. For the real-estate transaction with Philippe, see Willard, *Christine de Pizan*, p. 23, based on Jorga, *Philippe de Mézières*, 510 n. 5. For references to Bovet's appearing to Christine, see my Chapter 5 n. 1.

28. On the connections between the male writers of this group, see Hanly, "Courtiers and Poets."

literary forms an a priori resignation to their inability to influence the fate of the church and Europe, a taking refuge in an interiority "incapable of mastering the interplay of social, historical, and political forces"?[29]

Philippe de Mézières

When Philippe de Mézières began the redaction of his monumental *Songe du Vieil Pelerin* in 1388, he had physically withdrawn from the world of politics, yet his involvement continued.[30] He played a role in peace negotiations with the English, wrote a letter to King Richard II, continued to advocate and preach a crusade, and was a counselor to Charles VI and a mentor to the young cardinal Pierre de Luxembourg (1369–87), an important figure in the polemics of the Schism.[31] In the *Songe*, Philippe could thus draw on a wide range of experiences— his political functions, diplomatic missions, spiritual preoccupations—as well as on his extensive travel.

In 1388, from the convent of the Celestins in Paris, Philippe thus reenters the world of politics as the Vieil Pelerin, or Old Pilgrim, a figure who, as early as the prologue, is transformed into Ardant Desir. This multiplicity of incarnations corresponds to the multiplicity of voices, reflecting what Blanchard calls "a politics of different view points."[32] The *Songe du Vieil Pelerin* is an extreme case of allegory invaded by contemporary reality. Like most allegories, it refuses a univocal reading and is therefore at odds with most of the historical writing of the period.[33] Thus, for the question of the Schism it is indeed difficult to determine the precise attitude of the narrator.[34] At the end of book 1, for example, should

29. The first point is suggested by Blanchard, "Discours de la réformation," p. 403: "Mais c'est également une sorte de désaveu manifestant les limites du réformateur qui n'a plus les moyens de mettre en œuvre son rêve. . . . L'intellectuel se retire de la cité." The quotation is from Quillet, "Herméneutique," p. 1092.
30. Jorga, Philippe's most prolific biographer, comments: "Si l'on s'imaginait cependant que Mézières renonça pour toujours aux affaires de ce monde, on se tromperait. Bien qu'il n'ait peut-être jamais quitté le couvent des Celestins, son activité et son influence sont tout aussi grandes qu'auparavant" (*Philippe de Mézières*, p. 447). Pomian-Turquet places the beginning of the redaction of the *Songe du Vieil Pelerin* in December 1388, shortly after the majority of Charles VI. See "Philippe de Mézières: Carnaval romain ou révolte de Cola di Rienzo?" p. 124.
31. For Pierre, see above, Chapter 3.
32. Blanchard, "Discours de la réformation," p. 397.
33. Strubel notes that "une lecture documentaire ou polémique semble s'imposer" ("Le *Songe du Vieil Pelerin* et les transformations de l'allégorie au quatorzième siècle," p. 54). See also Blanchard and Mühlethaler, *Ecriture et pouvoir*, pp. 26–32.
34. Delaruelle et al. summarize the political message of the *Songe du Vieil Pelerin* by claiming that Philippe "invited this king [Louis II of Anjou] to invade the peninsula [Italy] to install Clement as the only legitimate pope" (*L'Eglise au temps du Grand Schisme*, p. 71). While this

we subscribe to the decision of Ardant Desir to support Pope Clement VII or go with Reine Verite (Queen Truth) and refuse to take a definite stance? What should our attitude be about the call for a general council in book 3? And are we justified in trying to extract a univocal message from this complex allegory?

The *Songe du Vieil Pelerin* consists of three parts of uneven length. The first book covers in eighty chapters a journey the protagonist and a large number of allegorical figures make across Europe (they also touch on other continents— they see India and Nubia—but not for long), where they encounter a variety of societies embroiled in political problems. The leading metaphor is that of "good money" that needs to be distinguished from forged coins. The terminology derives mostly from alchemy, but it also has connections to contemporary banking practices and concerns for uncorrupted coinage.[35] Book 2 takes us to France (in the shape of a metaphorical ship) and a consideration of all parts of society (up to chap. 177), while book 3 focuses on the young King Charles VI as a second Moses. Book 3, ending with chapter 321, is dominated by the allegory of the chessboard as a kind of organizing principle for the moral lessons addressed to the young king.[36] The Schism is treated in approximately thirty-seven chapters, mostly in book 1, but it crops up here and there in the other books. All in all, we have allegorical construct layered upon allegorical construct, a heavy machinery that threatens to collapse under its own weight.[37]

Clearly, Philippe was aware of the difficulties in extracting a coherent picture of history and a political message from his text. This is why he supplies a "Table figurée" listing the correspondences between the allegorical figures and terms he uses and actual historical personages and events, at the outset of his vast book. He states optimistically

> [The Table is supplied] so that the secular reader, ignorant of book learning, when reading stories and allegories that seem at first sight obscure can have recourse to the above-mentioned Table and explanation, which will be an easy thing to do; for once he has read the said Table, that is, the gloss on the names, he will easily and without any

---

idea certainly surfaces in the text, this summary seems too reductive, given the text's multivocal setup.

35. See Krynen, *Idéal du prince et pouvoir royal,* esp. pp. 194–97.

36. Book 3 is the longest, with 170 folios; books 1 and 2 have 121 and 80 folios, respectively. Coopland's edition is based on BnF fr. 22542, though he realized halfway through his edition that MS Arsénal 2682–83 was superior. See Badel, *Le Roman de la Rose au XIVe siècle,* for a critique of this edition (382 n. 44)

37. See Strubel, "Le *Songe du Vieil Pelerin,*" and Quillet, "Herméneutique," for efforts to bring some order into this excessive piling up of allegorical layers.

trouble or difficulty whatsoever, when reading this present book, be able to understand everything clearly.

[Et ce est affin que le liseur seculier, aucunefoiz non fonde en clergie, lisans les hystoires et misteres de primeface obscures . . . ledit lisant ayt son recours a la table et exposicion susdicte, qui sera assez legere chose a faire; car qui unefoiz aura leu ladicte table, c'est assavoir la glose des noms, legierement et sans ennuy ou difficulte aucune, lisant cestui present livre, il entendra clerement toutes choses.] (1:102)

The Table then explains that Ardant Desir and his sister Bonne Esperance are figures for the Vieil Pelerin, who in turn is the author of the book, which is in the form of a dream; the figures represent all those who are desirous of reform (1:106).

Somewhat earlier in the prologue, Philippe considered the form of the *songe*, or dream vision. In what strikes me as a fundamental statement about the reception and function of the political dream vision, Philippe suggests:

Those who will feel hurt in this book by the lance of Queen Truth and will feel displeased, if they do not want to reform themselves, they can calm themselves by saying that this book is only a dream. And those who gladly accept the doctrine of the good money and holy alchemy from Queen Truth and her three ladies Peace, Mercy, and Justice[38] will not consider the book a dream but will receive it as a moral doctrine and a new practice of reformation of all of Christendom.

[Ceulx qui se sentiront feruz en cestui livre de la lance de Verite la royne et auront aucune desplaisance, s'ilz ne se vouldront amander, pour eulz appaiser s'il leur plaira ilz pourront reputer cestui livre pour ung songe. Et ceulx qui prendront en gre la doctrine de la belle monnaie de la saincte arquemie de Verite la royne et les troys dames, Paix, Misericorde et Justice, ne le tindront pas a songe, mais le recevront comme morale doctrine et nouvelle pratique de la reformacion de toute la crestiente.] (1:95)

It seems that Philippe is preaching to the converted and that those who want to resist his teachings can do so easily by accentuating the negative—that is, fictional—nature of dreams.[39] But the part of his audience that is receptive to

38. Thus, Philippe's ladies are the Four Daughters of God of Psalm 85:10 (RSV). On this group in medieval allegorical literature, see Newman, *God and the Goddesses,* esp. pp. 44–47, 163–64.

39. This is a much-debated question, going back at least as far as Macrobius. See Kruger, *Dreaming in the Middle Ages.*

his doctrines will extract them from under the allegorical covering. Philippe seems intent on not offending anyone, not wanting to force his audience to swallow his moral and political lessons unless they are willing. He may also have been aware of the "social cost of dissidence," perhaps anticipating the string of failures that his various proposals, especially those concerning a crusade, would experience.[40]

What, then, are Philippe's views regarding the Schism of the church? About one-fifth of the *Songe du Vieil Pelerin* deals directly with this question—in particular, the chapters on the travelers' sojourns in Genoa, Rome, and Avignon, a passage that the *Songe*'s editor, G. W. Coopland, sees as an extraordinarily bold criticism of the Avignon papacy (1:37). Clement VII is targeted in the chapters on Avignon, but Urban VI does not fare any better in the chapters on Genoa, where he lived at that time. In the "Table figurée," Philippe in fact explains that "the horned shepherd or pastor" (le pasteur cornu) is Pope Urban VI and adds that "the big horned shepherd, called the Debonnayre, is a figure of Clement VII, whom his followers call the vicar of Christ" (le grant pasteur cornu, appelle Debonnayre, est prins en figure pour Clement VIIe, des siens appelle vycaire de Jesucrist; 1:110). Philippe echoes here the practice of such contemporary chroniclers as Michel Pintoin, who often refers to the "self-styled" or "so-called" pope.[41] The "Table," then, giving the explanation of things to come, does not advertise any partiality for Pope Clement.

Before our flying party touches down in Genoa and Avignon to visit the popes, they stop in Rome, where the inhabitants also get their share of biting satire. The treachery of the Romans was a common topos at the time and can be found, for example, in Vincent Ferrer's *Treatise on the Modern Schism* (1380), where, going back to Saint Bernard, he stresses their unreliability and duplicity.[42] Vincent uses the Romans' known bad character as a justification for the cardinals' mistrust of any promises the Romans made for their safety. These justified suspicions in turn serve as proof that the cardinals indeed elected Urban VI in fear and that therefore the election was invalid.

40. See Hanly, "Literature and Dissent in the Court of Charles VI," p. 273.
41. One formula is, for example, "Urbanus pro summo pontifice se gerebat" (1:636), suggesting that Pope Urban VI only played the role of the pope but was not truly so. Later on, in 1406, when things have deteriorated in the relationship between the French and Benedict XIII, Pintoin routinely refers to the Avignon pope as "Petro de Luna, quem nonnulle gentes in hoc miserabili scismate Benedictum duodecim appellant" (Pedro de Luna, whom certain people in this deplorable Schism call Benedict XII [an error for XIII]; 3:498). On Pintoin, see Millet, "Michel Pintoin, Chroniqueur du Grand Schisme d'Occident." See also Pierre Salmon's *Dialogues,* which always refer to Pope Benedict XIII as Pedro de Luna; the omission of the papal name advertises Salmon's partiality implicitly because he is navigating between Orléanist and Burgundian loyalties. See Hedeman, *Of Counselors and Kings,* p. 26.
42. Chap. 1, point three in the second objection (see Garganta and Forcada, *San Vicente Ferrer,* p. 428).

Philippe transposes recent political events into the framework of a beast fable, a mad carnival in Rome whose participants recap the events of the papal election of 1378.[43] Coopland rightly suggests that this scene may have the effect of a modern political cartoon; it is an "intense visualization" and dramatization (1:141). After visiting several churches, Reine Verite and her entourage settle in the papal palace for a consistory. Immediately, an unruly crowd appears, badly dressed and sporting animal heads. They seem to belong to Hellequin's horde and present a "travesty of a penitential cortège."[44] They are in fact strange penitents, showing themselves to be impious idolaters, unworthy of receiving the pope in their city but willing to tell their story to the queen. They choose Ysangrin the wolf to be their spokesperson, for they want someone simple and solid who will not use sophisms and double-talk but give a plain exposition of their ancient nobility (1:265). Renart, the fox, while also present, is rejected because of his passion for rhetoric and sophistry.[45]

Thus, a wolf-figure, dressed in the skin of a recently killed lamb, begins the Romans' discourse addressed to Reine Verite, confessing their malice and recognizing their guilt in the matter of the Schism (1:266). Ysangrin is the proverbial wolf in sheep's clothing, recalling for a late fourteenth-century audience the political theme of the bad ruler—both secular and ecclesiastical—as the bad shepherd or even a disguised wolf.[46] It is this multilayered personage, then, that offers a history of Rome and the papacy, emphasizing several times that at heart the Romans never abandoned their old idols, even though Reine Verite's "Great Master of Coinage" (Grant Maistre de la Monnoye)—that is, God— gave them "a wonderful alchemist, Saint Peter, badly dressed and without shoes, who forged very fine coins" (un merveilleux arquemiste saint Pierre, mal vetu et deschaux, qui forgeait tresfins besans; 1:266). The papacy's move to Avginon, Ysangrin continues, left Rome a widow "and the Romans stone cold" (et les Rommains froys comme une pierre; 1:268).[47] Pope Urban V at least came back to visit, and then Gregory XI returned, only to die in Rome. Hence the reproaches that the Romans caused the Schism.

43. Pomian-Turquet ("Philippe de Mézières") argues for a transposition of the revolt of Cola di Rienzo in 1347. See Mollat and Wolff, *Les Révolutions populaires en Europe*, pp. 99–104. But given that the beast figures recount the recent Schism, it would be difficult to see Cola di Rienzo in the senator who leads them.

44. See Williamson, "Ysangrin and Hellequin's Horde in *Le Songe du Vieil Pelerin*," p. 181.

45. Williamson discusses this distrust of rhetoric in "Ysangrin," pp. 176–77.

46. See, e.g., Christine de Pizan's *Livre du corps de policie* 1.9, "Commen le bon prince doit ressembler au bon pastour," for a lengthy development of this metaphor. See also her *Livre de la paix* 3.19.

47. The image of the city as widow appears at the beginning of the *Lamentations of Jeremiah:* "How like a widow has she become / She that was great among the nations" (1:1). See also fig. 1.

Philippe then has Ysangrin tell the story of the conclave and of the coercion of the cardinals by the armed Roman populace, a direct transposition of the reports of contemporary chroniclers, with an additional twist in the last phrase: "We surrounded the conclave and beat and screamed and threatened them that we wanted to have a pastor according to our will, *in order to resurrect the idols of our gods and exalt them*" (Le conclave avironnasmes, et feismes tant par batre et par hault crier et par menacier que nous eusmes pasteur a nostre gre, *pour redrecier les ydoles de nos dieux et pour les essaulcier;* 1:271, my emphasis). The crowd clamors for a Roman pope—or at least an Italian, and certainly not a French pope—in order to resurrect their pagan idolatry. So "our Apulian pastor" (nostre pasteur puilloys; 1:271) is elected, but then the cardinals escape (although Dam Renart, the fox, had barred the gates!) and create another sovereign pontiff "by whom we are deserted, and our laughter has turned into tears" (dont nous sommes desers et nostre risee est tournee en plour; 1:271). Now, Ysangrin insists, they would like to have their pope back, whether he is Italian, French, Burgundian, Scottish, German, or Hungarian.[48] At the end of this discourse the question arises whether the Romans should be extinguished as a punishment for their sins. Reine Verite addresses a long chastising sermon to them but agrees to spare them and to punish them only with poverty. The queen does leave some tokens, though, representing the hope of the party's return and a better fortune for the Romans.

Ysangrin's discourse, telling the official story accepted by the French in 1379 from the point of view of the perpetrators, effectively sets the stage for the chapters on Urban VI and Clement VII. Ysangrin, despite his protestations of being a simple and straightforward speaker, can be considered only an unreliable narrator: a wolf in sheep's clothing. The contexts of the beast fable and the mad carnival, linked to a vocabulary of the time denoting political irresponsibility, introduce elements of disorder and dislocation. Thus, although Ysangrin presents the events as they were told by many French chroniclers and polemicists after 1378, he leaves some doubts in the audience's minds. Who is the true pope cannot yet be determined.

Our travelers now move on to Genoa, the temporary home of Pope Urban VI, the "great horned pastor" (grant pasteur cornu; 1:283), who appears before them "clothed as a sovereign shepherd" (en l'abbit de souverain bergier; 1:284). Philippe shows the varying perceptions of this pope's legitimacy in a series of striking images:

48. In 1398, when the election of a new pope was being discussed (in case both reigning popes step down), the Avignon cardinals claimed in striking unanimity that they would be happy with any legitimate choice, be he African, Arab, or Indian, provided he is orthodox and not blinded by a passion to dishonor the church! (Pintoin, *Chronique du religieux de Saint-Denys,* 2:628.)

To some the above-mentioned cloak seemed to be beautiful and red, and the tiara on the head of the said shepherd made from three gold crowns; to others his cloak seemed of a pale, ashen black, and the tiara as belonging to a person made from smoke.

[Aux ungs ledit habit sembloit beaux et vermeilx et la chaere sus la tete dudit bergier de troys couronnes d'or couronnee, aux autres sembloit noir pale l'abit et cendreux, et la chaiere comme d'un parsonnage ou de fumee composee.] (1:284)

Around this "spectral pope"[49] are grouped the cardinals who wear "certain hats" (certains chapeaux; 1:284), which according to some observers are not quite what they should be. While to some the cardinals' cloaks seem as red as roses and true and "without a gloss" (sans glose; 1:284), to others they appear "dark, in pieces, dirty and yellow, woven from the fleece of an old sheep" (obscurs, derompuz, sales et jaunes, tissuz de la toison d'une vieille brebis; 1:284). Indeed, the color yellow evokes something else for the observers:

And the hats seemed to them to be made from old paper that had for a long time soaked in manure. How strange! said the above-mentioned observers, that if these cardinals were dressed in yellow like the Jews—for their faith was entirely corrupted by the great heat of avarice and ambition—they had by chance acquired the yellow color that could not be cured or washed away by all the water in the Thames.

[Et les chapeaux leur sembloient composez de vieil papier, qui longuement avoit trempe ou fum[i]er. Quel merveille! disoient les assitens dessusdiz, se ces cardinaulx estoient vestuz de jaune comme les Juifz, car de grant chaleur d'avarice et d'ambicion leur foye estoit entierement pourry, et par accident avoient acquis la jaunesse qui ne pourroit estre sanee ne lavee pour tout l'eauue de Tannisse.] (1:284)

The smoke and old paper perceived by one part of the observers suggest evanescence, a lack of stability of this papacy.[50] The bright-red color and the term *sans glose* are positive traits, emphasizing the legitimacy and straightforwardness

---

49. This term is David Nirenberg's (personal communication).
50. As we saw in Chapter 3, the visionary Constance de Rabastens associated Clement VII with smoke in a vision of just a few years earlier. See Constance de Rabastens, *Révélations*, p. 267.

perceived by some of the spectators. By contrast, the color yellow has only negative connotations, associated with corruption and, in expressions of antisemitic stereotypes, with avarice.[51] This brilliant tableau of changing colors and perceptions is undoubtedly one of the most dramatic images of the uncertainty, of the constant shifting of viewpoints characteristic of much of the literature engendered by the Schism.

Before proceeding to the judiciary hearing, Philippe offers his audience a long typological passage on the seamless tunic, an image of the church that spans the Old and the New Testaments. Joseph's tunic, spattered with the blood of sacrifice, is the Old Testament figure of Christ's sacrifice; the tunic stands for Christ and also for the Virgin, who adorns Christ with the seamless tunic (1:286). But the tunic—previously inviolate but now mutilated—also stands for the church "torn into two halves, and divided into two pieces" (en deux moitiez fendue, et en deux pieces divisee; 1:287). The terminology of the seamless tunic was of course also current in the learned discourses of the church, and it is interesting to note that at an extremely critical moment early in his papacy Benedict XIII had recourse to the same traditional image. In 1395, Benedict, who strongly advocated the *voie de fait* (armed conflict) to force Boniface IX to abdicate, tried to persuade the French king and dukes to support him in this enterprise. The French, of course, had already decided on the *voie de cession* (abdication) and were not willing to send troops to Italy. In a bull of that same year, Benedict claimed that until now he had directed all his efforts "to achieve and speed up the union of the shreds of the Lord's seamless tunic" (ad procurandum et accelerandum scisse dominice vestis inconsutilem unitatem)[52] but that now he must insist on military means to oust his rival. Going back to the *Songe du Vieil Pelerin*, it would be obvious to a learned audience that it was the Roman pope who had shredded the tunic in the first place. All the discourses of the Schism used the same vocabulary and thus established connections between different types of texts, whether "official," such as a papal bull, or poetic, such as Philippe's elaborate allegory laced generously with typology.

After this long typological excursus, then, the proceedings switch to a judiciary hearing on the merits of the Urbanist papacy. The allegorical figure of Compassion directly accuses Urban: "Here you have the creator of this horrible division, this horned pastor who calls himself sovereign shepherd" (veez cy

---

51. See Petzold, "'Of the Significance of Colours': The Iconography of Colour in Romanesque and Early Gothic Book Illumination." Pleij details the myriad negative meanings of the color yellow in chap. 6 of his *Colors Demonic and Divine*. They include "sorrow, covetousness, hunger, and death," as well as cruelty and lack of faith.

52. Pintoin, *Chronique du Religieux de Saint-Denys,* book 16, chap. 6 (2:287).

l'aucteur de ceste horible division, cestui pasteur cornu qui s'appelle souverain bergier; 1:287).The indictment is pursued by six cardinals, thin, sad, badly dressed in torn clothing (1:288). One of them, reputed like the other five to have died of Urban's cruelty,[53] admits the cardinals' initial anti-French sentiment but now voices the opinion that they repented of their wrong papal choice too late. They did not realize the murderous intentions of this frenetic pastor, who was more cruel than a serpent (1:289). The crazed tyranny of this pastor recalls the evil beast announced in prophecies, a clear reference to the biblical Book of Revelation and the end of times.[54] In response Reine Verite bitterly accuses Urban of having accepted "the tumultuous election" (la tumultueuse election) and to have "forged the Schism and the bitter division of my Father's cloak through which many a soul will descend into the abyss" (forgie le scisme et l'amere division de la cote de mon Pere, dont mainte(s) ame(s) en descendra en abisme; 1:291). She then goes on to speak of the pope who abdicated (Celestine V)—unlike Urban, who gained the papacy by force of arms and whom she calls the "pere de scisme" (1:292). Yet, when the queen is asked by the duke of Genoa to pronounce a judgment, she refuses, because she has not yet heard the arguments of the opponents (1:294).

In terms of subject matter and historical detail, these chapters reflect quite accurately a number of contemporary chronicles. But unlike the chroniclers, Philippe uses visionary elements, such as the brilliant opening scene in Genoa, to sow doubt and uncertainty, attitudes that are repeated in more straightforward terms at the end of this episode, when Reine Verite postpones any definite judgment.

From Genoa the travelers proceed to Avignon, the seat of Pope Clement VII. This stay is covered in thirty-three folio pages, more than three times the folios Philippe used for the stay in Genoa. While Urban himself sat on the bench of the accused in Genoa, here we find a much vaster battle of the vices and the virtues.[55] Three allegorical figures in particular are splendidly hideous: Orgueil, Avarice, and Luxure (Pride, Avarice, Lust). Each one has the human body of an old woman and a triple monstrous head. Orgueil, in a splendid silk robe with embroidered lions and eagles, sports the heads of a lion, a viper, and a serpent. She holds a pointed iron rod and leads a little hedgehog on a leash (1:308). Avarice wears an outfit so old that one can no longer make out its material; her heads are those of a griffin, a serpent, and a vulture. She carries a crystal vial full of gold pieces and, under her arm, a tamed black mole (1:308). Luxure, finally,

---

53. This is meant to be Adam Easton, who actually was the only one of the six cardinals to escape with his life. He died in England in 1397. See Valois, *La France*, 2:116–17.

54. See Deschamps on this image, below, and Chapter 6.

55. See Bell, *Etude sur le Songe du Vieil Pelerin*, chap. 3.

dressed in embroidered silk, has the heads of a siren, a marmot, and a sow. Her attribute is a vial made from a stained mirror filled with herbs; her pet is a weasel (1:309). Each wears a crown made from thorns and sulfur.[56] They represent "nothing," or the negation of all that is good, as they explain to Reine Verite: "Morally speaking, according to the doctrine of your Father's church, you could say that we are nothing" (parlant moralement, selon la doctrine des docteurs de l'eglise de vostre Pere, il se puet dire que nous sommes nyent; 1:315–16).

Philippe now exposes at great length how these Vices dominate the church, again echoing reproaches found in many chronicles and polemical writings. Thus, Michel Pintoin voices the same complaints in his *Chronique de Saint-Denys;* for example, in a chapter entitled "Quomodo papa Clemens gravabat Ecclesiam gallicanam" (How Pope Clement oppressed the French church; book 6, chap. 12), he describes how Clement squeezes the last penny out of his subjects and thinks only of gorging himself (and his cardinals) with good food. Book 6 covers the year 1385, but the theme is universal, and the attacks on the corrupt Avignon papacy continue throughout the chronicle into the reign of Benedict XIII.

Orgueil is in charge of an allegorical clock the different parts of which stand for her eternal life, and others, showing the zodiac, allow her to dominate people's lives. Vainglory and "superstitious vanity in gaining honors" (supersticieuse vanite des honneurs; 1:319) characterize the people she controls. As for Avarice,[57] simony aids in exerting dominance over the church, whose riches are safely stored in the papal palace in Avignon under the watchful eyes of her griffon—lest the poor and sick lay their hands on the church's treasures (1:332). Avarice is also the creator of wars, crime, and treachery.

Luxure, finally, is the most powerful of the three old women. She reigns everywhere, but particularly in the palaces of secular rulers and prelates and in monasteries. One day, she boasts, she created an especially precious coin, a female pope: "As vicar for your Father in this Roman court, I made reign a woman from England, which astonished the cardinals and all Christendom greatly" (pour lieutenant de vostre Pere en ceste court en Romme, je feiz regner une femme, qui estoit d'Angleterre . . . dont les cardinaulx et la Crestiente en fu moult esbaye; 1:338). Pope Joan cropped up a number of times in Schism polemics, and Philippe comes back to her later in the argumentation of Ardant Desir.[58] Here, Luxure accentuates the sexual aspects of Pope Joan, a temptation

---

56. For the negative connotations of all these animals, see Bell, *Etude,* p. 57.

57. Avarice (or Greed) was always seen as one of the causes the church's decay. Looking back on the Schism, the Council of Constance identified Avarice as its principal root. See Stump, *The Reforms of the Council of Constance,* esp. pp. 214–18.

58. See Boureau, *La papesse Jeanne,* pp. 174–79, and Gössmann, *Mulier Papa,* esp. pp. 59–61.

she managed to introduce among the highest prelates. The lengthy disquisitions of the Vices in effect present a whole history of the corruption of the church where detail after detail can be matched to historical events. In response to the testimony of these irrefutable witnesses—the very creators and embodiment of the vices they describe—church reform becomes more and more urgent. Indeed, this long exposé of the Three Vices is a dramatization of the call for reform, reiterating the points made in many polemical texts, such as Nicolas de Clamanges's *Tractatus de ruina Ecclesiae* (Treatise on the ruin of the church),[59] that the Schism is a punishment for the moral failings of the church and that only a thorough reform can heal the wounds of the Schism.

Reine Verite, consternated by this long recital of the church's sins, then begins the indictment of Clement VII. With great emotion she sums up the effect of the Schism on the faithful:

> The poor sheep, miserable and starved by their pastors, sheared, skinned, and scraped from all sides by the Schism, fight against each other because of the zeal of their mother the church and the desire they have to unify her, and they all believe they are doing the right thing.

> [Les pauvres brebiz chetives et toutes affames de leur(s) pasteur(s), tondues, et escorchees et reses de l'une part et de l'autre du scisme, par le zel de l'eglise leur mere et desir qu'ilz ont de l'union d'icelle, se combatent ensemble, cuidans bien faire chacun de sa part.] (1:354)

She then goes on to tell of virtuous popes and concludes that the church's growing temporal power is at the origin of her corruption. All along, councils were called to resolve ecclesiastical problems. Philippe embarks here on the conciliar project that he and his contemporaries, such scholars as Heinrich of Langenstein, Pierre d'Ailly, Jean Gerson, Simon de Cramaud, and many more, advocated for decades. It is clear that the Schism is not "an article of faith" (article de la foy; 1:365) but a power struggle between two strong-minded individuals. Philippe now turns to the image of a rhetorical tournament and has two champions, "Le Terrible" for Urban, and "Le Debonnayre" for Clement, make the cases for their popes.

Next, Ardant Desir, figuring Philippe himself, asks to take the floor, although he claims to be speechless with confusion. Nonetheless, he sums up the different attitudes toward the popes and argues convincingly that most of

59. See Coville's edition of this text, and Bellitto, *Nicolas de Clamanges*, pp. 42–43.

the faithful are acting in good faith, truly believing in the rightful election of their supreme pontiff. He then admits that he was swayed in Clement's favor by the cardinals' reports to the University of Paris about the rightful election of Clement. He adduces the legendary Pope Joan, already mentioned earlier by Luxure, in an argument that cardinals have the right to change their minds if they find they have been deceived; just as Joan deceived the prelates, hiding the fact that she was a woman, so Urban hid the illegitimacy of his election (1:370–71).

But there was also a more affective and spiritual motivation: the miraculous cure of Marie Robine at the tomb of the recently deceased Cardinal Pierre de Luxembourg (1369–87). Philippe had been a mentor of this eighteen-year-old cardinal, one of these *jeunes gens tristes* (André Vauchez's term) who had been elevated in the church hierarchy against his will.[60] Pierre d'Ailly had been one of his supporters, and it was this great writer and conciliar theorist who presented Pierre's case for canonization in 1388. The miracles that began to occur right after his death were instantly exploited for Clementist propaganda.[61] Marie Robine herself was enlisted as a spokesperson for Clement and set up handsomely as a recluse at the cemetery of Saint Pierre in Avignon.[62] Philippe, in the person of Ardant Desir, is a perfect example of the effectiveness of this propaganda, for in response to these miraculous proofs of Clement's legitimacy he concludes: "I confess humbly that the Debonnayre, Pope Clement, is the supreme vicar of sweet Jesus on earth and the supreme head of the church" (je confesse doulcement que le Debonnayre, pape Clement, est souverain lieutenant en terre du doulx Jesus et souverain chief de l'eglise; 1:374).

Ardant Desir's humility makes him add that he will submit to the judgment of Reine Verite, for little sheep and goats should not presume to inquire too deeply into the will of the big-horned goats who have the power to elect their sovereign shepherd. Reine Verite, however, refuses to pronounce a judgment. Her intent, she insists, was not to choose who is the rightful pope but to work for the reform of the church.

Philippe then abandons the question of the Schism for many folios and only returns to it in the context of the moral teachings addressed to the king in book 3. Chapter 247 contains an eloquent plea for a general council in order to

60. Vauchez, *La sainteté en Occident aux derniers siècles du Moyen Age*, p. 357. On Philippe and Pierre, see Jorga, *Philippe de Mézières*, pp. 460–62. See also above, Chapter 3.
61. See Valois, *La France*, 2:365. Pierre was used as a "counterweight" to the Urbanist Catherine of Siena (2:362). See above, Chapter 3.
62. See Tobin, "Le 'Livre des Révélations' de Marie Robine" and "Les visions et les révélations de Marie Robine d'Avignon dans le contexte prophétique des années 1400." See also above, Chapter 3.

resolve the Schism. One or the other pope, or even a third one to replace both of them, should be chosen by a council consisting of one-third nobles, one-third prelates, and one-third "le peuple groz" (the simple people; 2:293). Philippe thus has a more secular vision of the council than the contemporary conciliarists did. Some of them admitted that even though in early Christian times it was possible to include the ordinary faithful in church councils, today this is no longer feasible. Others argued that while simple people may be present at the council they will have no vote.[63] For Philippe, a full two-thirds of the council would be secular. The fact that this passage occurs in book 3 of the *Songe du Vieil Pelerin,* focusing on advice to the young king and placing the council in a wider framework that includes reform of the realm, can explain this vision of the council.

Further, a crusade should be organized that would unify Christendom and therefore automatically put an end to the Schism. As it had been for Catherine of Siena,[64] the crusade was one of Philippe's most cherished dreams, and he would return to it in the *Epistre au roy Richart II.* In the last part of the *Songe,* the Schism, then, appears in a more purely didactic context; the ideas expressed are identical to those coming out of the university milieux at the time.

Philippe's great achievement in the *Songe du Vieil Pelerin* is the mastery of so many different dramatic modes to present several sets of political problems. The beastly carnival procession in Rome serves the purpose of presenting the Romans as idolaters, unworthy of receiving a legitimate pope. The trial in Genoa, preceded by the hallucinatory vision of the pope and his cardinals, draws in imaginative ways on the judiciary tradition. And the extremely lengthy stay in Avignon, providing a history of the church's corruption through the accounts of the most hideous beings imaginable, ends with the queen's refusal to judge, thus calling for the convocation of a general council, an idea reiterated in a sober didactic voice toward the end of this monumental work.[65]

It is this voice, laced with a plaintive tone, that dominates in Philippe's *Epistre au roy Richart II.* Seven years have passed since the completion of the

63. See Heinrich of Langenstein's 1379 *Epistola pacis: Per omnium fidelium congregationem, sicut tempore ascensionis Christi erat possibile . . .* (cited by Sieben, *Traktate,* 120 n. 36) and Jean Gerson's later *De potestate ecclesiastica* (1416–17) in *Oeuvres complètes,* 6:210–50, esp. 6:240. On Heinrich's treatises, see Kreuzer, *Heinrich von Langenstein,* chap. 2. On Gerson, see Morrall, *Gerson and the Great Schism,* esp. pp. 100–108, on the *De potestate.* For an analysis of the contemporary definitions of the council, see Sieben, *Traktate,* esp. pp. 119–24. For the actual composition of the attendees and the vote, see the Conclusion of the present book.

64. See Cardini, "L'idea di crociata in Catarina da Siena."

65. In the best tradition of the allegorical dream vision, Philippe wakes up at the end of the book, consoled by Providence Divine and praying in front of the Virgin's altar in the chapel of the Celestins in Paris.

Songe du Vieil Pelerin, and the situation of the church has become worse instead of better. The death of Clement VII in 1394 had opened a brief window of opportunity for resolving the Schism (a window astutely perceived by Honoré Bovet, as we shall see shortly). But the quick accession of Pedro de Luna as Benedict XIII put an end to these hopes, for Benedict turned out to be the most stubborn, tricky, and power-hungry pope yet.

The letter to Richard II was probably both a real letter and what one might call an "open letter," a medium Philippe used publicly "to set forth his views and pleadings on the great issues of the day."[66] The Schism takes second or even third place, behind the wishes and strategies for a lasting peace between France and England (a truce was in effect then) and a grand design for a crusade;[67] it thus forms part of the general call for unity among Christians.

Unlike the *Songe du Vieil Pelerin,* which places the Schism in a variety of dramatic settings, the *Epistre* limits the metaphorics almost exclusively to wounds and healing, as well as familial images. The whole text, however, again features many allegorical systems (the kings as precious stones, the vineyards of Engadi, the terrible and the fruitful garden, and more) stacked on top of each other.

Addressing himself directly to Richard II, Philippe describes the open wound that Christendom is suffering from. Its poison has infected all the faithful. Up to now, it has been treated with *popilion* (p. 93), an ointment made from poplar blossoms.[68] But this remedy, which stands for the discourses of the flatterers, has prolonged the Schism instead of ending it. What is needed now is the "ointment of the apostles" (oingnement des apostres; p. 93), which is first corrosive and then soothing. Now the imagery switches to the church as the sick mother suffering from the wound of the Schism. Her sons, the two kings Charles VI and Richard II, are both descended from Saint Louis (d. 1270) and are therefore "brothers." They have left their mother torn to pieces and languishing; they have permitted the Schism that created "a two-headed monster of their mother" (un monstre de leur mere a .ii. testes; p. 94), a vision of the church also to be found in Deschamps and others. That is, initially a victim, the church has

---

66. Coopland, ed. and trans., in Philippe de Mézières, *Letter to King Richard II,* p. xxv. Perroy shows that this letter "a réellement existé dans les archives anglaises à la fin du XIVe siècle." See *L'Angleterre et le Grand Schisme d'Occident,* 364 n. 3.

67. See Tarnowski, "Unity and the *Epistre au roi Richart,*" and Brownlee, "Cultural Comparison: Crusade as Construct in Late Medieval France." The letter was written the year before the disastrous defeat of the European allies, including a French contingent, by the Turks at Nicopolis in 1396.

68. On this ointment and the entire medical vocabulary emloyed by Philippe, see Picherit, *La Métaphore pathologique et thérapeutique à la fin du Moyen Age,* chap. 9; pp. 77–78, for the remedies of the "popilion" and the "oignement des apostres."

turned into a monster herself and exerts monstrous influence on her children—
a truly vicious circle. The solution Philippe proposes here does not center so
much on a general council as on a lasting peace between France and England:
"The peace and true love shown publicly by you and your dearly beloved
brother Charles" (la paix et vraye amour monstree en publique de vous et du
roy Charles, vostre tresame frere; p. 97). At this time Richard II was coming
around to the French position of dealing with the Schism—though against the
feelings of his own subjects[69]—and Philippe, aware of these developments,
adopted a different strategy than he had in his *Songe du Vieil Pelerin*.

Thus, instead of the pan-European view Philippe took in the *Songe du Vieil
Pelerin*, here he shows the Schism to be a purely French-English problem. Echoing the words of the duke of Lancaster at the meeting of Amiens (April 1392)
that peace between England and France must be a precondition for the end of
the Schism, Philippe endorses the view that the two kings can abolish this
intractable division of the church simply by reconciling. This reconciliation will
be sealed by Richard's marriage to Isabelle of France (1389–1409), who was all of
six years old at the time.[70] This marriage did indeed take place the next year, but
a lasting peace remained elusive because Richard was deposed in 1399 and killed
the following year.[71] And the Schism was to last almost another generation.

Among Philippe's many political ideas, the Schism occupies an important
place. In the *travestissement* of allegory, he lucidly analyzed its causes and proposed solutions, such as a general council, also suggested by others and in
other genres. He avoided a clear-cut support of the Avignon papacy, in line
with the doubts already rampant in France at the time about whether
Clement VII and later Benedict XIII could be considered the true and only
pope. Armand Strubel suggests that, for Philippe, in the end "the relationship
between allegory and the real necessarily ends up, it seems, in an impasse."[72] It
is true that he is powerless to resolve the problem of the Schism, but is his language therefore "the language of impotence and defeat"?[73] His visionary texts
have their own force, I believe. They give his audience powerful images that
allow them to visualize the crises of their society and their church. They speak
in a poetic voice and appeal to the imagination—not the least powerful political

69. See Perroy, *L'Angleterre et le Grand Schisme d'Occident*, chap. 9.
70. Perroy points out that the problem that Isabelle did not adhere to the Roman pope, as did
Richard, was skirted by the archbishop of York ("c'etait tourner élégamment la difficulté")
by simply not mentioning it when he published "les dispenses pour la cérémonie nuptiale."
See his *L'Angleterre et le Grand Schisme d'Occident*, p. 379. For the words of the duke of Lancaster, see pp. 358–59.
71. Isabelle later married Charles of Orléans, nephew of Charles VI.
72. "*Le Songe du Vieil Pelerin*," p. 70.
73. Quillet, "Herméneutique," p. 1092.

weapons, to be sure, and not any less effective than the many theoretical tracts, polemic treatises, and diplomatic missions that occupied French scholars and politicians for two generations.

Eustache Deschamps

Philippe de Mézières clearly thought highly of Eustache Deschamps, also known as Eustache Morel, for he recommends his writings to the young Charles VI in his *Songe du Vieil Pelerin*. After advising Charles that he should have Saint Augustine's *City of God* (also studied by Charlemagne) and John of Salisbury's *Policraticus* read to him, Philippe continues (in the voice of Reine Verite): "You can also read and listen to the virtuous writings of your servant and official Eustache Morel" (Tu puez bien lire aussi et ouyr les dictez vertueulx de ton serviteur et officier Eustache Morel; 2:223). Deschamps's varied texts could certainly help the king get a better sense of what was going on in his kingdom. As royal official, military man, ambassador entrusted with various missions, and historiographer of the reign, Deschamps participated in the important events of his time. But he was more than a witness; he was a critic.[74] According to Thierry Lassabatère, he belongs to "this obscure and secret magma too often ignored that constitutes public opinion. . . . He reveals to us its profound beliefs, the craziest ideas, the way in which the people live what is happening around them."[75] His works are therefore particularly valuable testimonies to reactions to a wide range of social and political ills. While one cannot claim that Deschamps speaks exclusively for the "common people," he does give the impression that he was in the thick of things and did not hesitate to voice his opinions, many of them extremely negative. He did not prepare presentation copies of his manuscripts, but rather lost and scattered some of his works in his many travels; others were collected later.[76] The papal Schism is one of the topics that appear repeatedly in his vast oeuvre.

Unlike Philippe de Mézières, Deschamps did not choose to cast himself as a dreamer and traveler in the framework of an allegorical vision. Yet, many of his poems have a visionary, even hallucinatory, quality that creates indelible images of the monster of the Schism, the suffering church, or the evil moon in the shape of Pedro de Luna. The most common form Deschamps used was the

---

74. See Lacassagne, "Eustache Deschamps: Discours et société."
75. Lassabatère, "Le bon gouvernement selon Eustache Deschamps," p. 8.
76. The edition of Deschamps's works is based on BnF fr. 840, a huge collection not made under Deschamps's supervision. Most of his ballades cannot be dated precisely. All parenthetical references are to the edition listed in the Bibliography.

ballade, which, though fixed by poetic constraints, proved for Deschamps to be a wide-open form, receptive to just about any kind of subject matter. As Michèle Denizot-Ghil puts it, "The space of the ballade, restricted by the constraints of its fixed form, seems especially appropriate for the esthetic transfiguration of exemplary moments in history."[77] This transfiguration results in more dramatic evocations of the divided church than the rather standard but nonetheless moving allegorical representation we find in Deschamps's *Complainte de l'Eglise* (Complaint of the church) of 1393.

In 1380 Deschamps marks the changing of the guard in the papacy, the empire, and the French kingdom with a mournful ballade on the deaths of Pope Urban V (1370), the emperor Charles IV (1378), and the French king Charles V (1380) (ball. 165, 1:295–96). He moves from the Old Testament (David crying for Absalom) through myth (Hecuba lamenting the fallen Trojans) to the present; the triple loss causes cruel suffering to the church (vv. 1–8). It is interesting that Deschamps omits the death of Pope Gregory XI, who had died in Rome the same year as the emperor. Could this be seen as an implicit commentary on the Schism?[78] Was Urban V the last "true" pope for Deschamps? It is certainly possible that Deschamps inscribes himself here into the tradition of those who believed that Gregory's move to Rome marked the beginning of the Schism. This is confirmed by verses 21–22: "Alas! Urban's reign was very good. He led Christendom justly" (Helas! d'Urbain fut le regne tresbon / Crestienté tint en ses drois liens). It is as if Pope Gregory XI had never reigned. At this moment, then, Deschamps appears to toe the official line of the French monarchy and to support Clement VII, although he never militated in favor of the Avignon papacy.[79]

Several ballades can be tied to specific events in the development of the Schism and Deschamps's attitude toward it. In a ballade that can be dated rather precisely to 1381 (ball. 1012, 5:276–78), Deschamps seems to advocate the convening of a general council, a position that was then not yet favored by the university. The ballade begins with a general evocation of the corrupt state of the church and the conflicts between secular rulers. Bad bread has been distributed—a reference to the Antechrist[80]—and has been the cause of the discord. Now the Great Schism reigns and two popes want to be adored where a

77. Denizot-Ghil, "Poétique de la discontinuité dans l'œuvre lyrique d'Eustache Deschamps," p. 210.
78. This is suggested by Laurie, "Eustache Deschamps," p. 10.
79. See Boudet and Millet, *Eustache Deschamps en son temps*, p. 117.
80. See Boudet and Millet, *Eustache Deschamps*, p. 103, note to v. 22. Although in other chapters I use the spelling "Antichrist," here I prefer "Antechrist" because Deschamps spells it like this, highlighting the aspects of the Antechrist coming before (*ante*) the end of time, rather than his being the opposite (*anti*) of Christ.

single one should rule (vv. 21–27). Why do the kings not do their duty and convoke a council to determine which one should prevail? wonders Deschamps,
for one of the elections was surely inspired by the Antechrist. But which one? He
therefore exhorts "Colleges" and "Estudes" (vv. 35–36)—that is, the university—
to persuade the king in favor of a council. The refrain "A bad head causes pain
to the members" (Mal chief fait les membres doloir) evokes the concept of the
mystical body of the church that, like the body politic, can be corrupted from
the top down.[81]

In ballade 1012 Deschamps thus lays out a political agenda that came to be
adopted later on by the university and the monarchy.[82] The poetic form of the
ballade allows the interlacing of a number of themes, such as the role of the
Antechrist, that give support to his urgent message. But did anyone listen to his
message? It is difficult to say how much his poetry contributed to the *prise de
conscience* that would eventually lead to the university's forceful advocacy of a
general council, which would in any case take decades to come to fruition.
Meanwhile, Deschamps's frustration with the continuing Schism becomes
more and more evident.

This frustration—and even consternation—is visible in ballade 1208
(6:198–99), a direct response to a recent political event. Written in 1403, after
the French restituted obedience to Pope Benedict XIII, this poem begins with
an evocation of Solomon's wisdom: he always thought a project through to the
end, and he did not undo what he had previously approved of (vv. 1–10). Can
the French monarchy simply "thus do and undo" (ainsi faire et deffaire;
v. 21)—that is, flip-flop on its earlier decisions? Deschamps is baffled that the
withdrawal of obedience is not maintained even though the Schism has not
come to an end.[83] The withdrawal was meant to exert pressure on Pope
Benedict—moral pressure, but even more financial, because he had lost the
income from the French church and could no longer control appointments to
benefices.[84] Lifting the sanctions before the goal of "the perfection of unity" (la
perfection / De l'unité; vv. 28–29) is achieved is thus clearly a misguided move
on the part of the French king. It is also a move that is more in line with the

81. See also ballades 978 and 985 analyzed below.
82. See Kaminsky, *Simon de Cramaud,* for the development of the French position. Kaminsky
   does not mention Eustache Deschamps, however. For a detailed study, see also Millet,
   "Comment mettre fin au Grand Schisme d'Occident?"
83. Boudet and Millet rightly point out that Deschamps's title here ("Du restablissment de la
   sustraction") does not make sense because he here speaks about reestablishment of obedience to the Avignon pope (see Boudet and Millet, *Eustache Deschamps,* pp. 116–17). It is true
   that in 1405–6 the obedience was again withdrawn, but by that time Deschamps was probably
   dead.
84. See Kaminsky, *Simon de Cramaud,* p. 61.

position of Louis of Orléans, who had from the beginning been against withdrawing obedience. If Deschamps urges the king to hold firm and not to restore obedience, he at the same time rejects the position of his longtime employer, the duke of Orléans. It is remarkable how sober and in a sense "unpoetic" this ballade is. It is a *cri de coeur*, but an unadorned and straightforward one. Toward the end of his life Deschamps seems to be overcome by hopelessness in the matter of the Schism.

The contrast with the passion evident in earlier poems against Pedro de Luna is indeed striking. In Deschamps's eyes, as in those of almost all the French as the years progressed, the persistence of the Schism was in great part the fault of Pedro de Luna, who appeared on the scene as Pope Benedict XIII in 1394. As cardinal he had advocated the *voie de cession* (abdication of both popes) and spent his first years in office reiterating that promise but not acting on it.

Benedict XIII, for Deschamps, was "the bad moon" (la mauvaise lune), and the poet plays on the pope's real name in a number of ways. His ballade 948 (5:165–67) was "written about the division and the schism of the church, which is today much troubled by the moon" (faicte sur la division et cisme de l'Eglise qui est au jour d'ui moult troublée par la lune). The reign of the moon announces that of the Antechrist, "son of perdition" (le filz de perdicion; v. 16). A malefic conjunction of the planets (v. 6) has brought about this catastrophe.[85] Similarly, a Latin poem (*dictié* 1260, 6:281–82), written around 1398 when the French obedience was first withdrawn from Benedict XIII, begins with an evocation of the planets, identifying the reign of the moon as "the coldest and the worst, it is against charity" (frigidissimum, / Pessimumque contra caritatem; vv. 11–12) and as that of the Antechrist. *Dictié* 1261 (6:282–83), also in Latin, paints a dramatic picture of an earth shaken by quakes and haunted by eclipses of the sun (vv. 1–10). Here Deschamps compares the papacy to the solar system: as the sun is one, Saint Peter "obtained only one seat [papal throne] from God, not two" (solus obtinere solet / Sedem Dei, non duo; vv. 25–26). The singular papacy is thus supported by the very structure of the universe.

Deschamps plays on the theme of doubleness or duplicity in another ballade that targets Pedro de Luna (ballade 951, 5:170–71). It opens with a sarcastic statement parodying the charge that a hagiographer might define for himself: "I am charged with writing the Life of a saintly miraculous body who has a tongue in two parts and is as full of pity as is a wolf"[86] (Pour un saint corps miraculeux / Qui la langue a en deux parties, / Plain de pité comme est uns

---

85. Deschamps also wrote a number of ballades that incorporate contemporary prophecies. See Boudet and Millet, *Eustache Deschamps,* chap. 4, and below, Chapter 6.

86. Ballade 1195 (6:177–78) also plays with the theme of the wolf; here the cardinals, or the "chapeaulx rouges" (v. 22), are as rapacious as wolves and strangle the desolated church.

leux, / Suis chargiez d'escripre la vie; vv. 1–4). The ballade turns into a riddle with the refrain "Now guess who this could be" (Or devinez qui ce puet estre). The poet has already guessed that the person in question was a monk who has transformed a saintly place into a sumptuous palace; a master goldsmith who does not treat the gold of alchemy but that of the "common people" (commun peuple; v. 16). He is not a worthy descendant of Pope Silvester, nor would Saint Julien want to have anything to do with him. Among his miracles that one should record "in order to canonize our master" (pour canoniser nostre maistre; v. 33) is the one the poet describes in the *envoi:* "He makes his answers doubly, by doubling his tongue over in three knots" ([il] fait ses responces par deux / En doublant sa langue en trois neux; vv. 34–35).

This image of the twisted tongue captures perfectly the exasperation the French felt in face of Benedict XIII's constant excuses and delays in giving a response to the many embassies Charles VI sent to Avignon in order to get Benedict to abdicate. The chronicler of Saint-Denis, Michel Pintoin, describes for the year 1395 how Benedict refused an audience to the deputies of the university and how he would not yield to his own cardinals, who implored him to accede to the requests of the French king and the dukes: "They all kneeled down, and several cried and sobbed, supplicating that he should adhere to the *voie* of the king" (omnes flexis genibus, et plerique cum lacrimis et singultibus supplicarunt ut viam regis tenere; 2:315). But the pope remained intractable.

The victim of this stubbornness was, of course, the church. Like the other authors in this chapter, Deschamps presents the church as both monster and victim. The victimized church is the one who cries out in ballade 978 (5:219–20) that her head is being attacked from all sides and that the members bear the brunt. The cause of Eglise's fever and uneven heartbeat is the division caused by "convoitise" (greed; v. 21), a vice that has invaded the people's hearts and also the "chief" or head. The idea that the church herself has been invaded by greed, that the corruption made its way from the outside to the inside, shows Eglise to be both victim and incipient monster.

The most striking examples of the church as a full-blown monster can be found in ballades 950 (5:168–69) and 955 (5:176–78), which present the church as a two-backed and two-headed monster and as the Minotaur.[87]

---

87. The following discussion is indebted to Millet, "Le Grand Schisme d'Occident selon Eustache Deschamps: Un monstre prodigieux," which focuses on these two ballades. According to Millet, ballade 955 was written in the early 1390s, ballade 950 around 1399/1400. See also Combarieu du Grès, "Deschamps, poète de la fin du temps?" esp. pp. 172–73. In Antonio Baldana's 1419 chronicle *De magno schismate* the post-Pisan church is represented as a triple-headed monster holding a scroll and sitting among the participants at the council! See Guerrini, *Propaganda politica*, chap. 3, and her fig. 85c.

Ballade 955 creates both continuity and contrast between a mythological past and the troubled present. The Minotaur, who would be well known to a learned audience of the time through texts like the early fourteenth-century *Ovide moralisé*, was monstrous because he sheltered two natures, human and animal, in one and the same body. The *Ovide moralisé* poet allegorized the Minotaur as corrupted human nature, which led him to a long discourse on sins against nature.[88] Deschamps elaborates this theme of the unnatural when he tells us that nowadays there is a monster that is even more horrible than the Minotaur: a monster with two heads that presumes to rule over "reasonable animals" (raisonnables bestes; v. 7); its members fight against one another. Who is this perverse body? It is the church, two-headed because of discord and greed (vv. 11–15). Any creature, human or animal, born with two heads would be considered monstrous. And Deschamps goes on to spell out the effects of this unnatural state: schism and war. Only repentance can save us, but in truth it is the secular princes, cast in the role of Theseus, who must "throw this monster out" (mett[re] defors / Ce monstre ci; vv. 42–43). The *envoi* addresses the king, who is implored—in a tautology—to abolish the Schism by finding "the truth of the true opinion" (la verité du vray opinion; v. 53). This twofold use of "truth" and "true" seems to indicate that Deschamps believed at this time that the truth of the double papal election could still be retrieved—Clement VII was still alive—and used to resolve the Schism.

This hope is no longer evident in ballade 950, probably written after the withdrawal of obedience in July 1398. Neither of the popes originally elected in 1378 is alive at this point. Neither Boniface IX in Italy nor Benedict XIII in Avignon has any intention of stepping down. But not much can be done by the French about Boniface, so the French ire is directed against Benedict and culminates in the withdrawal of obedience. As we saw earlier, Deschamps repeatedly places Pedro de Luna in the context of the coming of the Antechrist. Apocalyptic imagery is also prevalent in ballade 950.

The bicephalic monster here has, like the wolf we encountered earlier, a double tongue; it is a poisonous snake, a precursor of the Antechrist, and it corrupts the world around it. Most interesting is the origin of this monster, which Hélène Millet traces back to the fifteenth and last prophecy in the *Ascende calve* series of the *Vaticinia de summis pontificibus* (Prophecies of the last popes) (fig. 2), used by Bernard Alamant, bishop of Condom, in his treatise (finished in February 1399) supporting the French withdrawal of

---

88. On the interpretive techniques of the *Ovide moralisé*, see Blumenfeld-Kosinski, *Reading Myth*, chap. 3, and specifically on readings of Pasiphae and the Minotaur Blumenfeld-Kosinski, "The Scandal of Pasiphae."

obedience.[89] Alamant had played an important role in the third Council of Paris (May 1398), where the withdrawal of obedience was discussed and finally decided on.[90] His *Tractatus* was thus a polemic justification after the fact.[91] Deschamps's ballade, then, is a poetic rendering of the striking images that emerged from the Pope Prophecies and entered the learned discourse of Bernard Alamant in the service of anti-Benedict XIII propaganda. This interpenetration of different types of discourses, their mutual fertilization, is one of the hallmarks of the *imaginaire* of the Great Schism.

Deschamps also used allegorical constructs to dramatize the suffering of the church. In ballade 1074 (5:373–74), for example, he calls on Charity, Pity, and Misericordia to meet with the kings and make clear to them the futility of war. Again greed is identified as the main culprit of discord. The rulers' responsibility is twofold, as the refrain states: "Restore peace to the world and the church" (Reformez paix au monde et en l'Eglise). As did Philippe de Mézières, Deschamps exhorts the kings to abandon their war of "disinheriting" (desheritement; v. 28)—that is, the Hundred Years War—and instead concentrate on reestablishing peace in the church. The "parlement" between these allegorical figures and the kings proposed by Deschamps also recalls the endless "consistories" Philippe staged between his personifications and popes and rulers in his *Songe du Vieil Pelerin*.

The church herself also appears as a personification, of course, as she does in many of the works considered in this chapter. Ballade 243 (2:75–76) begins with a complaint by Eglise evoking the opening of Jeremiah's *Lamentations:* "Alas! I complain, destroyed and desolate. Everyone has betrayed me. I used to be called Holy Church" (Las! je me plain, destruite et desolée: / Tout le monde me fait sedicion; / Je fus jadis saincte Eglise appellée; vv. 1–3). Like the fallen Jerusalem, Eglise looks back to better times, when martyrs and their mircales honored her. Now things are different. In typological terms she is figured by the Synagogue, "My subjects fornicate within me" (My sers en moy font fornicacion; v. 26).[92] This pitiful complaint is addressed to her "true spouse" (vray espoux; v. 29), Jesus Christ, and, significantly, not to kings and princes. This

89. See Schwartz and Lerner, "Illuminated Propaganda: The Origins of the *Ascende calve* Pope Prophecies," and Millet and Rigaux, "Ascende Calve: Quand l'historien joue au prophète," esp. p. 712, on Alamant's reading of the last Pope Prophecy as predicting the Great Schism. For more details on the Pope Prophecies and the Great Schism, see Chapter 6, below.

90. See Kaminsky, *Simon de Cramaud*, pp. 162–65. Alamant formulated the question to be discussed: whether pressure should be exerted on Benedict XIII through withdrawal of revenues and the like in order to accelerate his acceptance of the *voie de cession* (p. 163).

91. On this treatise, see Valois, *La France*, 3:207 n. 4. Valois knew of six manuscripts.

92. See Seiferth, *Synagogue and Church in the Middle Ages*.

FIG. 2 The two-headed monster from the *Ascende calve*. Vienna, Österreichische Nationalbibliothek, MS 13648, folio 8v

ballade thus evinces a certain hopelessness; it is a lament that does not advocate any specific means to end the Schism.

Christ is the spouse of the church, but in the Christian tradition so is the pope. Having two popes thus equals polygamy, or even marital rape, for the church. The Aragonese inquisitor Nicholas Eymerich, for example, presented Pope Urban VI as the rapist of the church in his treatise of September 1378.[93] The chronicler Michel Pintoin records for the year 1381 a Hungarian and Spanish embassy to the French king whose members insist that Urban VI is the only legitimate spouse of the church, a claim that leads the chronicler to the bitter conclusion that the church is pulled this way and that, as is a prostitute between two rival customers.[94] This theme and its variations is widespread in writings about the Schism and also appears in Deschamps's ballade 985 (5:230–32). Here Saincte Eglise is mournful because "two husbands took her so violently, while a single one should rule her in a sanctified manner as beloved consort in God's name" (.ii. espoux l'ont si violemment / Prinse, et un seul la deust sainctement, / Ou nom de Dieu, gouverner comme amie; vv. 14–16). Linked to the idea of the church as spouse is again the concept of her mystical body, whose members are dependent on the head. Corruption from above spreads to the lower parts, and the third stanza gives a vivid image of the chaos and moral degradation of contemporary French society. The *envoi* calls on the king to unify the church.

Deschamps combined a number of these themes and techniques in his only prose treatise on the Schism, *La Complainte de l'Eglise*, dated April 13, 1393. At that moment the continuation of the truce between France and England was being negotiated at Leulinghem. The Schism, of course, was one of the topics of discussion. Deschamps first wrote this text in Latin and then translated it into French at the request of the duke of Burgundy.[95]

The *Complainte* is designed as an official address to all Christian rulers by their "poor suffering mother, desolate and without comfort, whose entrails are

---

93. See Finke, "Drei spanische Publizisten aus den Anfängen des grossen Schismas," pp. 183–84. This image brings to mind a later illustration of Baldana's *De magno schismate* (fig. 12): The "first act of the Schism" is depicted as cardinals on horseback pulling the veil of the figure of Ecclesia with a lasso. Pope Urban tries in vain to protect her. The beginning of the Schism is thus shown as an act of male aggression against a female figure. See Guerrini, *Propaganda politica,* chap. 3. The image is also fig. 2 in Landi, *Il papa deposto,* with its caption, "Allegoria del Grande Schisma." See my Conclusion for more.

94. *Chronique du religieux de Saint-Denys,* 1:82, 90.

95. See Boudet and Millet, *Eustache Deschamps,* p. 116. Delaruelle et al. single out Deschamps (particularly in this text) as more effective in offering a solution to the Schism than Juan de Mozon or Bernard Alamant, whose "mediocre works intend by futile and diffuse lamentations to speed up the resolution" of the Schism (*L'Eglise,* 1:76).

cut into pieces and divided into two parts by the sin and abomination of her children, led astray from the path of justice" (povre mere tresdolente, desolée et desconfortée, de laquelle les entrailles sont tranchées et divisées en deux parties pour le pechié et abhominacion de ses enfans forlignans la voie de justice; 7:293). In her detailed indictment Eglise calls on standard ancient and biblical *exempla,* such as the pride and greed of Alexander the Great or the fate of the city of Niniveh. Deschamps uses the Eight Beatitudes as a structuring device to express Eglise's desire for the reform of her children's morals. At present, abomination reigns, but Eglise proposes several strategies to remedy the situation: a crusade to liberate the Holy Land, and convocation of a general council to resolve the Schism.

Eglise specifies the rationale and goal for this council: so that "I have only one true husband and that the division of the Schism that so detestably wants to make me into an adulteress should cease" (je n'aye que un seul et vray espoux; et que la trencheure du cisme qui si detestablement m'a voulu et veult faite adultere, cesse du tout; 7:307). She has been invaded and ravished like booty; her veil has been ripped in two, and she has been accused of adultery. Her children should feel compelled by nature to put an end to the violence and avenge the only mother they have (7:309). As repentance saved the city of Niniveh, so it can save the Christian realm. Spiritual and moral reform will lead to the church's union.

To end the treatise, Deschamps reminds us both of the allegorical nature of his text and of its official character by having Eglise affix her signature:

> Written in my poor palace, besieged by discord and dangerous division, waiting for your help by means of prayer . . . the thirteenth day of April after Easter, in the year of Our Lord 1393.

> [Escript en mon pauvre palays, assiegé de discorde et de division perilleuse, attendans vostre secours par le moyen de oroison . . . , le .XIIIe. jour du moys d'avril après Pasques, l'an de grace Nostre Seigneur mil .CCC..IIIIxx.et treize.] (7:311)

Deschamps certainly saw the negotiations of the truce as a propitious moment to propose convening a general council. Like the other writers of the time, he was well aware that only a united front of the English and French kings could exert the pressure necessary to get both popes to abdicate. And this meeting was indeed the beginning of a rapprochement between the English and French positions, though the plans never came to fruition. At the latest, with the deposition of Richard II in 1399 any idea of concerted action had to be abandoned.

Deschamps wrote about the Schism in a number of voices: as the desolate church, as a stern accuser, as an apocalyptic prophet, as a creator of monsters, and as a conciliar scholar. He composed ballades, *dictiés*, and even a prose treatise around the central problem of the divided faith, offering not only indictments and apocalyptic visions but also concrete solutions. But, like his poetic colleague Philippe de Mézières and the French rulers, he was destined to be defeated by the popes' intractability.

$$\mathcal{F}ive$$

POETIC VISIONS OF THE GREAT SCHISM II:
HONORÉ BOVET AND CHRISTINE DE PIZAN

In Chapter 4 we saw that the poets who were concerned about the Schism were all part of the same milieu, even if their social ranks differed considerably. While we know of the personal connections between Eustache Deschamps, Philippe de Mézières, and Christine de Pizan, we do not know whether Honoré Bovet had ever met Christine. But they did meet in a vision: at the beginning of her *Book of Deeds of Arms and Chivalry,* composed around 1410, just after Bovet's death, Christine tells us that she saw a man in "solemn clerical garb" who inspired her and offered his help. She responds to this generous offer by letting Bovet know that she has always admired his work and that his "haunting and virtuous presence" has already aided her in completing many works.[1] It is thus fitting that they make a joint appearance in this chapter.

Honoré Bovet

Honoré Bovet tackled the problem of the Schism in a number of different and quite distinct genres: in the prologue to his lengthy and sophisticated treatise on chivalry, the *Arbre des batailles* (Tree of battles; 1386–89); in an allegorical

---

1. See *The Book of Deeds of Arms and Chivalry,* 3:1, pp. 143–44. Fig. 182 in Schäfer, "Die Illustrationen," shows Bovet standing at the side of Christine's bed.

dream vision, the *Somnium super materia scismatis* (Dream on the subject of the Schism; June–October, 1394); and, somewhat more peripherally, in the *Apparicion de maistre Jehan de Meun* (The apparition of master Jean de Meun; Summer 1398), a dream vision featuring not only the venerable author of the second part of the *Roman de la Rose* (and a translator of Boethius) but also several speakers at the margins of society who debate the sorry state of affairs in France. These texts were composed while their author was on constant diplomatic missions, crisscrossing much of Europe in quest of peace and an end to the Schism.

The *Arbre* was an immensely successful composition, with seventy-three manuscripts surviving to this day.[2] A first redaction was completed in 1386–87; a second and longer version was finished in 1389 and dedicated to King Charles VI. It was largely inspired by Giovanni of Legnano's *De bello, de represaliis et de duello* (On war, reprisals, and the duel), but Bovet created nonetheless a new type of text, less judicial in character and full of historical anecdotes. Legnano, "one of the juridical glories of Bologna," as Noël Valois refers to him,[3] was also the author of *De fletu Ecclesiae* (On the tears of the church), one of the first salvos in the polemics of the Schism launched in August 1378—that is, between the election of Urban VI and that of Robert of Geneva as Clement VII. Legnano supported the election of Urban VI, and we shall see that in his *Somnium* Bovet attempted to refute this text while exploiting Legnano's treatise on warfare to the fullest in his *Arbre*.

Bovet's interest in the history of the papacy is especially evident in what Coopland calls "the historical interpolation." Present in three manuscripts, it is a treatment of European history from 1159 to 1334 (the year Queen Joan of Naples was born). In this passage he does not arrive at the Schism. By contrast, the prologue insists on the importance of the Schism, and part 1 leads up to it.

The prologue, addressed to Charles VI, explains the reasons for the text's composition: "First of all, the condition of Holy Church today is one of such tribulation" (tout premierement l'estat de sainte Eglise est aujourd'huy en telle tribulation; p. 1)[4] that God must provide a remedy as quickly as possible. Only then does Bovet go on to speak of the many wars raging in the kingdom, from the conflict with England to more localized wars, especially in Provence, Bovet's homeland. This hierarchy of conflicts, represented by "a tree of mourning" (un arbre de dueil; p. 2) with the warring popes at the top, is shown in several of the frontispieces of the earlier *Arbre* manuscripts.

---

2. Ed. Nys, trans. Coopland. On the manuscripts, see Richter, "La Tradition de l'Arbre des Batailles."

3. Valois, *La France*, 1:127. For a brief biography of Giovanni and a study of the *De Bello* as a source, see Coopland's translation of the *Tree of Battles*, pp. 25–34.

4. Ed. Nys. All parenthetical page references will be to this edition. Translations are my own.

In these images the Schism is conceptualized as a war between two papal armies, recognizable by the arms of each pope. Thus, in manuscript BL Royal 20 C VIII, which belonged to the duke of Berry, the left standard features the checkerboard of Clement VII and the right one shows Urban's eagle.[5] The figures of the popes are more or less effaced, but another manuscript, BnF fr. 1266 (fig. 3), showing the same heraldic devices, reveals by the clever device of placing the papal cross either right-side or wrong-side up who in Bovet's eyes is the legitimate pope: the pope on the left, identified again by the checkerboard as Clement VII, holds the cross correctly, while the pope on the right holds his upside down.[6] The same scheme is used in a manuscript, Pierpont Morgan Library MS M 907 (fig. 4), that must have been produced after 1394, the date of Pedro de Luna's election. Here the pope on the left with the cross right-side up is supported by a little army showing the flag with Pedro's half-moon, while the army on the right now must fight for Boniface IX, whose eagle standard, however, is identical to that of Urban VI in the duke of Berry's manuscript.[7] Violent battle is thus the hallmark of the Schism, while the suffering church, featured in Bovet's later *Somnium,* makes no appearance here.

It is interesting to note that although Bovet's frontispieces identify the Avignon papacy as legitimate and the Roman one as illegitimate, the explanation of his striking tree imagery emphasizes the pain caused by the papal Schism rather than a disputation on who is in the right: "Now, since you see that on the tree of suffering are two between whom there is great discord and a great war over the holy pope of the Roman church" (Maintenant puis que vous voiez comment sur l'arbre de douleur sont deux entre lesquels est grande discorde et grant guerre sur le saint pape de l'eglise de Romme; BnF MS fr. 1274, folio 7r).

It is the tree of *suffering* that structures the different levels of warfare in Bovet's time, a tree that in several manuscripts features at its bottom two men or a group of clerics obviously discussing current events through lively gestures

5. See Galbreath, *Papal Heraldry,* p. 42, fig. 83, for Clement; and p. 79, fig. 138, for Urban. On these frontispieces, see Hindman, *Christine de Pizan's "Epistre d'Othéa,"* pp. 157–62 and figs. 62–64. For the British Library manuscript, see fig. 62.

6. The pope on the right has a double eagle here, which rather identifies Urban V. But because he is opposed to Clement VII he is clearly Urban VI. Hindman errs when she claims that this manuscript shows the arms of Pedro de Luna (*Othéa,* p. 161.) For Pedro's arms, see Galbreath, *Papal Heraldry,* p. 43, fig. 89. A note on the device of showing arms (or crosses) upside down: in 1408 the French, exasperated with Benedict's refusal to abdicate, shamefully exposed the representatives that he had sent to Paris on a public scaffold, mitered and dressed in garments with Pedro's arms upside down. On the miters was written "They are disloyal to the church and the king." See Delaruelle et al., *L'Eglise,* 1:141.

7. The arms of Boniface are "Gules a bend checky silver and azure." See Galbreath, *Papal Heraldry,* p. 80 and fig. 140.

FIG. 3 Frontispiece of Bovet's *Arbre des batailles* showing popes Clement VII (left) and Urban VI (right) and their armies on the upper level. Two figures are debating to the left of the bottom of the tree. Paris, Bibliothèque nationale de France, fr. 1266, folio 5r

(see figs. 3 and 4). These political commentators embody the growing interest in public opinion in the era of the Schism, a development that has recently been analyzed by Bernard Guenée for the chronicle of Michel Pintoin.[8] The many comments one finds there on the suffering caused by the Schism to ordinary people highlight that this Schism was not merely an affair between rulers

8. Guenée, *L'opinion publique.* See also Miethke, "Die Konzilien als Forum der öffentlichen Meinung."

FIG. 4 Frontispiece of Bovet's *Arbre des batailles* showing Popes Benedict XIII (left) and Boniface IX? (right; with Pope Urban VI's arms) and their armies on the upper level. A group of clerics is debating to the left of the bottom of the tree. New York, Pierpont Morgan Library, MS M. 907, folio 2v

but a moral and emotional burden for every Christian. The laypeople at the foot of the tree, overwhelmed by the multiple armies on the upper branches, thus dramatize the effects of the Schism, of the Hundred Years War, and of civil war on those at the bottom of the totem pole.[9]

Returning to the structure of the tree, it is evident that the Schism is at the top of Bovet's agenda, and it is King Charles's task to lead France to its resolution. Ancient prophecies, Bovet claims, clearly predicted Charles's salvific role. There were many prophecies swirling around at the time; here Bovet may refer to Telesphorus of Cosenza, whose *Libellus* played an important role in the polemics of the Schism.[10] But Bovet does not pursue the path of prophecy concerning the French king; instead, he turns to the Apocalypse, another favorite theme of prophetic writings.

In part 1 of the *Arbre* Bovet thus clothes the Schism in apocalyptic imagery, but not before giving us a lengthy history of a large number of previous schisms that forms part of a chapter on the origin of battles. Schisms, Bovet tells us, are as old as the Old Testament. We need look no further than the division between Moses and the idolaters of the golden calf. Indeed, were Bovet to recount all the schisms in the Old Testament and the whole Bible he would never finish his book (p. 7). He therefore skips the sacred Scriptures and proceeds to the history of the papacy and its many schisms, couched in the visionary language of the Apocalypse.

What Bovet offers his audience is an exegesis of the biblical Book of Revelation in terms of church history—or more specifically, the history of the papacy. Though he was no theologian and did not play a particularly high-profile role in the Schism,[11] this exegetical mode ensures his authority and justifies his public voice, as will the visionary framework for the *Somnium*. Bovet could not have foreseen the huge success of his *Arbre,* which was diffused and translated all over Europe, but he could not have chosen a better forum for the wide dissemination of his views on the Schism.

In Bovet's exegesis of the Apocalypse the seven angels signify the seven ages of the world; they also stand for the popes who lived in these ages (p. 8). The fifth angel takes us into the author's own lifetime; he stands for Urban V, a saintly

---

9. The illustrator of the extremely beautiful MS BnF fr. 1274, produced in 1456 for Jean de Bourbon, managed to place what looks like hundreds of little soldiers, in addition to warring popes and cardinals, on the branches of the tree. The tree, on a deep-blue background, is surmounted by three haloed angels stabbing three devils with lances—an additional pictorial comment on the apocalyptic aspects of the Schism in part 1 of the *Arbre,* analyzed below.

10. See Millet and Hanly, "Les batailles d'Honorat Bovet," p. 154. On Telesphorus, see Donckel, "Studien über die Prophezeiung des Fr. Telesforus von Cosenza"; Rusconi, *L'attesa della fine,* pp. 171–84; and below, Chapter 6.

11. See Bovet, *Tree of Battles,* trans. Coopland, p. 18. He was engaged in Schism politics but not on the high level of a Gerson, a Cramaud, or a d'Ailly.

pope, whom Bovet followed to Rome in 1368. Skipping over Gregory XI, as did Deschamps in ballade 165, he arrives at the exposition of the falling star Saint John saw in his vision: this is "Barthelemy archevesque de Bari" (p. 26)—that is, Bartholomeus Prignano or Urban VI. To this star is given "the key to the pit of the abyss" (la clef du puys d'abysme; p. 27), which signifies avarice, the hallmark of Urban's usurpation. Those in the thrall of the abyss lose all ability to do good—indeed, they lose free will. The creation of Urban's own college of cardinals is figured by the opening of the pit, and the nefarious color red is linked to his cardinals, who in order to acquire worldly honor "did not refuse the red hat—and what made it red? The blood of schism and sacrilege" (ne refuserent mie le chapel rouge, voire mais de quoy rouge, du sang de scisme et de sacrilege; p. 27).

Smoke rises from the pit, signifying the preaching of Urban's cardinals, those who accepted dignities and benefices from him and declared him the true pope. The sun of the church (that is, the pope) is hidden by the smoke (that is, the Schism); the air, representing all Christendom, is no longer clear but dark (p. 28). This striking imagery paints a troubling picture of the state of the church and all her faithful. Philippe de Mézières, as we saw above, also associated Pope Urban with smoke, and a very similar image of a pope standing in a temple full of smoke appeared at just about the same time in the visions of Constance de Rabastens, only there it is Clement VII in Avignon.[12] During the period of 1384–86, when Constance had her visions, Bovet spent some time in her region, composing a history of the counts of Foix, including Gaston Fébus (d. 1391), who appeared as a savior figure in several of Constance's visions and who may have helped her to avoid prosecution, at least for a while.[13] Though no acquaintance between Constance or her confessor Raimond de Sabanac and Bovet can be ascertained, there is a certain coincidence of images that is intriguing.

After giving us the dramatic scene of a church obscured by smoke, Bovet goes on to explain what the locusts and scorpions stand for. The former stand for the treacherous Romans who intimidated the saintly college of cardinals. Scorpions, Bovet informs us, are, according to the opinion of the "natural scientists" (les maistres naturiens; p. 28), as smooth as earthworms; they gently scratch a person's flesh while all the time ready to inflict a fatal sting. Just so did

---

12. See *Le Livre des révélations,* chap. 48, p. 267. See above, Chapter 3. We can also think of Hildegard of Bingen's church complaining that her crown is "darkened" by the schism. See Chapter 1.

13. On Bovet's admiration of Gaston Fébus and his history of the counts, see Millet and Hanly, "Les batailles d'Honorat Bovet," pp. 150–53. See also Tucoo-Chala, *Gaston Fébus,* p. 22, who shows that the fifteenth-century chronicler Michel de Bernis relied on Bovet's account. That Fébus may have aided Constance is suggested by Charpentier, "La fin du temps," pp. 158–59.

the Romans, who gently comforted the cardinals after the death of Gregory XI and then violently broke the conclave (p. 29). Like Vincent Ferrer and Philippe de Mézières, Bovet appeals to Saint Bernard for testimony on the evil nature of the Romans. Returning to the apocalyptic vision, Bovet now tells us that the locusts were forbidden to damage any hay and verdure, which stand for the simple faithful who were deceived by Urban's false doctrine and for the clerics who should know better. It is important to note here that Bovet does not blame ordinary people for believing in Urban, and that he stresses that it is not malice that makes them adhere to the wrong pope. The only rescue can come from the trees, representing the secular rulers, in particular the kings of France, who, as anyone who has read any chronicles knows, have never tolerated schisms, antipopes, or heresies (p. 31)—a clear admonition to Charles VI.

Bovet closes part 1 by insisting again "that the war of the church and of the faith is more dangerous and more harmful than that of kings or princes or other secular lords" (que la guerre de l'Eglise et de la foy est plus perilleuse et plus griefve que n'est celle des roys ou des princes ou des aultres seigneurs terriens; p. 32). The entire *Arbre des batailles* is therefore set under the sign of the Schism, and the military advice and intricate rules of battle, meant to perfect the young king's martial comportment, should also contribute to his diplomatic skills in resolving the Schism.

How difficult any diplomatic mission in matter of the Schism was is amply evident in Bovet's *Somnium super materia scismatis* of 1394. It was not a propitious moment for Bovet: "How could a foreigner [from Provence], ill and almost disgraced, succeed in making his voice heard in high places?"[14] Which voice should he choose in order to be heard? And to whom should the text be addressed? Bovet chose to couch his message in the form of a dream vision that featured himself, coming to the aid of Ecclesia, and twelve kings and dukes, two of them men to whom he sent copies of the *Somnium*: Charles VI and the duke of Berry. Bovet also sent a copy to the newly elected pope, Benedict XIII, who, for reasons that will become clear below, certainly could not appreciate this particular work.[15] The *Somnium* was written in 1394 and can be dated rather precisely through a reference to the death of Clement VII on September 16 of that year, followed by the election of Benedict XIII about ten days later. For a brief time there was only one pope, Boniface IX in Rome, who some people hoped might be persuaded to abdicate. The French king, in any case, tried

14. Millet and Hanly, "Les batailles d'Honorat Bovet," p. 166. In 1393 Bovet fell seriously ill and did not recover for about a year.

15. For background and a commentary, see Valois, "Un ouvrage inédit d'Honoré Bonet."

hard to dissuade the Avignon cardinals from electing another pope in their obedience—to no avail, of course.[16]

Bovet opens his *Somnium* with a classic scene: the visionary (it is not explicitly stated that he is asleep) lies in bed, in this case a *grabatum* (p. 69),[17] a miserable bed that provides the perfect backdrop for his anguished mind. As he is pondering "the damage of the current schism" (jactura scismatis nunc currentis; p. 69), a magnificent, beautifully dressed woman appears to him. Her face is covered with tears, and it does not take long for our prior to begin crying as well. He inquires about her name, the cause of her pain, and the remedy she is seeking. She identifies herself as the mother of the faithful, Ecclesia. Beautiful from the front, she is worm-eaten from the back, a view she invites Bovet to contemplate.[18] She bemoans the contrast between former times, when she was honored and bathed in light, and the present, which sees her in lacerated garments; forsaken by her friends, she has been made a widow (p. 70).

This mournful figure of course evokes Philosophy at the beginning of Boethius's *Consolation of Philosophy*. But even more apt is the opening of Jeremiah's Lamentations, dramatically showing us the degradation of Jerusalem: "How like a widow has she become / she that was great among the nations! / . . . / She weeps bitterly in the night, / tears on her cheeks; / among all her lovers / she has none to comfort her; / all her friends have dealt treacherously with her, / they have become her enemies. . . . Jerusalem sinned grievously, / therefore she became filthy" (1:1–2, 8). Jerusalem is thus a sinner, but also a victim and an object of pity. In response to Ecclesia's lament Bovet offers to rally her unfaithful friends. Ecclesia points out a nearby palace, but before our poet can get any more instructions, she vanishes. The vision of Ecclesia thus has the twofold nature we have observed before: like the fallen Jerusalem, she is shown to be both a victim and the embodiment of moral failure.

Bovet now is "shaken by terror" (terrore percussus; p. 70) and wants nothing more than to forget this whole vision. However, after a brief rest, he does approach the palace, where he is greeted by two guards, who respond to his clamoring at the bridge of Ceca Ignorantia (Blind Ignorance). They are Guerra and Oppinio (War and Opinion), who have replaced the previous guards, Pax and Concordia (Peace and Harmony; p. 71). Fortunately a guide appears,

16. See Pintoin, *Chronique*, book 15, chaps. 6 and 7. Pintoin insists on the king's repeated efforts to prevent an election.

17. Ed. Arnold. All parenthetical references will be to this edition.

18. For an example of this motif in medieval sculpture, see "The Prince of the World" at the Sebaldus Church in Nuremberg (plate 4 in *Gothic and Renaissance Art in Nuremberg, 1300–1550*).

Dulceloquium (Sweet Talk) who, unlike our prior—who is clothed in prosaic garments—can easily gain access to the palace and helps Bovet to do the same. Once inside, he proceeds from court to court, discoursing with kings and dukes about the Schism, reliving in fact a number of his real previous journeys and diplomatic missions in the framework of a vision. All along, the most important arguments of the Schism polemics appear in various guises. As Hélène Millet and Michael Hanly point out, Bovet constructs a kind of utopia here, uniting all these rulers, some of them mortal enemies, under the same roof.[19]

Bovet's *Somnium* resembles in its setup Philippe de Mézières's *Songe du Vieil Pelerin,* but it is much more compressed, both in geographical scope and in its cast. While the Old Pilgrim travels with a huge cortège, Bovet travels alone; each episode consists of a conversation, so there is none of the formal virtuosity of Philippe's inventions. Yet, the poetic voice comes through as sincere and eminently reasonable. Bovet, as several scholars have noted, was an independent spirit, a "candid critic" of his times, but also in the *Somnium* "a prudent censor."[20] The framing of the account of his diplomatic failures—and the rulers' moral failures—by a vision allows him to be both frank and protected, and lends his voice the authority of an inspired visionary.

Our prior now ascends step by step through the different courts,[21] each time appealing to the ruler in power and receiving basically nothing but excuses for his efforts. The refrain at the end of each discussion is "We can do nothing, ascend higher" (Non sumus potentes. Altius ascende). The discussions Bovet has with each ruler clarify both his own and his interlocutor's positions on the Schism. Valois comments on each encounter and evaluates its historical accuracy, showing that Bovet in fact reproduced the state of affairs in the fall of 1394.[22] I shall concentrate on a different aspect here: the *mise en scène* of the

19. Millet and Hanly, "Les batailles d'Honorat Bovet," p. 167.
20. Valois, "Un ouvrage inédit," p. 204; Bovet, *Tree of Battles,* trans. Coopland, p. 19; Valois, *La France,* 2:418.
21. They are in order: Charles III of Navarre, Jean le Grand of Portugal, Robert III of Scotland, Juan of Aragon, Henri III of Castille, Jacques I of Cyprus, Sigismund of Hungary, Louis II of Anjou, Richard II of England, the dukes of Berry and Burgundy, and the French king Charles VI. In the planned (but never executed) illuminations for one of the manuscripts (BnF lat. 14643) each king and duke was to be individualized. For example, the king of Cyprus was to be shown *parvus et antiquus, sedens in cathedra dolens* (small and old, sitting mournfully in a seat), and the duke of Berry listening to mass in his chapel. See Ouy, "Une maquette de manuscrit à peintures," p. 51. Ouy attributes these instructions to the hand of Gerson.
22. See "Un ouvrage inédit." One of the major themes is, for example, the refutation of Legnano's *De fletu Ecclesiae,* in which the author neglected to take into account the testimony of the cardinals regarding the circumstances of Urban VI's election. See Millet and Hanly, "Les batailles d'Honorat Bovet," p. 165. This discussion occurs at the court of Sigismund (see p. 86 of the Arnold edition).

narrator figure. How does Bovet construct his authority, and how does he represent the suffering inflicted on the ordinary faithful (of whom he is one, because he is not a prelate or ruler) by the Schism?

We saw that the major authorizing framework is that of the vision and the mission given to him by the figure of the church. Another means Bovet uses is that of the recognition scene—that is, his interlocutors recognize him from some previous event or comment on some personal issue. The king of Portugal, for example, tells him, "I was a religious just like you not that long ago" (sicut tu, religiosus fuerim non est diu; p. 72), while the king of Scotland admires him for his enterprising spirit even though "you are already advanced in years" (jam es annorum plurium antiquatus [Bovet was in his mid-forties at the time]; p. 72). And although admired by King Robert, Bovet fares no better with him, for the king tells our prior at the end of their discussion: "Leave us in peace and ascend higher" (nos in pace relinquas . . . et altius ascende; p. 74).

Especially amusing is Bovet's encounter with the duke of Lancaster, who says to him, "Are you not that prior who some time ago talked to me about this subject in Amiens?" (Nonne tu es ille prior qui dudum Ambianis de hac materia fuisti mihi loqutus? p. 92). And indeed, Bovet had been at the peace negotiations in Amiens in 1392, where the duke had told him that first peace between the kings must be established and then "we shall have one pope, not before" (haberemus unicum papam, ante non; p. 92). This reenactment of a previous "real" discussion creates multiple layers of authority, for Bovet himself and for the political positions he lays out in his *Somnium*.

A further authorizing technique Bovet employs repeatedly is the retelling of his vision in order to authenticate his mission. Thus, he reveals to the king of Navarre how he saw Ecclesia in lacerated garments, how he saw her putrid back, and how she appealed to him for help: "All this the good king listened to with compassion" (quae omnia bonus rex condolenter audivit; p. 71). But in response Charles of Navarre tells his own troubles and begins the refrain "We are incapable. Ascend higher" (Non sumus potentes. Altius ascende; p. 72). Similarly, Bovet tells the king of Cyprus that he was lying in his bed in his house outside Paris (the house that used to belong to Jean de Meun, as we shall see shortly) when on the morning of the feast day of Saint Augustine a most anguished figure of the church appeared to him and begged for his help. The king answers evasively that he will follow wherever the French king leads (pp. 77–78).

Bovet is clearly ready to suffer for his church, as is evident in the longest visit of his whole mission at the court of Sigismund, the king of Hungary, though some of his account is tongue in cheek, I suspect. The sound of trumpets and great agitation everywhere tells our prior that Sigismund is about to depart on a military campaign against the Turks and therefore too busy to converse with him. Timidly and full of fear, he cowers in the corner of a vast hall where he can see no vendors of bread or wine, and what is worse, even if there were a vendor he would have no money (nec habebam denarium neque bursam; p. 78) to buy anything, although he did send his servant to fetch the pension given to him by his king.[23] Thus, poor Bovet is reduced to asking for alms among thirsty paupers. Finally, unable to find a bed, he rests his tired head on some stones and stretches out on the ground (p. 79).

Instantly Ecclesia appears to him and reprimands him for his complaints, reminding him of Christ's poverty and suffering. She cites her martyrs and saints, who gladly suffered for her, and concludes her rebuke with the incontrovertible argument "It certainly is evident to me that you were raised in France, where monks live delicately" (Certe bene apparet michi quod tu fuisti nutritus in Francia, ubi vivunt monachi delicate; p. 80). She adds that clearly he loves the world more than her and that he is unworthy of her. Bovet's *mise en scène* of himself as a man not capable of great suffering (the lack of wine, bread, and a soft bed are enough to reduce him to despair) highlights, despite its comic aspects, the gravity of humans' fault with regard to the church. While they worry about creature comforts, riches, and power, the church has written her history with the blood of sacrifice, a sacrifice of which the warring papal parties and their adherents have proved unworthy.

Fortunately, after Bovet wakes up, King Sigismund returns, and he can show his love for Ecclesia in a lengthy discussion about the Schism. Sigismund knows that "if Christendom were united the Turks would never presume to invade this realm" (si Christianitas esset unita Turci non presumpsissent invadere istud regnum; p. 83). Bovet again trots out an account of his entire vision (totam visionem; p. 83) in order to implore the king to aid Ecclesia. But Sigismund's allegiance to the Roman pope cannot be shaken, despite Bovet's eloquent recapitulation of the lengthy inquiries in Spain and Portugal that ended with the support of the Avignon papacy. His analysis of the situation in Naples, which adheres to Avignon even though the first Roman "antipope" (antipapa; p. 84), Urban VI, was from Bari, also fails to persuade the king.[24] The king rigidly (prerigide; p. 84) answers that the Roman side also has brilliant

23. In 1392 Bovet was awarded an annual pension of one hundred francs by Charles VI, but it is not certain that he actually received it before 1398. See Millet and Hanly, "Les batailles d'Honorat Bovet," p. 144. See also Hanly, "Literature and Dissent in the Court of Charles VI," p. 284.
24. In 1379 Joan of Naples briefly declared for Urban VI, only to revert to Clement VII a few months later.

clerics, such as Giovanni of Legnano and Baldus of Ubaldis,[25] who made a convincing case for Urban. But, Bovet counters, should we not believe the eyewitnesses? A long discussion on the merits of the respective cases follows, summing up in fact what Walter Ullmann presents in his chapter titled "The Opinion of Legal Experts." In response, Bovet once again tells about his vision of the ailing Ecclesia (here he mentions the twenty-two schisms the church has already endured[26]), but to no avail; for the moment, Sigismund accepts that prelates as well as rulers are divided and will remain so—and besides he cannot busy himself with this cause right now (p. 86).

In the English court, Richard II complains of the French preponderance in the recent history of the papacy. After his election, Richard recalls, Clement immediately sent three cardinals to the French king, who opted for Clement but neglected to consult all the other kings. So now England and France are on opposite sides while in the past they presented a united front in several schisms and, most important, against threats of the Saracens.[27] He insists that he sees Rome as the true seat of Saint Peter, although admittedly life is sweeter in Avignon (p. 91). As we saw earlier, Bovet also converses with the duke of Lancaster, his old acquaintance from the negotiations in Amiens. This is a lengthy discussion that touches on a number of standard points in Schism literature: Who can compel a pope to do anything against his will? What is the motivation of those who believe in the wrong pope, just ignorance or is it malice? Would it not be best to convoke a general council? (pp. 94–95). The death of Clement VII (September 16, 1394) now opens a window of opportunity for a speedy new election of one pope (p. 94). But alas, this was not to be, and as before Bovet's visit ends inconclusively and our prior is pained at the icy response of the English.

At the court of the duke of Berry, Bovet is impressed by the splendor of the duke's collections. Once again he reveals his vision of the suffering Ecclesia as an authenticating device. The duke, emerging from attending mass, delivers a well-constructed apology of Charles V's comportment early in the Schism, similar to what we shall find in Christine de Pizan's biography of that ruler. But the duke is unwilling to embark on any particular solution to the Schism at

25. See Ullmann, *Origins of the Great Schism*, chap. 8, "The Opinion of the Legal Experts" (including a photograph of the effigy of Baldus between pp. 146 and 147).

26. This number seems to come from the list the Italian prophet Telesphorus of Cosenza established. See Millet, "Ecoute et usage," p. 446. On Telesphorus, see Chapter 6.

27. These are the same themes Philippe de Mézières concentrated on in his 1395 letter to Richard II. See above for the rapprochement between England and France at this moment and for the plans for Richard's marriage to the French princess Isabelle.

this point, though he does recall a story he just read in Bovet's *Arbre des batailles* that urges him to act, a clever reference that adds Bovet's identity as famous author as part of the *mise en scène*. Bovet has not much more luck with the duke of Burgundy, who appears fresh from a sumptuous dinner in the company of the duke of Orléans and the duke of Bourbon. The prior praises the duke of Burgundy for having forced the Flemish to adhere to Clement and for having had ancestors that settled previous schisms, but it soon becomes clear that hunting, theater, and feasting—not the resolution of the Schism— are at the top of Burgundy's agenda (p. 100).

This leaves the king of France, who greets him like a long-lost friend. Bovet immediately tells the king about the terrifying vision of Ecclesia and of the many labors he has undertaken on her behalf. Their discussion centers on the *voie de fait,* or military conflict. They conclude that arms will never subjugate anyone for long, and Bovet, in his role as trusted adviser—he compares himself to the fool in a chess game who may be more skillful and tell the truth better than his learned compatriots—to the king, rejects this solution. This appeal to Bovet's informed opinion on the part of the king is one more, and very important, authenticating device. In his fiction our poet assumes the role that he could not quite attain in real life.[28] Finally, Bovet concludes that concerted action of all rulers is the key to ending the Schism and suggests that Charles VI should write to other kings and the Roman pope; he even supplies the letters in question. He then exhorts the king to wake up from his sleep and think about ways to remove the Schism. The traditional end to a visionary narrative—the waking up of the dreamer—is replaced here skillfully with an exhortation to his audience to wake up and take action.

The *Somnium* presents in a dramatic and entertaining way the principal arguments in Schism polemics current in 1394. It is a *mise en scène* of an affecting character whose mission to aid the divided church has both emotional and intellectual strengths. In Bovet's insistence on concerted action, he refuses to fully endorse any of the *voies* that were in vogue at the time. He does lean toward a general council, but at this point he is still a true Clementist, and it is only when Clement's successor, Benedict XIII, proves to be completely

---

28. In a letter of November 2, 1394, Bovet wrote: "Verum Rex super scisma quesivit meam pauperem opinionem, et eam sibi dedi, *et copiam per capellanum meum Domino nostro mitto.*" That is, the cordial personal discussion may very well be only part of Bovet's literary imagination. For the quotation, see Bovet, *Apparicion,* ed. Arnold, p. ix n. 2 (my emphasis). The new edition by Hanly also includes a transcription of the many marginal notes in Latin (lacking in the Arnold edition), which provide Bovet's own commentary and contextualization of the *Apparicion.* My thanks to Michael Hanly for sending me the manuscript of his edition before publication.

intractable that Bovet comes around to the position of the University of Paris and advocates withdrawing obedience from the Avignon papacy.

This is the position we find in the *Apparicion maistre Jehan de Meun*, a text that, like the *Songe du Vieil Pelerin*, "poses . . . the great political questions of the end of the century."[29] Bovet himself calls it "a little thingy" (une petite chosette; p. 4), but as Millet and Hanly point out, "the 'little thing' was in reality a great political offensive directed at the Orléans clan. A rhymed and illuminated envelope delicately covered a large quantity of critical observations on the state of French society."[30] Two of the manuscripts were dedicated to, though not commissioned by, the Orléans family: one to Louis, the other to his wife Valentina Visconti. A third copy was presented to Jean de Montaigu, a former *Marmouset* or counselor to Charles V and for a time to Charles VI. Belatedly, a second redaction was offered to Philippe of Burgundy in an ill-fated attempt to garner his favor.[31] The year was 1398 when in the month of July France withdrew its obedience from the recalcitrant Benedict XIII in Avignon. Two years earlier the French, coming to the aid of the Hungarian king, had suffered a cruel defeat at the hands of the Turks at Nicopolis. Charles VI was still plagued by long bouts of madness; physicians and charlatans offered their help in vain. The Dominicans (or Jacobins) were in disgrace because the Dominican theologian Juan de Monzon did not endorse the Immaculate Conception of the Virgin, which was championed by the university.[32] This complex situation, then, colored and determined the themes of what Bovet would offer to his three dedicatees.

Scholars who love the *Roman de la Rose* have always been intrigued by the title of this work, although Jean de Meun plays a minor role in it. Yet, he cuts an imposing figure as he appears to Bovet in the garden of the house he used to inhabit, albeit more than one hundred years earlier.[33] Whether our prior is asleep or not is not quite clear, because he is taken over by an "ymagination" that may have put him to sleep early (en bonne heure; p. 5). In any case, he sees Jean de Meun approach; clad in a fur coat, he begins to speak to Bovet in rhyme. The thirteenth-century poet reproaches him with his taste for easy living and his general uselessness: "And you, sir, are stuffing yourself [in my house] like a pig, without doing any good to anyone" (Et vous sire, . . . /

29. Badel, *Le Roman de la Rose au XIVe siècle*, p. 398.
30. Millet and Hanly, "Les batailles d'Honorat Bovet," p. 158.
31. Hanly, "Literature and Dissent in the Court of Charles VI," p. 286.
32. For a concise account of this conflict, see Guenée, *Between Church and State*, pp. 159–69 ("The Juan de Monzon Affair" [1387–89]).
33. The house is 218 r. du faubourg St. Jacques. A plaque alerts us to Jean de Meun's occupancy, but Bovet remains unmentioned.

Mengiez ceans comme pourcel / Sans faire prouffit a nully; vv. 14–16; p. 6). The times are perilous, the year 1400 is near, and with it all sorts of dire events.[34] He then indicts the disorderly state of French society at the time. Bovet answers in prose, claiming that his abilities to utter verse are nil for he never had a chance to study like Jean de Meun, being "from a foreign land, a simple person of little importance" (d'estrange pays, petite personne et de petit affaire; p. 8). While he is explaining himself, a physician, a "false Jew" (faulx Juif), a Saracen "as black as coal" (aussi noyr comme charbon), and, trailing behind, a mournful Jacobin appear on the scene (p. 9). The debate between these four "outsiders" dominates the rest of the text.[35]

While each discussant represents a certain position, his discourse does more than represent only one point of view, for each of them speaks about a variety of topics. As I suggested earlier, the Schism is not at the center of this text, but in a sense it lurks behind everything else, as Jean de Meun makes clear when he attributes civil wars to the division of the church (p. 13). The Saracen, widely traveled and a true linguist ("car je say parler tout langage"; v. 305, p. 18), tells about his trip to Rome, where the French are branded as schismatics, a fact that surprises the Saracen, who asks whether all Christians are not of one faith (pp. 19–20). He sees things from the perspective of what is good for Muslims: discord among Christians is good because it weakens them, but great wars are bad because they give too much practice to Christian warriors. On the whole, the French favor soft living and do not represent a serious threat to the Muslims—as was shown recently at Nicopolis. In particular he ridicules the pomp that accompanies the departure for a crusade, masking the weakness of the troops (p. 26). He also indicts the luxury of the Roman papacy: Boniface IX and his cardinals seem to him to be emperors and kings rather than men of the church (p. 39).

Later on, the Jacobin agrees that discord among Christians gives joy to the Saracens (p. 41). Juan de Monzon's position of rejecting the idea of the Immaculate Conception, he claims, was also that of Thomas Aquinas, and therefore the Dominicans are unjustly defamed at this moment (pp. 41–42). He then revisits the history of the church, the beginnings of Islam (Muhammad was chosen as a leader in the wake of the divisions in the church; p. 50), the split between the Eastern church and the Western church, and the nature of papal elections and concludes that it is avarice that engenders schisms. To end

---

34. See Rusconi, *L'attesa della fine*, for expectations of disasters around the year 1400. Bovet's note in the manuscript mentions Arnold of Villanova, who predicted the coming of the Antichrist.

35. See Batany, "Un Usbek au XIVe siècle," for a reading of the work from the perspective of "outsiders" judging French society. Batany concentrates on the Saracen.

schisms, and in particular this one, there is only one way: "la voie de cession" (vv. 1318–19; p. 55). But because this solution has proved so far unsuccessful, France has taken the right initiative by subtracting obedience from the Avignon pope Benedict XIII (p. 55).

At the end of this long discussion—which also touches on the theme of marriage, where "as easily as choosing a cheese one marries a woman" (aussy legier com de frommage / Prent on femmes de mariage; vv. 1492–93, p. 60)—Bovet is asked to put the debate in writing, either in verse or in clear prose (p. 61). Bovet agrees, but not before filling in some of the gaps: the recent history of his homeland Provence, torn apart by civil war and, for twenty years now, by the effects of the Schism (pp. 61–66).[36] The wars have made him an exile. His long and doleful account ends with a call to reform and a rhymed dedication to Valentina Visconti.

In his varied works Bovet shows great imagination in dealing with the problem of the Schism. In the *Arbre des batailles* he prefaces his chivalric treatise with an involved exegesis of the Book of Revelation, focusing on the Schism and condemning Urban VI. As time passes and the Schism persists, the apportioning of blame becomes less clear-cut, though in the 1394 *Somnium* Bovet is still a Clementist. Here he chooses the form of the dream allegory where his modest role as royal adviser is transfigured into that of trusted confidant of a number of rulers. A series of personal and considerate face-to-face discussions, endorsed by the ailing Ecclesia who seeks his help, forms the bulk of this thoughtful text. Bovet here leans in the direction of the *voie de cession* and a general council. With Benedict XIII's speedy election and tenacious occupation of the papal throne, things look different again in 1398. The biting criticism of French society and the church is now put into the mouths of outsiders who speak the bitter truth but are already protected by their marginal or disgraced status. Bovet now has come around to the position of the University of Paris and the French king: withdrawal of obedience is the only means to pressure Benedict to resign. The following year Bovet was sent to Prague to the king of the Romans and Bohemians, Wenceslas IV, to try to persuade him to join the French cause—in vain, of course. Bovet worked for the end of the Schism in his literary productions as much as in real life. He thus followed the moral imperative to take action that he put in the mouth of Jean de Meun at the beginning of the *Apparicion*. His success was limited,[37] but then so was the success of every ruler and theologian until the Council of Constance.

36. For the complicated events involving Louis of Anjou and Raymond Roger de Beaufort, see Bovet, *L'apparicion*, 62 nn. 1 and 2 and 63 n. 2.

37. On Bovet's fading away and constant struggle to obtain a livelihood, see Hanly, "Literature and Dissent in the Court of Charles VI."

Christine de Pizan

Unlike Philippe de Mézières and Honoré Bovet, Christine de Pizan was not herself a politician or diplomat, nor did she receive a salary from any employer, as did Eustache Deschamps. Although she spent a number of years at or near the royal court, as a nonnoble laywoman her possibilities for any intervention in secular or religious politics were limited to her writings, which in turn were the only source of her income. In her many works, she engages almost all contemporary political problems in forceful and imaginative ways.[38] In addition to the Hundred Years War, it was the French civil war (starting in earnest after the assassination of Louis of Orléans, Charles VI's brother, in November 1407) that preoccupied Christine.[39]

Though Italian by birth, Christine's loyalties always lay with France, and it was this internecine war that caused her the greatest distress. But the civil war cannot be separated from the development of the Schism, as Christine was well aware. Louis's continued support of the recalcitrant Benedict XIII angered the duke of Burgundy and contributed to his fateful decision to have his cousin murdered. The Schism was thus not always at the forefront of Christine's political thought, though it does appear in a variety of interesting contexts. Christine's view of the clergy was not very flattering; in fact, in the *Livre du corps de policie* (Book of the body politic), finished in 1407, she indicts the greed of bishops and priests and calls them not human beings but "true devils and infernal pits" (droiz deables et gouffres infernaulx).[40] In part, this disillusionment must have been because of the Schism. The chronicler of Saint-Denis, Michel Pintoin, bemoans again and again the demoralization of the faithful and the lack of confidence in ecclesiastical leaders caused by the division of the church,[41] and Christine was no exception.

Christine de Pizan had more temporal distance from the early controversies of the Schism than the other authors in Chapters 4 and 5 when she began to

---

38. For an overview, see Mombello, "Quelques aspects de la pensée politique de Christine de Pisan," and Blumenfeld-Kosinski, "Christine de Pizan and the Political Life in Late Medieval France."

39. On this incident and the troubles preceding and following it, see Guenée, *Un meurtre, une société.*

40. Christine de Pizan, *Livre du corps de policie* 1.7, p. 11. Her sentiments about the corruption of the clergy echo those of other would-be reformers at the time.

41. For the year 1381, for example, we find: "Ubique negligenter Deo serviebatur; minuebatur fidelium devocio" (1:84); for 1390: "Inde rectus zelus populi christiani intepuerat" (1:692); for 1406, when Christine wrote the *Corps de policie:* "Et qualiter occasione [that is, because of the Schism] ipsius diu zelus intepuerat populi christiani" (3:372).

treat this problem in a number of texts. Nonetheless she was very informed on Charles V's early policies, which she analyzes in the *Livre des fais et bonnes meurs du sage roy Charles V* (The book of the deeds and good conduct of the wise King Charles V; 1404), a biography commissioned by the late king's brother, Philippe le Hardi of Burgundy. The *Charles V,* however, was not the first text in which Christine tackled the thorny question of the Schism.[42]

She had lamented the Great Schism already in the *Chemin de longue étude* (Path of long study) of 1402, the year before France resumed, at least for a while, obedience to Benedict XIII. The work is dedicated to King Charles VI, and he is designated at the outset as the judge who will have to decide the debate Christine is about to lay out "in a poetic manner" (par maniere poetique; v. 42). Like Philippe de Mézières's *Songe du Vieil Pelerin,* the *Chemin* recounts an imaginary journey across Europe (and parts of Asia and North Africa), but, unlike in Philippe's work, here the protagonists go all the way into the heavens, where a council of allegorical ladies debates the origins of the world's troubles and possible solutions. Christine, led by the Sibyl of Cumae, witnesses this council and is chosen, at its end, to return to earth to transmit a message to the French princes. The setup is quite reminiscent of the *Judicium Veritatis in causa Schismatis* (The judgment of truth in the matter of the Schism), an anonymous text dating from before 1389,[43] except that in the *Chemin* it is Christine who seeks the remedies to the world's woes and not the figure of Ecclesia herself. Also, the focus is squarely on secular problems, although initially Christine's woeful reflections also include the Schism.

At the beginning of the *Chemin,* Christine lies in bed reminiscing about the misfortunes of her own life and sleepless with worry about the desolate state of the world. She reads Boethius, but even he does not provide sufficient consolation. Passing in review wars and other tribulations, Christine indicts the schismatic popes in emotional terms: "God's church is desolated and more afflicted than ever before. The pastors have been stricken and the lambs have lost their way, scattered and distraught" (L'Eglise de Dieu desolee / Est plus qu'oncques mais adoulee; / Or en sont ferus les pastours, / Et les brebis vont par destours / Esperses et esperdües; vv. 371–75). She considers the problem of the Schism within the context of human destructiveness but does not assign blame to any particular party, nor does she propose any specific solutions. Indeed, she does

---

42. For a quick overview of Christine's writings on the Schism, see Mombello, "Quelques aspects," pp. 74–85.

43. In *Judicium Veritatis,* France is also chosen as the site for a tribunal to decide who the true pope is (Clement VII). See Valois, *La France,* 1:370.

not explicitly return to the Schism at the end of the book, although the Schism is of course subsumed into the set of problems the French king is expected to solve.

The imagery of the pastor and the lambs points clearly to those who are to blame: both leaders of the divided church have abandoned their duties toward their flock. Christine uses the same metaphorics later on when she speaks of the duties of rulers toward their subjects in the *Corps de policie* and the *Livre de la paix* (Book of peace) of 1412–13, clearly linking the requirements for virtuous secular and religious conduct.[44] After the ruminations on the Schism, Christine goes on to wonder why animals show hostility toward each other. She concludes that "evil or unnatural desires" (divers appetis; v. 389) push animals to destroy each other. Like Honoré Bovet, then, Christine sees the Schism in the wider framework of unnatural warfare and, like Philippe de Mézières, she indicts both popes.

In 1403 Christine writes a prayer to the Virgin Mary in which she begs the mother of Christ to supply a "a good shepherd" (bon pastour; v. 22) to the church so that peace and tranquillity may reign.[45] It also includes a stanza devoted to "all the prelates of Holy Church, that you may defend them against the snares of the devil" (tous les prelaz / De saincte Eglise que des laz / De l'anemi tu les deffendes; vv. 31–33). This may be an allusion to the Schism, but only in the vaguest terms.

In the same year, however, Christine creates the memorable image of the "highest seat" (plus hault siege), a common term for the papal throne, on which the two papal contenders sit more or less comfortably (fig. 5).[46] The passage that this miniature illustrates occurs in the *Mutacion de Fortune* (Fortune's transformation) of 1403, a vast universal history whose first part is an allegorical account of Christine's own life. Interwoven into the history of the world, we find a moral evaluation of society that indicts all social classes for their failings. Her remarks on the Schism form part of this indictment. Christine tells us that on this "plus hault siege" she sees two powerful men sitting. She is not sure whether goodness or good sense reside in them because they both want to be pope. Led on by Fortune, the "lady of false dealings" (dame de faulx affaire; line 4303), the two are induced to seat themselves on this narrow seat that was made for one person, not two. Yet, "two in fact occupy it" (II. si l'occupent de fait; line 4312). And although they are somewhat uncomfortable,

---

44. For some examples on sheep and shepherd metaphorics, see Chapter 4 n. 46.
45. Christine de Pizan, *Oeuvres poétiques,* ed. Roy, 3:2.
46. For slight variations in this scheme, see the miniatures of this scene reproduced in Meiss, *French Painting in the Time of Jean de Berry,* plate volume, figs. 23–28.

FIG. 5 Two popes on one throne in Christine de Pizan's *Livre de la mutacion de Fortune*. Paris, Bibliothèque nationale de France, fr. 603, folio 109r

this place pleases them so much that not one of them wants to hear of leaving it or moving to a lower seat. And yet, everyone knows that only one person can sit there, but neither of them wants to leave, and each one of them says he has a right to it. Whether the Holy Spirit put them there, I do not know. Nor do I know by which path they ascended nor how they placed themselves there. I can only refer to things as they are now, but I know well that great evil comes from this, for, from the argument between these two results such evil and such grief that many people harbor vengeful feelings toward this congregation that should be united, and this Schism makes a great part of the people go astray.

[Tant leur agree et plaist la place
Que cil n'y a, a qui il place
D'oïr parler de la laisser,
Ne en plus bas siege abbaisser;
Et toutefoiz scet bien chacun
Qu'il n'y en peut seoir fors qu'un
Mais nul d'eulx partir n'en vouldroit
Et chacun dit qu'il y a droit.
Se le saint Esprit sus ce pas
Les assist, ce ne sçay je pas;
Le chemin, par ou ilz monterent,
Ne sçay, ne com la se bouterent;
Je m'en attens a ce qu'en est,
Mais bien sçay que grant mal en naist,
Car, pour le debat de ces .II.
S'en en suit tel mal et tel deulz
Que grant part de gens en rancune,
Pour la congregacion, que une
Ne Doit estre, sont en ce Scisme
Des gens errer fait plus du disme.]

(lines 4315–34)

Christine here starts with the strong image of the two popes squeezed on one narrow seat, blaming each of them equally for his unyielding hunger for power. While she refuses to comment here on the double election and claims ignorance about how these men came to be on the papal throne, she does insist on the evil caused by the Schism, in particular the grief ordinary Christians experience because of it. The two popes, with the help of certain kings—who themselves are in discord because of these two—lead the entire world astray. Any intervention on the part of the princes remained futile (lines 4339–48), perhaps an allusion to the embassy of 1395, as we shall see below.

Christine then goes on to indict the cardinals, who resemble wolves more than shepherds, finally exclaiming that if such people are the world's heads it is no wonder that the members are infected and contorted (lines 4335–80). From this image of the infected body politic Christine moves on to a real beheading, alluding to the cruel murder of some of Urban VI's (Berthelemi; line 4400) cardinals in 1386, ordered by the pope himself.[47] The chapter ends with Christine's praise of the good members of the clergy, those who desire "that the

47. See Valois, *La France*, 2:112–17, for details of this episode.

Schism be removed and peace brought about, and this pestilence be taken away" (Que soit Scisme osté et paix mise / Et tel pestilence desmise; lines 4475–76).

In the illuminations of this chapter of the *Mutacion*, the painful and troublesome aspects of the Schism period do not appear. Rather, we see two prosperous-looking men sitting rather peacefully together on a throne (fig. 5), apparently engaged in a debate, which is exactly the term Christine uses in line 4329 to designate the Schism. Barbara Wagner analyzed the illustrations of the two popes in the *Mutacion* manuscripts as if they represented the situation of 1403,[48] but, as we just saw, in the text Christine speaks of "Berthelemi"—that is, Urban VI (and not Boniface IX, who became pope in 1389). The exact time period targeted in the illustrations thus remains ambiguous.

The analysis of Christine's chapter showed that the political specifics are rather vague; the double election of 1378, for example, is consciously elided, and responsibility of the secular rulers in propagating the Schism is summarized in the brief phrase "with the consent of some kings" (par l'assentement d'aucuns roys; line 4346). Nor does Christine propose a practical solution to the Schism. I agree with Wagner's assessment of the scene as a council or discussion but would argue that the rather peaceful coexistence of the two popes—they are not engaged in the warfare visible, for example, in Bovet's frontispieces to the *Arbre des batailles*—more likely points to an earlier period. The fact that the popes are not wearing tiaras (their garments are a purplish red in fig. 5) and are not holding any insignia of their office suggests that they are engaged in negotiations that perhaps included abdication, the goal of French policy for most of the time Christine was writing. Given that Christine offered this text to the brother of the late Charles V, one can conjecture that this miniature is supposed to represent an earlier and more hopeful phase of the Schism, reflecting Charles V's approach of negotiation and thus exonerating him of the disastrous consequences that his decisions produced but that he could not foresee before his death in 1380.

The lack of in-depth political analysis of the Schism in this text also points to Christine's desire here to depict an earlier and somewhat less problematic

48. Wagner argues that the miniatures of the presentation copies, probably produced under Christine's supervision, to a certain extent contradict the text. The popes are shown in a discussion rather than fighting, which seems to suggest that they are meeting in a council. Christine sees her role as that of a mediator, according to Wagner. See "Tradition or Innovation?" For a similar argument regarding papal predominance during the Schism (post-Pisa) in the miniatures of Pierre Salmon's *Dialogues* in MS BnF fr. 23279 (produced by the Master of the Cité des Dames, also employed by Christine), see Roux, *Les Dialogues de Salmon et de Charles VI*. There, for example, the Pisan pope Alexander V is depicted as a gigantic, majestic figure seen from the front, while his rival Benedict XIII is shown in another image as a tiny cardinal hidden away in a tiny castle (Roux, color plates x and ix). The text is far less clear-cut.

period of the Schism. Her vague allusions to the attempts at intervention by
some princes (lines 4348–49) do not evoke the elaborate but unsuccessful
embassy of the French dukes to Benedict XIII in 1395 that led to the withdrawal
of obedience, for example. Instead, Christine goes on to a conventional indictment of a corrupt clergy. This lack of precise political references is surprising,
since 1403 marked the moment when the French monarchy reestablished its
obedience to the Avignon Pope Benedict XIII. Its withdrawal in 1398 was an
issue that divided the ducal houses, with Louis of Orléans staunchly supporting Benedict. The purpose of the withdrawal, as we saw above, was to force
Benedict XIII to abdicate and, in what was hoped would be a bilateral renunci-
ation of both popes, to bring about a new unified papal election. From 1403 to
1406 France again adhered to Benedict—with all the financial obligations this
entailed.[49] When the obedience was again withdrawn in 1406, Louis's continued approval of Benedict helped set the stage for his assassination. Of all these
intricate and eventually fateful diplomatic activities, there is no direct trace in
the *Mutacion*. In the context of this allegorical universal history, then, Christine presents the Schism primarily as one of the countless disasters caused by
Fortune and by humans' moral failings. In contrast, in the *Charles V* Christine
shows great insight into the king's attitude early in the Schism and into the
political wrangling that ensued.

Ten chapters of part 3 of the *Charles V* are devoted to the Schism. Christine
begins by describing the death of Pope Gregory XI in Rome in March 1378. The
cardinals assembled in April to elect the new pope. The lodgings meant for
them were hit by thunder and lightning, presaging the disasters to come: "a
remarkable fact in view of what was to come" (laquel chose fait moult à noter
par ce qu'il s'en est ensuivi; part 3, chap. 51; 2:136), observes Christine. Around
the conclave, pandemonium reigned. Rome's populace, armed and enraged,
threatened the cardinals within by shouting, "We want a Roman"—or else!
The new pope, Urban VI, was not a Roman, but at least an Italian, Bartolomeo
Prignano, the archbishop of Bari.[50] It was not until May that the French king
learned of Urban's election, and initially he adopted a wait-and-see attitude,
wanting to ascertain the facts of this contentious election (part 3, chap. 51).
Shortly after Urban's appointment the cardinals realized that they had made a
huge mistake. The new pope instantly showed himself to be autocratic and not

49. On the ups and downs in France's relationship with the Avignonese papacy, see Kaminsky,
Simon de Cramaud.

50. According to witnesses, the Romans screamed "Romano, romano! Romano lo volemo o italiano!" (Valois, *La France*, 1:39). Christine's account corresponds in most details to what Valois has gleaned from a variety of chronicles. See *La France*, 1: chaps. 1 and 2. For a dramatic
account of the events surrounding the conclave, see also Ullmann, *Origins of the Great
Schism*, chap. 1.

deferring in the least to the cardinals, who saw their role as becoming more and more important in the governance of the church, reflecting a general trend in Europe for more political control by councils and "parlaments."[51]

Christine then reports on the missives from the cardinals in which they described the circumstances of the election: they had voted in fear and under duress, and therefore the election was invalid. In September the cardinals, by now outside Rome in the more pleasant surroundings of Fondi, proceeded with "the election of a true pope" (l'election de vray pape; *Charles V*, part 3, chap. 56; 2:146) in the person of Robert of Geneva, a powerful Frenchman, as Clement VII. In November 1378 Charles called a council in Paris, and after hearing reports of a number of witnesses, he concluded that Clement VII was indeed the true pope. Hoping to sway other European rulers in Clement's favor, Charles sent out various teams of ambassadors but did not succeed in persuading the king of Hungary or the Flemish of Clement's legitimacy (part 3, chap. 57). This is where Christine leaves things, except to add a violent lament that reflects the state of affairs in 1404:

> This painful schism and poisonous, contagious plant that was thrust into the bosom of the Holy Church at the instigation of the devil. Oh, what a scourge! What a painful calamity, which now has lasted twenty-six years; this pestilence is not close to being extinguished unless God in his holy compassion brings a remedy, for this wound has become purulent and one has become accustomed to it . . . ; there is a danger that sudden death will result from this one day in the Christian faith, that is, such a deadly divine vengeance that at that moment we will all have to cry: "Miserere mei, Deus!"

> [Ce doloureux sisme, et envenimée plante contagieuse, fichée par instigacion de l'Anemi ou giron sainte Eglise. O quel flayel! O quant douloureux meschief, qui encore dure et a duré l'espace .xxvi. ans, ne taillée n'est ceste pestillence de cesser, se Dieux, de sa sainte misericorde n'y remedie, car ja est celle detestable playe comme apostumée et tournée en acoustumance . . . ; si est grant peril que mort soubdaine s'en ensuive quelque jour en la religion crestienne, c'est assavoir une si mortel de Dieu vengence que à celle heure faille tous crier: "Miserere mei, Deus!"] (part 3, chap. 61; 2:155–56)

The period between 1378 and 1404 brought to light the grievous consequences of the Schism. Christine's metaphors of the contagious plant, the festering

---

51. See Ullmann, *Origins,* p. 7, and Bautier, "Aspects politiques du Grand Schisme," p. 459.

wound,[52] and the idea that the Schism represented God's vengeance on Christianity recall other texts, such as Philippe de Mézières's *Letter to King Richard II*, but this passage is nonetheless extremely powerful, especially in its contrast to her sober and approving tone when describing Charles's policies regarding the Schism. In the *Charles V* Christine stressed the careful deliberations leading up to the king's decision to support Clement, a decision that in hindsight could be seen as one of the major factors in creating the Schism and dividing Europe. As historian/biographer looking back at the year 1378, Christine approves of Charles's policies, but as the writer living in 1404, she cannot but bemoan the heavy price paid for Charles's course of action.

Christine was aware of the intricate relationship between secular politics and the division of the church. She begins one of her most complex works, the *Advision Cristine* (Christine's vision) of 1405, with a preface explaining how her allegory should be interpreted. For part 1, chapter 12, we find these intriguing instructions:

> The twelfth chapter, which speaks of the two birds of prey that sprang up from the entrails of the preceding (that is, Charles V), can signify the occupants of the papal throne for the past twenty-eight years or so. The seeming praise said of one of them can be interpreted by a figure of rhetoric named "antiphrasis," by which is understood the opposite of what is said. What is said of Fortune, who by her wind brought the noble falcon down, can be understood as the ruin of the church, which church is so noble that she makes her circle throughout the world, which is to say that she should encompass the entire world.

> [Le .xij.e chappitre qui parle des .ij. oysiaux de proie qui sourdirent des entrailles du devant dit peut notter les .ij. aucuppa[n]s le pappé qui ont continué environ l'espace de .xxviij. ans. La louenge qui semble estre dicte d'aucun d'i[c]eux se peut entendre selon une reigle de gramaire que on dit par antifrasis, c'est a dire au contraire de ce qui est dit. Ce qui est dit de Fortune qui par son vent trebuscha le noble faucon se puet entendre de la ruine de l'Eglise, laquelle Eglise est si noble que elle fait sa roe par tout le monde, c'est a dire que tout le monde doit comprendre.][53]

---

52. See Picherit, *La Métaphore pathologique.*
53. *Le Livre de l'advision Cristine*, p. 10.

But at the same time, the two birds of prey can stand for "body and soul together," or they can signify Charles VI (and his illness) and his brother, the duke of Orléans. How exactly does this interpretive scheme work, and what does it mean for Christine's views of the Schism?

The *Advision* begins, like Dante's *Commedia,* with the protagonist at the midpoint of her life, fatigued and desirous of sleep. Christine then embarks on a three-part dream journey that takes her from the belly of Chaos to the weeping figure of France, thence to the University of Paris, and finally on to a long dialogue with Lady Philosophy (later transforming herself into Theology) in which she wants to be comforted for all the misfortunes life has inflicted on her.

In part 1, the allegorical figure of France presents her complaint, which is essentially a history of France plus tearful commentary, to her patient scribe Christine. In chapter 12 she tells of two golden butterflies that transform into two birds of prey, one of which has a crown on his head, like a hoopoe. This is the peregrine falcon, Charles VI, whom Philippe de Mézières had already called a falcon (*Songe du Vieil Pelerin* 1:110). Fortune's evil wind blows him off course, and he falls to the ground and is torn asunder, requiring continuous care. The fierce noble bird can thus no longer defend France, which now becomes vulnerable to every greedy bird.

But how can the Schism be figured in this chapter? The most important effect of this passage, I believe, is the highlighting of the interconnectedness of secular and religious politics. If the birds are Charles VI and Louis of Orléans, then one of them, as the French king, is placed higher (this is the "praise" Christine refers to in the preface), but if the birds are the popes, we must discount the laudatory remarks and convert them into their opposite (by antiphrasis): blame. The Schism, which Christine later presents as the creation of "Fraud," a nefarious creature with sharp fingernails (1.27), is thus seen as part and parcel of France's downfall. Indeed, returning to the beginning of chapter 12, we find that the butterflies, or the two popes, emerge from Charles V's entrails and are thus presented as his offspring. In sharp contrast to her praise of Charles V's policies during the first months of the Schism in the *Charles V,* finished when she was already working on the *Avision,* Christine here metes out blame for Charles's creation of the Schism. In 1404–5, hindsight had clarified what Charles's rapid approval of Clement VII had meant for Europe. But her accusation is hidden under multiple veils of allegory, while her praise of Charles V is clearly laid out on the literal level of a biography and mirror for princes. Some of the ideas on the uses of dream visions and allegories as protective devices, which we considered at the opening of Chapter 4, are thus amply confirmed.

Finally, in Christine's *Sept psaumes allégorisés* (Seven allegorized psalms) we find another, more hopeful, reference to the Schism. Written in 1409–10, when the Council of Pisa promised a solution to the impasse, this text provides allegorical readings of the seven penitential psalms.[54] In the allegory of Psalm 101:18 (102:17)[55] we find a prayer for "the Holy Catholic Church, from whom it seems that You have withdrawn Your holy hand for a long time now" (sainte Eglise catholique, de laquelle par lonc temps il a semblé que tu eusses retrait ta sainte main; Rains ed., p. 127), and for Pope Alexander V, elected in June 1409 at the Council of Pisa. Christine prays that he may repair "past ruin" (la ruine passee; p. 127) of the church. This prayer was in vain, as it turned out, for the other two popes refused to step down and Europe remained divided, now with three popes instead of two. In the allegory of the next verse, Christine commends the souls of her dead family members, as well as those of Charles V and Philippe le Hardi, to the Lord. The loss of the first of these two powerful patrons had changed the life of Christine's family irrevocably for the worse; the death of Philippe in 1404 brought on the scene his son Jean sans Peur, an ambitious, ruthless man who contributed in no small measure to the ruin of France. That Christine sees a small ray of hope in 1409–10, just when civil war begins to tear France apart, is attributable to the Council of Pisa. Christine hoped to see at least one of the major crises she was preoccupied with resolved in her lifetime.

The Great Schism did come to an end before Christine's death around 1430. And yet, in her last work, *Le ditié de Jehanne d'Arc* (Tale of Joan of Arc), written just two weeks after Joan had crowned the dauphin in Reims (July 1429) and eleven years after the end of the Council of Constance, Christine assigns the role of pacifier of the church to Joan: "In Christendom and in the church harmony will reign through her. She will destroy the unbelievers one talks about and the heretics with their vile ways" (En Christianté et l'Eglise / Sera par elle mis concorde. / Les mescreans dont on devise, / Et les herites de vie orde / Destruira; stanza 42, vv. 329–33). The dream of a crusade still had not died at this time[56]; the reference to the heretics may be a reminiscence of Johann Hus, who had been burned for heresy at the Council of Constance. But was there still a schism?

54. In the Vulgate these are Psalms 6, 31, 37, 50, 101, 129, and 142; in the Revised Standard Version they are Psalms 6, 32, 38, 51, 102, 130, and 143. For an analysis of this text in the context of Christine's oeuvre and the culture of the time, see Walters, "The Royal Vernacular."

55. Psalm 101 (Vulgate) begins "Domine, exaudi orationem meam, et clamor meus ad te veniat" ("Hear my prayer, O Lord; let my cry come to thee"; RSV Ps. 102). Verse 18 (Vulgate) reads "Respexit in orationem humilium, et non sprevit precem eorum" (He will regard the prayer of the destitute and will not despise their supplication, RSV 102:17).

56. See Jorga, *Philippe de Mézières,* for ideas on crusade in the later Middle Ages.

In a letter of April 1429 the count of Armagnac is said to have asked Joan's opinion on which one of the several popes that still made claims to the papal throne was the right one: Martin V, elected at Constance and adhered to by all of Europe; Clement VIII, who resides at Peñiscola (he abdicated July 26, 1429); or Benedict XIV, whose whereabouts are unknown.[57] Jean of Armagnac, linked to the king of Castile, had long supported the Spanish popes; he had been declared schismatic and heretical by Martin V and consequently been excommunicated in March 1429. Noël Valois portrays him as an indecisive and overly cautious soul who hoped to see the light with the help of the saintly young girl.[58] It is possible that the count wanted to find the way back to Rome via Joan's advice. Marina Warner speculates that "if Joan had answered that Martin V was without doubt the true pope, he probably would have felt honourably released from his previous vows of fealty and changed sides, thus regaining his possessions."[59] The Maid of Orléans, however, sent an evasive answer. Too busy with warfare at the moment to concern herself with this issue, she asked the count to wait for her arrival in Paris in order to receive an answer. The letter and response are part of the trial transcript.[60] Asked at her trial whether she indeed gave any advice to the count, Joan claims to remember little but states that she never pronounced herself on the three popes and that in any case the only true pope is the one in Rome. Nonetheless, she is accused of having denied the legitimacy of Pope Martin V.

Did Christine have any knowledge of this letter? She must have been aware that the election of Martin V had not eradicated the claims of several other popes, even though they had hardly any support except for a few close followers. Seeing in Joan the pacifier of church and kingdom was for Christine part of the fulfillment of all the dreams she had had for France and for the role of women. Whether she knew of this letter or not is finally immaterial: Joan's role needed to be complete—and that included her destruction of the last traces of the Schism.

Until the end of her life, then, Christine could not help but be confronted with the problem of the Schism and its aftermath. In the *Ditié* her tone is hopeful: Joan had already unified France and was about to chase the English from French territory; she would lead a crusade and put an end to the Schism once and for all. Or so Christine thought.

---

57. See Duby and Duby, *Les procès de Jeanne d'Arc,* pp. 51–53. The Dubys state that some scholars consider this letter apocryphal. But see Wood, *Joan of Arc and Richard III,* p. 126.

58. See Valois, *La France,* 4:467–68. Valois characterizes the count as follows: "Le comte d'Armagnac était une de ces âmes perplexes, insuffisamment éclairées, qui refusaient de prendre un parti avant d'avoir vu la lumière" (p. 468).

59. Warner, *Joan of Arc,* p. 92.

60. Quicherat, *Procès,* 1:82–83. See also Tisset, *Procès de condamnation,* 3:114–17, for a contextualization.

Conclusion

The four authors considered in Chapters 4 and 5 cast their ideas on the Schism in many different forms that appealed to their contemporaries' reason as well as to their imagination. They created powerful images and discourses to express Christians' anxieties and frustrations in face of the long-lasting division of the church. In some texts, the Schism was treated in the context of a didactic treatise. Both Philippe de Mézières and Honoré Bovet, for example, appear to have believed that the perfect education of the ruler would necessarily lead him to end the Schism.[61] They therefore wove condemnations as well as proposed solutions into texts that addressed a variety of topics, from precepts for warfare to the prince's reading matter. In other works, secular and religious leaders were featured in dream visions, our poets clarifying for them the roots of the Schism and writing a script for its abolition. For Deschamps the ballade was the preferred form, a concise way to lay out horrifying visions as well as sober political reflections. Christine saw the Schism mostly as a stage in the history of the world, as part of a set of political problems to be deplored and solved by those divinely elected for this purpose.

The ideas on ending the Schism we find in our texts were eminently reasonable, exactly what was needed to solve this intractable problem. But were our authors heard by those capable of executing these ideas? It is difficult to evaluate how much real influence they may have had. When finally events occurred that could be construed as a response to their proposals—such as the Council of Constance—our three male authors were long dead, but in any case their influence had faded even earlier, mostly through badly chosen alliances in the power struggle that would lead to the French civil war.[62] Christine was perhaps more skillful in this respect, managing to keep several alliances alive at once, over the years dedicating her works to the king, the dauphin, and several of the dukes. But her voice, as well, was mostly silent after Agincourt (1415), even before she had to seek refuge in a convent after the fall of Paris in 1418.[63]

The achievement of our four authors, then, was not so much their actual political intervention but rather the creation of an *imaginaire* of the Great

---

61. Similar concerns can be found in other contemporary texts, such as Gerson's sermon *Adorabunt eum,* addressed to Charles VI on January 6, 1391. A long discourse on the ruler's necessary qualifications and duties leads up to an exhortation to end the Schism, this "rotting wound" (Gerson, *Oeuvres,* 7:2, p. 533).

62. For de Mézières and Bovet, see Hanly, "Literature and Dissent in the Court of Charles VI," and for Deschamps, see Laurie, "Eustache Deschamps."

63. Christine finished the *Epistre de la prison de vie humaine* in January 1418. In many ways it represents a farewell to her attempts at political intervention. See Blumenfeld-Kosinski, "Two Responses to Agincourt."

Schism. They spoke for those whose voices could not be heard, the masses of Christians whose religious zeal was flagging, whose hopes for a united church had been dashed again and again. They showed kings and popes where their duty lay; and they visualize for us what it meant to live in a time when the church could be considered a two-headed monster or a suffering mother victimized by her children. It was certainly not due to a lack of poetic imagination or because of deficient rhetorical powers that our authors' programs met with little concrete political success and that their advice was not heeded by the secular and religious leaders capable of ending the Schism. No poet or prophet can sway those who are truly determined to hang on to power.

Six

PROPHETS OF THE GREAT SCHISM

Prophecy as propaganda, prophecy as an expression of public opinion, prophecy as inspired literature or moral indictment, as social radicalism or political revolt—the definitions of prophecy are as varied as the characters of the prophets.[1] Despite its frequently predictive character, prophecy is anchored in contemporary reality and responds to the challenges and changes of a given period. Paul Alphandéry takes into account the mutations of medieval political and religious life when he states: "To these new forms . . . of the events in social, political, and ecclesiastical life correspond new manifestations of prophecy that are modeled on them, and thus we see, with a singular force, the emergence of prophet figures linked to a city, a nation, a national church, a monastic order, or a party or faction in a church or an order."[2] The dramatic developments in the division of the church, and the appearance of the new factions or parties evoked by Alphandéry, were thus reflected in the prophetic activities of a number of individuals. Prophecies often acquired a national character—indeed, many historians of this period speak of a battle or compe-

---

1. These definitions come respectively from Niccoli, *Prophecy and People,* p. xv; Rohr, "Die Prophetie," p. 29; Wojcik and Frontain, *Poetic Prophecy,* introduction. On political prophecy as a genre, see Coote, *Prophecy and Public Affairs,* chap. 1.
2. Alphandéry, "Prophètes et ministère prophétique," p. 342.

tition of prophecies,[3] each supporting through prophetic discourse the position of a given nation or party.

In this chapter I shall give just a few examples of the prophecies that emerged at the time of the Great Schism or were reinterpreted as having presaged this traumatic event. While political prophecy existed at all times, it was at the time of the Great Schism that it became most explicit and militant. Rather than surveying the vast prophetic literature of this period,[4] we shall look at a few key moments and texts in order to understand how prophecy fits into the *imaginaire* of the Great Schism and to see which functions these particular prophecies had, keeping in mind the varied definitions of the term "prophecy."

The most important theme will be the association of the Great Schism, the Antichrist,[5] and the end of times, an apocalyptic conceptualization of the Schism that was not a major issue with the saints and visionaries in Chapters 2 and 3, although we did see it appear in the preface to Honoré Bovet's *Arbre des batailles* in Chapter 5. Other points that will come to the fore are the nationalistic impulses, mostly pitting France against the Empire, that are discernible in some of these texts. In addition we shall explore which interpretive criteria distinguish this type of prophetic activity from most of the visionaries we considered earlier. We shall see that the male prophets of this chapter appeal much more to exegetical and hermeneutical models for their prophecies than did female prophets or visionaries. Since for women the scrutinizing of Scripture was not an accepted activity, generally exegesis was not explicitly constructed as an authority-giving topos. Finally, the use of images in prophecy, conceptualizing the popes and the Schism in a variety of different ways, will also be of special importance here.

We begin not with specific prophets but with the mysterious text-image tradition of the anonymous *Vaticinia de summis pontificibus* (= *Vaticinia;* Prophecies of the last popes).

The Pope Prophecies and the Great Schism

One of the most popular texts of the Middle Ages, the *Vaticinia de summis pontificibus,* was also one of the most obscure. There are about one hundred

---

3. See, for example, Kampers, *Kaiserprophetieen,* p. 167, and Alphandéry, "Prophètes," p. 355, who also uses the German term *Weissagungskampf.*
4. Rusconi has done this admirably in *L'attesa della fine.*
5. Emmerson observes that "the polemical interpretation of Antichrist . . . became a typical feature of late medieval controversies" (*Antichrist in the Middle Ages,* p. 72).

manuscripts and about twenty early printed editions of this intriguing artifact.[6] Strictly speaking, the *Vaticinia* are not a text but rather a text-image combination similar to emblems: each page is devoted to one pope, who is represented with a series of often strange attributes, beasts, and personages; above there is a quotation or motto, below there is a usually impenetrable prophecy. Often the name of a real pope, varying in the different manuscripts and editions, is added. As Bernard McGinn points out, the *Vaticinia* constituted a new genre in medieval culture.[7]

To complicate things, there were two distinct series of prophecies, created at different periods, which were subsequently joined together, albeit in the reverse order of their dates of creation. The first series is generally referred to as *Genus nequam,* or the origin of evil, derived from the first words of the first prophecy. It was probably created between 1280 and 1305. The second series, or *Ascende calve* (Arise, bald one), came about some years later (ca. 1328–30). The two were joined together sometime between the Council of Pisa (1409) and the Council of Constance.[8] Eventually, they were falsely attributed to the abbot and prophet Joachim of Fiore (1135–1202).[9]

The earliest group was derived from a Greek text of about 1180, the so-called *Leo Oracles,* consisting of sixteen symbolic images and captions; they were just as obscure as the Pope Prophecies but dealt with emperors. A general message emerges despite the obscurity: "it seems that the original series embodied a revolutionary change from corruption and ruin to spiritual revival through the revelation of a saviour-ruler."[10] A look at one of the most interesting manuscripts

6. I am counting here the manuscripts that contain either one of the two or both versions together. See below. For a list, see Millet, *Il libro delle immagini dei papi,* pp. 260–62.

7. McGinn, *Visions of the End,* p. 188.

8. The first extensive study was done by Grundmann in 1929 in "Die Papstprophetien des Mittelalters." The *Genus nequam* group was studied and edited by Fleming in *Late Medieval Pope Prophecies.* Lerner, in "Recent Work," surveys the different opinions on the creation and dating of this group and arrives at the date of 1280–1305 (p. 156). On the *Ascende calve,* see esp. Millet and Rigaux, "Ascende Calve," and Schwartz and Lerner, "Illuminated Propaganda" (for the arguments leading the authors to the date of 1328–30, see pp. 166–70), which also contains an edition of the *Ascende calve.* See also Millet and Rigaux, "Aux origines." There is considerable disagreement between Lerner and Millet and Rigaux on the origins of *Ascende calve.* For a recent comprehensive study of many of the different versions and manuscripts, see Millet, *Il libro delle immagini dei papi,* and for a briefer introduction, Millet, *Le Livre des prophéties des papes.*

9. To this day auction and other catalogs list the many printed editions of the *Vaticinia* under Joachim of Fiore (generally the title *Vaticinia de summis pontificibus* is reserved for the conjoined text).

10. Reeves, "Some Popular Prophecies," p. 111. Reeves also shows illustrations of the *Leo Oracles* from a variety of printed editions. A table on pp. 132–33 compares the *Leo* illustrations with those of the Pope Prophecies.

containing the *Genus nequam,* MS Yale Marston 225, reveals the context in which this prophecy may have been read and used. This anthology, put together probably between 1327 and 1328 at the Avignon court of Pope John XXII, had a definite thematic thrust. In addition to the *Genus nequam* it contained the oracle of the Tiburtine Sibyl, a group of twenty-six anonymous prophecies, and a 1347 revision of the so-called Tripoli prophecy, all pointing toward the same myth, namely, "that of the savior-emperor. In addition [the anthology] presents an early example of the two motifs: last world emperor and angelic pope."[11] We shall see shortly how popular this combination became in later prophetic texts.

It seems that initially the group contained only six prophecies, which were applied to five cardinals from the house of Orsini and can be read as "a work of propaganda, taking sides against the Orsini faction in the curia" and trying to prevent the election of a candidate from the camp of Boniface VIII, who had been arrested at Anagni in September 1303.[12] Thus, from their inception these prophecies had a relation to the political reality of their time, but that relationship constantly changed and at times became quite incomprehensible.

Whatever the origin of the early shorter group, it appears that its message appealed to the Spiritual Franciscans, advocates of strict evangelical poverty who were at odds with the mainstream Franciscans, for it was in this milieu that the *Genus nequam* apparently took shape. By 1305 "the prophecies were circulating as Pope Prophecies reflecting a Spiritual Franciscan point of view."[13]

The *Genus nequam* group features popes from Nicholas III (1277–80) all the way to the last angel pope.[14] The seven real popes go up to Benedict XI (1303–4); they are followed by a number of positive figures of future popes. Among the real popes, Celestin V (1294), who had espoused true Franciscan poverty and abdicated after a few months, is the only one who is not sharply attacked. The rest are taken to task for their supposed crimes. After Benedict XI a turning

11. Fleming, *Late Medieval Pope Prophecies,* p. 15. See pp. 70–77 for a detailed study of the manuscript. On the Tripoli prophecy, see Lerner, *Powers of Prophecy.* On the theme of the World Emperor and related prophecies, see the comprehensive study by Möhring, *Der Weltkaiser* (esp. pp. 260–91).

12. Lerner, "Recent Work," pp. 154–55. The "cardinal hypothesis" was put forth in 1991 by Rehberg ("Der 'Kardinalsorakel-Kommentar'"), who, following some earlier clues and based on his reading of a commentary on the first six oracles, concluded that these represent different Orsini cardinals. Lerner's meticulous examination of this thesis confirms it ("Recent Work," p. 149). Yet, as Fleming points out, it is not necessarily the case that the early commentator accurately interpreted the intentions of the *Genus nequam* group's creator, whose identity and true purpose remain unknown (*Late Medieval Pope Prophecies,* p. 8).

13. Lerner, "Recent Work," p. 145. On the ideals and persecution of these Franciscans, see Burr, *Spiritual Franciscans.*

14. On the tradition of the angel pope, see McGinn, "'Pastor angelicus.'"

point when there will be "no more simony" (ninth prophecy), "unity" (tenth), and "true charity" (twelfth) is anticipated. Indeed, Marjorie Reeves suggests that the creators of *Genus nequam* may have wanted to influence the election of Benedict XI's successor as well as call for a wide-ranging reform of the church and society.[15] But whatever their original purpose may have been, the prophecies were sufficiently vague to open them up to many different interpretations. This feature ensured their popularity, for they were never out of date; they just needed to be adapted to new circumstances.

The *Genus nequam* group thus circulated widely, and around 1328–30 a second group was created on their model, beginning with the words *Ascende calve*. As did the earlier group, this one begins with Pope Nicholas III (1277–80) but ends its series of nine real popes with a later pope, John XXII (1316–34). Again, only Celestine V is viewed in a positive light. Units ten and eleven may also refer to real popes; the remaining ones are future popes, with the thirteenth being an "angel pope," the fourteenth "portrayed as standing on the edge of disaster," and the fifteenth depicted as the *bestia terribilis* of the Apocalypse (fig. 6). This group of prophecies, then, sees history as a sequence of bad and good popes followed by a "time of tribulation, probably the time of Antichrist."[16]

Orit Schwartz and Robert E. Lerner have shown that at the heart of the pictorial program is the fight between the dove and the crow—that is, the Franciscan and Dominican orders. Pope John XXII, for many Spiritual Franciscans the incarnation of Antichrist because of his opposition to true poverty, "is given the motto 'This most disgraceful image of clerics will fight against the dove.'"[17] But the scourge with which this pope threatens the dove disappears after the two earliest manuscripts, confirming that the most heated pro-Spiritual polemic was limited to these two manuscripts and that later versions convey vaguer messages.[18] Schwartz and Lerner also show convincingly that *Ascende calve* must predate the arrival on the papal throne of Jacques Fournier (Benedict XII [1334–42]), a zealous persecutor of heretics and thus no protector of "the dove," as the last real pope in the series was supposed to be (pp. 168–69). Created between 1328–30 in a specific polemical context, *Ascende calve* was merged with the *Genus nequam* group probably around the time of the Council of Constance, and like that first group it acquired a variety of new meanings.

15. Reeves, *Influence of Prophecy*, pp. 401–3.
16. Schwartz and Lerner, "Illuminated Propaganda," pp. 158–59.
17. Schwartz and Lerner, "Illuminated Propaganda," p. 161. For the images, see this article and Millet, *Il libro*.
18. Schwartz and Lerner, "Illuminated Propaganda," p. 161.

FIG. 6 The "terrible beast" often depicting Pope Urban VI. Plate xv from the Pope Prophecies, ed. Pasquilino. Venice: H. Porrus, 1589

For our purposes the most interesting image of *Ascende calve* is that of the *bestia terribilis* (fig. 6),[19] a variation on the dragon from Revelation 12:3–4: "And there appeared another wonder in heaven: and behold a great red dragon, having seven heads and ten horns, and seven crowns upon his heads. And his tail drew the third part of the stars of heaven, and did cast them to the earth." Instead of the seven heads, however, this dragon has a human head, and in most versions its tail is in the shape of a snake or another dragon holding a sword in its mouth. Frequently the monster sits on a bed of fire.

The motto reads *Terribilis est, quis resistet tibi?* (You are terrible, who can resist you?), echoing Psalm 76:7: "But thou, terrible art thou! Who can stand before thee once your anger is roused?" (Revised Standard Version [RSV]). The text itself in a way "explains" the image: "Haec est ultima fera, aspectu terribilis, quae detrahet stellas. Tunc fugient aves, et reptilia tantummodo remanebunt. Fera crudelis, universa consumens, infernos te expectat"(This is the last beast, terrible to look at, which pulls down the stars. Then the birds will flee and only the reptiles will remain. Cruel beast, devouring all things, hell awaits you). The apocalyptic associations are clear.

We have an intriguing testimony to the power of this image in a letter that the Franciscan Giovanni delle Celle wrote to his Florentine friend Guido del Pelagio in 1374—that is, during the papacy of Gregory XI—asking for some more information on the end of times. Speaking of a book he believed to have been authored by Joachim of Fiore, he describes our Pope Prophecies. On the whole he interprets them according to the "canons of traditional eschatology."[20] However, figure fifteen troubles him more than the others and in "anxious puzzlement" he tries to decipher this particular emblem.[21] For him the beast is the Antichrist, but, he says, someone told him that the hideous creature is meant to represent another pope. So one of two things must be true: either the book he saw is corrupt, or someone just added this meaning on his own. He then tries to describe the beast to his friend, urging him to picture the "most terrible things he can imagine."[22] This witness thus reveals the cryptic nature and frightening effect this dragon had for a contemporary audience. But for Giovanni, writing in the pre-Schism period, this monster could not

19. This illustration, taken from the Venice 1589 edition by Pasquilino Regiselmo in my own collection, has brown-ink superscripts that identify this image as Gregory XIII (1572–85), another testament to the text's openness to varying interpretations. In this copy the thirty popes are identified as ranging from Sixtus IV (1471–84) to Alexander VIII (1689–91) by handwritten additions.

20. Rusconi, *L'attesa della fine*, p. 59.

21. Reeves, *Influence*, p. 215. The following paraphrase is based on Reeves's quotation from this letter.

22. See Rusconi, *L'attesa della fine*, p. 59.

represent the current pope, Gregory XI. We have to wait until the perfect candidate for identification with the terrible beast appears.

In a number of later manuscripts the *bestia terribilis* is designated as Pope Urban VI, who for many was the originator of the Great Schism. He would indeed be the fifteenth pope after Nicholas III, the first pope in both series, an interpretation that could be activated only after 1378, of course. Thus, in the Northern Italian manuscript Vatican Library Rossiano 374 (1410–17), of which there is a beautiful facsimile edition prepared by Lerner and Robert Moynihan, figure fifteen is identified as Urban VI by both a subscript and a superscript. The superscript also features the term *fera ultima* (the last beast). This beast, though believed to represent a pope here, wears a crown rather than a tiara, perhaps reminiscent of the last image of *Genus nequam,* showing a lion-like animal with a crown that was thought to represent the Antichrist. In some images the animal is accompanied by a figure holding a papal tiara (fig. 7), in others it is featured alone.[23] For the *bestia terribilis,* or Urban VI, Lerner and Moynihan explicate the arrangement and number of stars (seven in the tail, three above, and five in the half-moon on top) as an allusion to the fifteen cardinals that Urban saw as pro-Clementist and therefore disloyal to him. Five of them were eventually tortured and killed on his orders.[24] Thus, in this particular version we find here an *ex eventu* (after the fact) prophecy related to one of the most controversial incidents of Urban's reign. In addition, the snake holding a sword in its mouth can be seen as a cruel reversal of the Son of Man holding a sword in his mouth in Revelation 1:16.

Equally dramatic are the dragons in a number of manuscripts of German origin. One of the most beautiful of the *Vaticinia* manuscripts is BnF lat. 10834, possibly made in Cologne just before the Council of Constance.[25] Here the dragon on folio 6v is bright green, with red ears and a gold crown surrounding

23. See, for example, picture XVI for prophecy 15 (this is prophecy 30 in the combined series) in Fleming, *Late Medieval Pope Prophecies* (no pagination); figs. 13 and 14 in Millet, *Il libro.* For a beast wearing a headdress reminiscent of American Indians next to a pope holding his tiara, see MS Firenze, Bibl. Riccardiana 1222/2 (Millet, *Il libro,* fig. 11). More beasts can be seen in Guerrini, *Propaganda politica,* figs. 1–3.

24. On this incident, see Valois, *La France,* 2:113–16, and below. By far not all manuscripts feature fifteen stars, however. See, for example, the manuscript from St. Gall (Kantonsbibliothek [Vadiana] 342), in which the beast's tail contains sixteen stars with three above the tail; at the bottom left one can see a scorpion, a symbol of fraud. The connection with the cardinals is made explicit by Paulus Scalichius in the 1570 Cologne edition. See Guerrini, *Propaganda politica,* p. 15. In some manuscripts from the fifteenth and sixteenth centuries the beast wears a pointed cap linking it to heretics (Guerrini, *Propaganda,* p. 13).

25. See von Wilckens, "Die Prophetien," p. 173, and illus. 188; the image is also in Millet, *Il libro,* fig. 6. Other manuscripts of this period feature the same identification. See Guerrini, *Propaganda politica,* figs. 2 and 3.

a Reuerentia, & deuotio augumentabitur.
a al. pro titulo. Bona uita.

VATICINIVM
XXX.

XXX

VATICINIO
XXX.

a La Riuerenza, e deuotio s'aumentarà.
a al. per titolo. Buona vita.

FIG. 7 Pope and crowned beast. Plate xxx from the Pope Prophecies, ed. Pasquilino.
Venice: H. Porrus, 1589

the pointed cap often identifying heretics. He sits on a bed of horrific red flames. The superscript identifies this monster as Bartholomeus, the bishop of Bari, or Urban VI, *Scisma incepta* (At the beginning of the Schism), which could also imply that he, rather than Clement VII, was the originator of the Great Schism.

This conceptualization of the role of Urban VI in the Great Schism rejoins the Book of Revelation and thus places the events of the reign of Urban into the scheme of the Apocalypse. These manuscripts postdate the reign of Urban VI himself—that is, they represent retrospective interpretations of the origins and the first decade of the Schism, invariably faulting Urban. Was the beast ever designated as Clement VII, Urban's adversary? Hélène Millet and Dominique Rigaux point to MS Vatican lat. 1264, where a different hand juxtaposed the name of Clement VII to the *bestia terribilis.*[26] But this is a rare occurrence, for almost all the prophecies were applied to the Roman line of the papacy only.

In later Reformation propaganda the beast reappears, this time designating the papacy *tout court.* Andreas Osiander's 1567 version of the Pope Prophecies, for instance, reuses the monster and explains that the pope's rule "is the beast or the animal. . . . He has in front an honest face, but behind with the tail secretively, viciously and with cunning it bites into the sword of the Word. . . . Then his adventure is discovered, that he is a monstrous abomination."[27] Thus, the connection between the beast of the Book of Revelation and a specific pope that gained prominence during the Schism was exploited later on in the movement to abolish the papacy altogether.[28]

In addition to the depiction of Pope Urban VI as a dragon we find other monsters, of which two in particular are interesting for our understanding of the different conceptualizations of the Schism. Both have been studied in detail by Hélène Millet and Dominique Rigaux; I shall give just a brief indication on how they might serve to illuminate further the realm of the *imaginaire* of the Great Schism.

We saw in our analysis of Eustache Deschamps's poetry that the image of the schismatic church as a monster with two heads gained ground at this time.[29] In addition to seeing the church as victim, Deschamps also emphasized its division as an internal monstrosity expressed by two warring heads. Figure 2 comes from a manuscript of the *Ascende calve* that most likely predated the Schism (ca. 1362–70) and may have come from Germany.[30] In a prescient image

26. Millet and Rigaux, "Un puzzle prophétique," p. 159.
27. See Heffner, "'Eyn Wunderliche Weyssagung,'" p. 160.
28. Scribner points out: "Thus, the evangelical propaganda did not break with the pre-Reformation apocalyptic feeling, but rather exploited it." See *For the Sake of Simple Folk,* p. 147.
29. See above, Chapter 4.

the last prophecy, usually depicting the apocalyptic dragon, here features a winged monster with two furry heads, one of which sports a pair of curved horns. A scorpion, representing fraud, can be seen on the left. Because this last image was often interpreted in the post-1378 period as Urban VI, one can regard this image as one more of the possible figural representations available to the *imaginaire* of the time and as picked up by poets like Deschamps and writers like Bernard Alamant, bishop of Condom. In 1399 Bernard was asked by the French king Charles VI to write a treatise supporting the recent withdrawal of obedience from Pope Benedict XIII, in which he depicts the Schism as a horrifying dragon who continuously punctures the church, presumably with his fangs and horns.[31]

In a manuscript today in Madrid there is yet another conceptualization of the schismatic popes. This manuscript, probably created between 1390 and 1410 in the Aragonese circles in Avignon, represents an original assemblage of the Pope Prophecies, as Hélène Millet and Dominique Rigaux have shown.[32] Here there are two beasts depicted in prophecy fifteen: a bear on the left whose large mouth—perhaps evoking the mouth of hell—is held open by a strange hybrid dragon with horns, griffin claws, and a fishtail surrounding the familiar stars. In another prophetic text in this manuscript Pope Clement VII is identified as the bear of the *Oraculum angelicum Cirilli* (Cyril's angelic oracle), while Urban VI, as we saw, was frequently seen as the *bestia terribilis*.[33] Thus, we have a different image of the Schism here, one recalling the warring popes (though not in animal shape) in the manuscripts of the *Arbre des batailles* (figs. 3 and 4). In these images the illuminators' partisanship was often evident in the placement of the papal cross: wrong side up indicated illegitimacy, and vice versa. In the Madrid manuscript it is more difficult to discern the *parti pris* of its creator: given the probable Avignonese origin, the bear takes on a more benign nature—indeed, he looks rather stunned to be clawed by this strange winged creature. Urban's nature, described by the very cardinals that elected him as characterized by a "truculent rabies,"[34] is mirrored in the aggressive pose of the hybrid dragon.

30. For a description, see Millet and Rigaux, "Ascende calve," p. 714. The authors believe a German origin more likely than the Italian one indicated in the library's catalog.

31. See Millet, "Le Grand Schisme d'Occident selon Eustache Deschamps," pp. 218–19.

32. For a detailed study of this manuscript, Madrid, Biblioteca Nacional 6213, see Millet and Rigaux, "Un puzzle prophétique." All fifteen illustrations are reproduced in this article.

33. See Millet and Rigaux, "Un puzzle prophétique," p. 157. The reference to the mouth of hell is suggested by Millet and Rigaux on p. 159. The bear in the *Oraculum* (ca. 1290s) is described as "wondrous . . . , moved by the Spirit, who comes forth from the rock and hastens to the Queen of Feathers and the New Seer." See McGinn, "Angel Pope," 163 n. 29.

34. This judgment was made by the cardinals in a letter to King Charles VI even before the second papal election of September 1378. See Delaruelle et al., *L'Eglise*, 1:16.

Perhaps the strangest and most enigmatic figuration of Urban VI appears in a manuscript at Corpus Christi College in Cambridge.[35] Put together by Henry of Kirkestede, a librarian and administrator at Bury Saint Edmunds, between the 1350s and his death (probably around 1381), the manuscript is a fascinating anthology of prophetic texts ranging from the Sibyl and Methodius to Hildegard of Bingen and pseudo-Joachimite texts, a letter by Jean de Roquetaillade, and a selection of the Pope Prophecies between folios 88 and 96. As Robert E. Lerner points out, once the Great Schism had begun and Henry realized that the fourth pope after Clement VI (1342–52) was Urban VI (who had also caused some trouble at Henry's very own abbey), the identification of the *bestia terribilis* became clear: it must be Urban VI. But unlike the other images associated with prophecy fifteen that show terrifying dragons, or in one case the dreadful two-headed monster, Henry's collection is adorned with a mild-looking beaver (fig. 8), who is identified as the Roman pope in what Lerner aptly calls "a hand that shows the quaver of age."[36] And indeed, according to the *Physiologus* the beaver is "extremely inoffensive and quiet," although he has the gruesome habit of biting off his own testicles if he is hunted. The reason: his organs are supposed to have medicinal powers and are therefore desirable to hunters; without them he thinks he is safe. In the same way, a sinner should shed his sinfulness in order to be safe from the devil.[37]

It is interesting that most medieval images of beavers bear little resemblance to the actual animal or the very realistic beaver in Corpus Christi 404. Of the thirteen beavers reproduced by Debra Hassig, most look like dogs; some have cloven hooves; a few have a broad tail.[38] Only one, a manuscript from London or Oxford created between 1265 and 1270, illustrating Guillaume le Clerc's *Bestiaire* (BnF fr. 14969, folio 28v; Hassig fig. 87) has the broad tail, webbed hind feet, and clawlike front feet of our papal beaver. Given that monastic communities made ample use of beavers, especially for their fur, it is clear that realism was not one of the concerns of the illustrators.

Replacing the dragon of prophecy fifteen with the beaver must have had some significance for Henry of Kirkestede. Perhaps the moral message of the beaver's story—that to reach spiritual perfection you must exercise penance—should be applied to Urban VI, whose reputation was quickly going downhill

35. This is Cambridge, Corpus Christi MS 404. For the table of contents, see Reeves, *Influence,* p. 541; for a brief description, see Millet and Rigaux, "Ascende calve," pp. 717–18; for a study, see Rouse, "Bostonus Buriensis"; Lerner, *Powers of Prophecy,* pp. 93–101; and Millet and Rigaux, "Un puzzle prophétique," pp. 148–49.
36. Lerner, *Powers of Prophecy,* pp. 96–98; quotation on p. 97.
37. *Physiologus,* trans. Curley, p. 52.
38. See Hassig, *Medieval Bestiaries,* chap. 8, on the beaver, and figs. 78–91.

FIG. 8 Pope Urban VI identified as a beaver. Plate xv (details) from the Pope Prophecies. Cambridge, Corpus Christi College, Parker Library, MS 404, folio 95r

in the early Schism years? In the manuscript of Le Clerc's *Bestiaire* we find an image of monastic penance just above the beaver (Hassig, fig. 86) that spells out the moral lesson to be drawn from this story. So in some by now perhaps lost ways the animal must have signified the pope's nature and the possibility of his moral reform for Henry.

Our last monster, created around 1390, comes from Northern Italy and now resides at the Pierpont Morgan Library in New York (fig. 9).[39] Millet and Rigaux suggest that this empty mantle may signify the power vacuum under the divided papacy,[40] but they also concede that the symbolism of the mantle is

39. MS M. 402. For a brief description, see Millet and Rigaux, "Ascende calve," p. 715. The authors suggest that the manuscript originated in the milieu of the Visconti family, who did not support the Urbanist faction strongly enough. See also Millet, *Il libro*, p. 162.

40. Millet and Rigaux, "Ascende calve," p. 712, though an empty tunic does not seem to be a common image for this vacuum. In relation to the idea of the power vacuum, one should rather think of the rites of the *sede vacante* (the empty papal see) that were activated at the

multivalent in medieval iconography. In my view, the dragon's sharp claws attached to the mantle (which is mauve, the same color as the popes' outfits in the *Mutacion de Fortune* manuscripts; see fig. 5) suggest that Urban VI is puncturing the seamless tunic of the church. The image of a united Christianity as a seamless tunic was current at the time (we encountered it, for example, in Philippe de Mézières) and appeared in a variety of contexts.[41] Thus, both the sword pointing in the direction of the mantle and the claws about to rip it dramatize the destructiveness of the *bestia terribilis* in the shape of Urban VI.

Except for our last example, any symbol of the victimized church is notably absent from the *bestia terribilis* images. For the most part, Urban VI is shown as a destructive and horrifying dragon, evoking various monsters of the Book of Revelation. The internal strife of the church, its division into two obediences, is figured mostly poetically, as in the ballades of Eustache Deschamps, but this conceptualization may have predated the Schism, as can be seen in the monster from Vienna. Henry of Kirkstede's beaver remains mysterious, confirming again the finally unresolvable nature of many medieval prophecies.

From their inception the Pope Prophecies circulated widely in different forms and influenced a number of the prophets, to whom we shall now turn.

Prophets and False Prophets

The southern French prophet Jean de Roquetaillade (Johannes de Rupescissa) was as prolific as he was controversial. Although he died before the outbreak of the Great Schism (sometime after 1365), he seems to have made accurate predictions about its nature. A Friar Minor in 1332 (the year he had a vision about his combat with the Antichrist), he was also a theology student in Toulouse, a hotbed of the Spiritual Franciscans, from about 1327 to 1338. He was a follower of Peter John Olivi (d. 1298), embracing the ideal of absolute evangelical poverty.[42] Already in his youth he had visions and revelations that he soon

---

time of the Schism during the French withdrawal of obedience beginning in 1398. See Rollo-Koster, "*Castrum Doloris*." The empty See was sometimes represented as an unoccupied pillow. See the interesting illustrations in Ulrich Richental's chronicle of the Council of Constance. In one image the empty pillow is being transported to the Council of Constance so that it can be occupied by the new legitimate pope (see fig. 8 in Cramer, "Bilder erzählen Geschichte").

41. See, for example, Pierre d'Ailly's *Epistola diaboli Leviathan*, p. 187.
42. On Roquetaillade, see the classic studies by Bignami-Odier, *Etudes sur Jean de Roquetaillade*, and an updated, though often shortened version, "Jean de Roquetaillade." See also Kerby-Fulton, *Reformist Apocalypticism*, pp. 187–91. On Olivi, see Burr, *The Persecution*. The brief sketch of his life is indebted to the entry by Pommerol in the *Dictionnaire des lettres françaises*.

FIG. 9 The "terrible beast" with the empty tunic. Plate xv from the Pope Prophecies. New York, Pierpont Morgan Library, ms M. 402, folio 8v

translated into prophecies, indicting the vices of the clergy and the luxurious way of life at the papal court at Avignon. In 1344 he was arrested and thrown into jail in Figeac, then transferred to other prisons, ending up in Avignon in 1349. His horrible existence there is described in vivid detail in some of his texts. Though seen as part of a threatening network of prophets challenging authority, no concrete indictment allowed the church to condemn and execute him. In fact, the authorities considered him to be *fantasticus* rather than *hereticus*.[43] After 1365 there was no more trace of him. His numerous works were widely diffused—a significant fact considering his status as a long-term prisoner—but are only now appearing in critical editions. We shall zero in on one tiny part of his vast literary production.

Prophecies of the end of times usually involved the appearance of a tyrant accompanied by demonic armies, false popes, or Angel Popes, as well as of one or several Antichrists who would precede the final savior/king/emperor and who in turn would usher in the Last Judgment in an apocalyptic battle. Older Antichrist traditions, inaugurated by Adso de Montier-en-Der (ca. 950), held that the "son of perdition" (2 Thess. 2:3–4) would be born from the tribe of Dan and come from "the East" as a perverse imitator of the life of Christ to destroy the human race.[44] Omitting a host of fascinating details, I would just highlight the fact that Adso and his successors posited the emergence of one Antichrist in the future, although the existence of many antichrists, based on 1 John 2:18 in the present was also acknowledged.[45]

This idea was modified significantly by Joachim of Fiore, the foremost medieval "prophet of the Antichrist" who "believed in the advent of many Antichrists, with particular emphasis on two superlatively terrible Antichrists still to come." Specifically, Gog (Rev. 20:8) was now posited as the last Antichrist in a series, "and with that stroke the abbot effected the first major departure in medieval Antichrist thinking since the days of the Fathers."[46] Joachim insisted that the Book of Revelation "revealed the entire history of the church—past, present, and future," thus rejecting Saint Augustine and his commentators' tenet that the thousand-year reign of Christ is in fact "a figure for the life of the church in the present"—that is, the Book of Revelation cannot

---

43. See Lerner's "Historical Introduction" to Johannes de Rupiscissa, *Liber secretorum eventuum,* p. 30.
44. See Emmerson, *Antichrist,* chap. 3; Möhring, *Der Weltkaiser,* pp. 144–48, 360–68; and my *Not of Woman Born,* pp. 131–35.
45. See Lerner, "Antichrists and Antichrist," p. 554.
46. See Lerner, "Antichrists and Antichrist," pp. 553, 554, 560. See also Emmerson and Herzman, *Apocalyptic Imagination,* chap. 1.

be applied to future events. For Joachim, the reign of the Holy Spirit was to arrive "between the demise of Antichrist and the Last Judgment," and it was to occur on this earth.[47]

Joachim's prophetic texts, with their innovative view that the Book of Revelation presaged an earthly future, provided a kind of template for later prophets. Thus, unlike most previous prophecies, the texts authored by Jean de Roquetaillade could contain precise references to contemporary historical events and personages—for example, the tyrannical ruler, this staple of prophetic literature, will be Louis of Sicily; and the false pope, another typical figure, will be Nicholas V (1328–30), the antipope supported by Louis.[48] This fits in with Jean's claims that he is not, properly speaking, a prophet—that is, someone who would say "this will happen"—but rather an exegete or someone skilled in hermeneutics. The verse from Daniel 10:1 "In visione opus est intelligentia" (the [true] work in a vision is its understanding), stressing that the deciphering of a vision's significance is the true task of a prophet,[49] could be seen as Jean's job description.

While one of Joachim of Fiore's prime contributions to Antichrist thinking was that the Antichrist "represent[ed] the embodiment of the worst imaginable Western corporate dangers—a depraved royalty and a depraved papacy," one of Jean's most important contributions to the development of prophecy in the fourteenth century was that he highlighted "the schism of the church as a constitutive element of the eschatological-apocalyptic chronology."[50] Thus, among Jean's many dire predictions concerning the arrival of the Antichrist, as well as countless wars and disasters, his prophecy of a coming schism in the

47. Lerner, "Antichrists and Antichrist," pp. 557, 559; and Lerner, "Refreshment of the Saints," pp. 97, 100. In the latter article Lerner traces the idea of chiliasm from the church fathers to the fifteenth century, demonstrating that Saint Jerome was "the originator of the tradition of expecting a period on earth between the destruction of Antichrist and the Last Judgment" (p. 101). For a study of how Joachim arrived at his position on the "earthly Sabbath" at the end of time, see Lerner, "Joachim of Fiore's Breakthrough to Chiliasm."

48. See Torrell, *Recherches sur la théorie de prophétie*, p. 233, and Lerner, "Historical Introduction," p. 53. On the influence of Hildegard of Bingen on Jean, see Bignami-Odier, *Etudes*, pp. 193–94, and for that of Robert of Uzès (d. 1296), whose prophecies also featured an Angel Pope, see Kerby-Fulton, *Reformist Apocalypticism*, pp. 97–102. See also Reeves, *Influence*, pp. 321–23.

49. See Torrell, *Recherches*, pp. 241–46, here 243. In the *Liber Ostensor* (1356) Jean claims he has no right to say "hoc erit" (this will be). See Torrell, *Recherches*, 243 n. 17. Torrell's quotation from the Book of Daniel does not exactly correspond to the biblical passage. The end of Dan. 10:1 reads in the Revised Standard Version "And he understood the word and had understanding of the vision."

50. Lerner, "Antichrists and Antichrist," p. 568, and Rusconi, "Il presente e il futuro della Chiesa," p. 196.

1349 *Liber secretorum eventuum* (Book of secret events), his second great prophetic work after the *Oraculum Cyrilli,* stands out.[51]

Conceived while its author was imprisoned in Toulouse (as he tells us), the *Liber* and its ideas, as suggested above, fit into well-established patterns, such as that of the Antichrist's reign preceding the end of times or the coming of a world emperor.[52] But Jean, as we saw, more than preceding prophets, clearly identifies the persons involved. With a pronounced bias in favor of France, the *Liber* portrays—in thirty "intellections"—events in three successive eras[53]: the period from 1349 to 1366, characterized by the rise of the Antichrist (he would have been born in 1337); the Antichrist's reign from 1366 to 1370; and finally a millennium of peace between the Antichrist's destruction in 1370 and the arrival of Gog in 2370. The fourteenth-century events would be masterminded by a member of the "viper brood" of the Hohenstaufen, Louis of Sicily. Louis would also help to bring about a schism, with only a small fraction of the Franciscans remaining faithful to the true pope. The pseudo-pope will triumph and reign together with the Antichrist in the shape of Louis of Sicily. Through a General Council he would deprive the church of its temporal goods. Extending his reign to the East, worshiped by the Jews as the new Messiah, Louis will finally meet resistance through the French, who in a great battle with Christ's help will defeat the Antichrist and the pseudo-pope, throwing them into a lake of fire. Unlike most texts that signaled the end of the world shortly after the Antichrist's death, Jean saw a 700-year period of peace, ruled by the Holy Spirit, beginning in 1415. In ca. 2115 things would start to go downhill again. Even the Franciscans would "sink by degrees from purity to laxity to sodomy to blasphemy and heresy."[54] As in other Antichrist texts,[55] Gog and Magog would then appear in order to inflict the last punishment, exactly 1,000 years after the death of the Antichrist, before being destroyed by God, who will finally enact the Last Judgment.

As mentioned above, the Schism was not usually part of the scheme of the end of times. But Jean gives us a detailed picture of this signal event. Beginning in his nineteenth "intellection" Jean "understood" (*intellexi:* the word highlights his hermeneutic rather than prophetic skills) that there would be "in the

---

51. On this text, see Bignami-Odier, *Etudes,* chap. 2, and the "Historical Introduction" by Lerner in Johannes de Rupescissa, *Liber secretorum eventuum.* The prophecy is in paragraphs 19–26, pp. 146–50. Jean was also aware of the *Ascende calve* prophecies and seems to have written a now-lost commentary on them. There are several precise references to the prophecies in his *Liber ostensor.* See Schwartz and Lerner, "Illuminated Propaganda," pp. 165–66.

52. On this theme, see Kampers, *Kaiserprophetieen und Kaisersagen;* on Jean, see esp. pp. 156–59.

53. The following summary is indebted to Lerner's "Historical Introduction," pp. 33–35.

54. Lerner, "Historical Introduction," p. 35.

55. Generally, on the Antichrist tradition, see Emmerson, *Antichrist in the Middle Ages.*

center"[56] of the universal Roman church a "scandal so incredible, so vast and horrible, so dangerous and ruinous that one cannot conceive of its violence or in words fully express the poison that will flow." Before the arrival of the Antichrist there will be an empty papal seat for a year and a half because of the discord among the cardinals. While the cardinals are in the conclave, violence erupts all over Italy. Eventually, the cardinals succeed in electing—according to the canonical rules—a saintly man, not one of their own ranks.

A later reader would recognize already here some similarities with the situation of 1378: though the papal See was not vacant for eighteen months, there was certainly violence outside the conclave, and Bartolomeo Prignano, the future Urban VI, was not one of the cardinals. But it gets even better: "Sanctioned by God's just judgment, it will happen that at the suggestion of a double-tongued traitor involved in dark machinations—to the outrage of Christ and the true pope—another son of ambition and pride will assume a pseudo-pontificate with the help of many cardinals who will defect from the true pope. They will try to annul the canonical election of the true pope for fanciful reasons and through false arguments" (rationibus fantasticis et sophismatibus fictis; p. 146). While harking back to Peter John Olivi's prophecy that "[the false pope] will not be canonically elected but put in by schism,"[57] this passage is also applicable to the beginnings of the Great Schism. In fact, any post-1378 reader who progressed this far in Jean's text must feel transported to the situation between April and September 1378 when Urban's regime was questioned by the cardinals who finally moved to Anagni to elect Robert of Geneva. The term *rationibus fantasticis et sophismatibus fictis* foreshadows arguments used in later tracts on the disputed election, notably the letter of Catherine of Siena reproaching the three Italian cardinals who had voted for Robert of Geneva. She calls their claims that they had voted under duress false and ridiculous and, as did all defenders of the Roman pope, repeatedly terms Urban's election "canonical."[58] Annulment of the first election and proving that this election had not been canonical had indeed been the cardinals' goal. Further, the term *pseudo pontificium* (or *pontifex*) is exactly the one employed in the polemics of the Great Schism to designate the "other" pope. The introductory idea—namely, that God sanctioned these impious acts—also fits into a common conceptualization of the Schism: the division of the church, as we have seen, was often interpreted as a divine punishment for human, especially clerical, depravity.

56. The Latin word is *ventre* (p. 146), alluding to the mystical body of the church.
57. The quotation is from Olivi's *Commentary on Revelation*. See McGinn, *Visions of the End*, p. 211.
58. This letter is T 310. See above, Chapter 2, for an analysis of this letter.

The forced abdication of the true pope that Jean evokes in the next few paragraphs had no precise counterpart in the events of the Great Schism, although abdication of one or the other pope was a constant theme of many of the texts we encountered in the previous chapters. However, the linking of schism and the Antichrist will become a major preoccupation during the Great Schism. Jean lays out this connection in paragraph twenty-six, citing 2 Thessalonians 2:3–4. Here Paul tells his audience that the day of the Lord will not come "unless the rebellion (discessio) comes first and the man of lawlessness is revealed, the son of perdition."[59] Jean explains in the same passage that "hoc est principalis discessio quam intendit Apostolus, postquam venit ibidem Antichristus" (this is the principal schism that the apostle speaks of, after which comes the Antichrist). As we shall see shortly, this connection will be worked out in much greater detail by the star prophet of the Great Schism, Telesphorus of Cosenza.

Given all these intriguing parallels between Jean's "intellections" and the events of the Great Schism some thirty years later, it is not surprising that Jean was considered a prophet of this particular event. Hélène Millet identified passages from Jean's *Liber* in the famous collection of Schism documents that the Avignon cardinal Martin de Zalba (d. 1403) left to Pope Benedict XIII and that are now in Armarium LIV in the Vatican Archives.[60] Volume 31 contains three prophecies, of which the first is by Jean. Zalba anthologized a number of prophecies relating in his mind to the Great Schism—representing both the Clementist and the Urbanist sides—and Jean features prominently there, a proof that even in the inner sanctum of the Avignon papacy the strange and *fantasticus* Franciscan prisoner of a previous generation enjoyed a privileged prophetic afterlife. His emphasis on the French role in combating the Antichrist in the shape of Louis of Sicily also fed into the national preoccupations that came to the fore at the time of the Great Schism.

In a more negative vein, Jean was also evoked by the well-known inquisitor Nicholas Eymerich, one of the first polemicists of the Great Schism. Even before the second papal election in September 1378, Nicholas wrote an acerbic treatise against Urban VI, depicting him as a poisonous snake coming out of its lair, a second Saul full of venom, perversity, and deception. He determined that the election of Urban, although seemingly canonical, was in fact illegitimate because the *elegendi libertas* (freedom in the election) was missing. Anticipating a whole series of arguments that later became standard elements of Schism polemics, Nicholas condemned, in four conclusions, the election and

---

59. "Rebellion" is the translation of *discessio* in the Revised Standard Version; "falling away" in the King James. "Separation" or "schism" would be more accurate.
60. See Millet, "Le cardinal Martin de Zalba," pp. 267–69.

called for punishment of the new pope and his followers.[61] In July 1379 Nicholas delivered a speech before the Castilian king in which he tried to determine who was authorized to make a decision in a case of serious discord, such as the Schism. He rejected the solution of a general council, and he did not accept that kings or prelates should be the arbiters in this conflict. How about a duel or an ordeal by fire to determine the truth? No, he says, these things are forbidden. Maybe one should trust visionaries? After all, there are plenty of *bégards* and those who call themselves holy who claim that "that they see visions and in their sleep (*sompnia sompniare*) get messages from an invisible Christ. Do they have the authority to make these decisions? No way! (*Absit!*)." Should we believe Arnold of Villanova, brother Johannes de Rupescissa of Toulouse, the abbot Joachim the Italian, or Merlin, "who in their visions and in their writings intone with wide-open mouths this and that [hec et illa]"? This is not reasonable faith. "They were pseudo-prophets who in their made-up prophecies spouted many lies and gave bad advice."[62] Nicholas concludes that only the College of Cardinals that elected both popes can resolve the conflict.

This polemical discourse is an excellent example of the distrust of visionaries that came to the fore at this particular time. The more precise the prophecy, the more likely the rejection, especially if repeated prophecies, often with precise dates attached, did not materialize. By 1379 it was clear that Jean de Roquetaillade's prediction of the Antichrist's reign from 1366 to 1370 had not literally come true. Nor was the Antichrist destroyed in 1370. But by then Jean was dead and could not suffer from the lack of fulfillment of his prophecies. For a French monk in Germany it was another story. The following anecdote taken from Heinrich of Langenstein's treatise against false prophets, while meant principally as an indictment of fanciful visions and revelations,[63] also dramatizes the anguish caused by the Great Schism that we have traced throughout this study.

Heinrich of Langenstein (1325?–1397), also known as Heinrich of Hessen or Henricus de Hassia, was vice chancellor of the University of Paris from 1371 to 1381. He was one of the great personalities of the early Schism years and the author of a number of ecclesiological treatises, of which one of the most important was the 1381 *Epistola concilii pacis* (Letter on the peace council), laying

---

61. See Finke, "Drei spanische Publizisten," p. 184.
62. I am paraphrasing and citing here from Finke, "Drei spanische Publizisten," p. 185. Finke believes that fr. Pedro of Aragon's visions may have prompted this outburst. On Pedro, see above, Chapter 2. Nicholas went on to fall out of favor with the Castilian king (he also persecuted Raymond Lulle and at one point Vincent Ferrer) but ended up at the Avignon papal court to work for Benedict XIII.
63. See Vauchez, "Les théologiens face aux prophéties."

out in detail the conciliarist theory that finally came to fruition at the Council of Constance.[64] A short time after writing this treatise, Heinrich left Paris because he did not want to live in an area of Clementine obedience. After a stay at the Cistercian abbey of Eberbach, he was appointed to the University of Vienna in 1384, where he eventually became dean of the Theological Faculty (1388) and rector (1393–94). He died 1397 in Vienna.[65] Among his many works is one that is especially intriguing in the context of prophets and false prophets: his 1392 treatise *Liber adversus Thelesphori eremitae vaticiniae* (Book against the prophecies of the hermit Thelesphorus).[66] In a moment we shall encounter this strange eremitical personage from Calabria, but let us first analyze the story of the unfortunate prophesying monk.

Heinrich provides one of the clearest examples of the connection between the different polemical activities at the time of the Great Schism; like Jean Gerson he was a conciliar theorist and a skeptic when it came to visions. In chapter 8 of his lengthy treatise Heinrich decries the proliferation of prophets in his time (diebus istis; col. 516). What do they prophesy about? The origins, progress, and end of the present Schism, and they do so with their voices and writings. It is significant that this is the same expression used by Nicholas Eymerich; it alerts us to the assumed mode of consumption of these prophecies: a prophet was one who spoke aloud, presumably in public, and not necessarily to a learned audience. But he was also someone who wrote, disseminating his prophecies and revelations to a more literate public. Going back to Nicholas Eymerich and his examples, we can see that some of the prophets he lists were certainly not able to prophesy "in voice" (voce)—namely, the legendary Merlin as well as Jean de Roquetaillade, who was imprisoned for most of his prophetic life. Yet, *voce et scriptis* is the common expression used to describe prophetic utterances, undoubtedly harking back to the way Old Testament prophets communicated their warnings.

Heinrich mocks people who consult the stars and, based on astrology, predict the victory of one pope and a rapid end to the Schism.[67] For Heinrich, these predictions are nothing but superstition. But what about those who are called prophets in our world? Going back to the classical biblical topos "by

---

64. See the edition in Kreuzer, *Heinrich von Langenstein.* On conciliarist theory, see Tierney, *Foundations of the Conciliar Theory.* For more on Heinrich and his interest in Hildegard of Bingen's prophecies, see the last section of this chapter.

65. For a concise biography and analysis of his works, see Hohmann and Kreuzer, "Heinrich von Langenstein."

66. Edited by Pez, in *Thesaurus,* vol. 1. All references will be to this edition.

67. On the problem of prophecy and astrology, with a focus on Pierre d'Ailly, see the excellent study by Smoller, *History, Prophecy, and the Stars.* On Heinrich and Jean Gerson, see also Guerra, "Il silenzio di Dio e la voce dell'anima."

their fruits you shall know them,"[68] Heinrich proceeds to tell an anecdote that is meant to illustrate the iffiness of these "fruits."[69]

About nine or ten years earlier (that is, in the very first years of the Schism) a certain French monk in Eberbach (monachus quidam gallicus; col. 516) named Wilhelm, a learned man of great saintly and religious accomplishments, was often visited by Heinrich. This monk claimed to be the recipient of many revelations, among them those that told him the present Schism would not last much longer. "But what happened? Ten years went by and the Schism was in no way diminished, but is in fact even more serious (acutum; col. 516) than before." The monk, undeterred, scrutinizes the Scriptures (believing himself to be a true erudite) and comes up with another date for the end of the Schism. Here we see that visionary experience has been replaced with hermeneutic activity. Jean de Roquetaillade, and even Joachim of Fiore, had placed a similar emphasis on interpreting Scripture rather than on claiming continuous revelations. Nonetheless, the new date proves as faulty as the previous predictions had been: "the Schism remained entrenched and vigorous" (col. 516). At that point the monk loses his mind, tears off his religious habit, and, "in a vile secular tunic" (col. 517), he begins to roam in the mountains surrounding his monastery. From this story we can see, Heinrich admonishes us, that God's just judgment punishes the sin of presumption and curiosity. God permitted his spirit to be invaded by errors and to be deceived by revelations, presumably in the good cause of exposing false prophets.

What are we to make of this story? It dramatizes better than any theoretical refutation of prophecy the dubious results of people's anguished questioning of the development of the Schism and their vain efforts to find a solution. We should not forget that the monk is French and that he, being in Eberbach, finds himself in a territory of Urbanist obedience, while most of France adhered to Clement. Furthermore, Heinrich highlights in this story several important means of accessing prophetic knowledge: messages from Christ—that is, revelations, astrology, and exegesis. The sequence of the monk's efforts to determine the precise date of the Schism's end perhaps indicates a progression toward the most reliable means: exegesis. Yet, even here the monk fails, which I take to be more an indictment of his presumptuousness than an indictment of his methods.

This story forms part of the polemic against one specific and influential prophet: Telesphorus of Cosenza, who wrote his extremely popular Libellus on

---

68. On this topos, see Caciola, *Discerning Spirits.*
69. This anecdote is mentioned briefly by Smoller, *History,* p. 93, and by Guerra, "Il silenzio," p. 396.

the tribulations of the church in 1386. In several manuscripts the *Libellus* and the Pope Prophecies appear together, and we shall see that Telesphorus was certainly inspired by the notion of the Angel Popes featured in the Pope Prophecies.[70]

Telesphorus's text, starring no fewer than three Antichrists, is rather confusing and in parts contradictory. Bernard McGinn has provided a cogent summary that outlines Telesphorus's major schemes and can serve as a basis for more detailed analyses:

> Telesphorus thought that the *Mystical Antichrist* had been born in 1365 in the person of a coming Emperor Frederick III, who would be associated with a False Pope of German origin. Satan was to be released, and a period of great conflict between good and evil would last until 1409. The forces of good would be led by the French king, fittingly named Charles, who would help the True Pope, the *pastor angelicus,* to defeat Frederick and the False Pope. The Angelic Pope would then crown Charles emperor, ending German claims over the empire. The two messiah figures would also do battle against the *Great Antichrist,* who was set to appear in 1378 and who would lead the Church into schism. They would defeat him and end the schism in 1391 or 1393, and would then reform the Church before setting out on crusade to conquer the Holy Land. This messianic breathing space (which was to include four Angelic Popes in all) was to end in 1433 with the advent of the *Final Antichrist,* or Gog, at which time the Last Emperor Charles would lay down his crown at the Holy Sepulcher. Another earthly time of peace, however, the coming seventh age, would follow the defeat of the Final Antichrist.[71]

Though Telesphorus's text was widely diffused in manuscripts and printed editions, little is known about this intriguing personage, except that he was a "poor priest and hermit" and hailed from Calabria.[72] The initial scene shows us

70. See Donckel, "Studien über die Prophezeiung." In BnF lat. 10834, for example, which contains twenty-six of the thirty Pope Prophecies, a reference to Telesphorus appears at the bottom of folio 7r in connection with Pietro Tomacelli, who became Pope Boniface IX (1389–1404). This pope has a little bear on his head and two bears on either side. For another example, see BL MS Arundel 117, folio 114v (table 16 in Millet, *Il libro*).

71. McGinn, *Visions,* p. 247; my emphasis. The scene of the emperor laying down his crown and scepter in Jerusalem can be found already in the mid-twelfth-century German *Play of Antichrist* (p. 79).

72. The quotation and the following details come from the passage on Telesphorus in the Life of Joachim of Fiore, *Acta sanctorum,* May VII, p. 137b and 137c. On the Life of Joachim by Daniel

Telesphorus, "sad and suffering from the evils of the current Schism," as he begs God, with fasting and copious tears, to tell him about the causes and the anticipated duration of this disaster. He also wants to know who is the true pope and who is the pseudo-pope. It is important to note here the emotional distress caused by the Schism. As we saw in Chapters 4 and 5, emotional turmoil is often a trigger for an allegorical dream vision. Thus, for example, both Honoré Bovet and Christine de Pizan were overtaken by grief at the opening of their respective visionary texts, the *Somnium super materia scismatis* and the *Chemin de longue etude*. We can certainly posit here a mutual fertilization of the different types of prophetic discourses, whether poetic and "fictional" or meant to be understood as "real," divinely inspired experiences.

After his prayer for elucidation Telesphorus has indeed a dream vision, on Easter morning 1386, in which an angel, two cubits tall, dressed in an ankle-length tunic and with two large shiny wings, gives him precise instructions on which bookish sources to scrutinize (essentially all major prophetic texts of his time) in order to find answers to his questions. Then, "waking up from sleep, I called my dearest friend Eusebius of Vercelli," and the two set out on their research mission.[73] As can be seen from this setup, Telesphorus's *Libellus,* preceded in many manuscripts by a dedicatory letter to the doge of Genoa, is presented as an anthology plus commentary of some of the best-known prophetic traditions of his time, but, as we shall see, there are also some innovations.[74]

Noting Telesphorus's geographic location of Calabria, Noël Valois highlights the French political interests in this area: "The program of political and religious hopes of the house of France was clothed in prophetic shape in a corner of Italy where the French influence made itself markedly felt."[75] Furthermore, the dedicatory letter is addressed to Antonio Adorno, doge of Genoa, the very city where the Roman pope Urban VI had taken refuge at this troubled

---

Papebroch, see Reeves, *Influence,* pp. 121–25. The fact that Telesphorus's story forms part of the Life of Joachim of Fiore shows that he is meant to represent a kind of guarantee of Joachim's divine inspiration. Joachim certainly was controversial, and his inclusion the *Acta sanctorum* was somewhat problematic, as Reeves shows very well.

73. *Acta sanctorum,* May VII, p. 137b.

74. Following Donckel, "Studien," scholars for a long time adopted his curious idea that the authors of the dedicatory letter and the text were not the same. Furthermore, based on a tortuous stylistic and numerical analysis, he argued that the letter dates from 1356 and the text proper from 1386. These arguments were effectively refuted by Spence in "MS Syracuse Von Ranke 90." I thank Robert Lerner for this reference. About fifty manuscripts (in both Latin and French), many of them beautifully illustrated, survive, together with several printed editions. On the illustrations, see Guerrini, *Propaganda politica,* chap. 2.

75. Valois, *La France,* 1:372. Valois adds in n. 3 "Il y avait dans cette région du royaume de Sicile de puissants seigneurs du parti de Louis d'Anjou, qui pouvaient contribuer à y répandre la foi en Clément VII et le respect de la France."

moment. Urban's situation in Naples had become untenable in the wake of conflicts with Charles III and the uprising of some of his cardinals against him. In fact, Urban arrived in Genoa accompanied by five of them, now his captives, who were being brutally tortured and eventually murdered at Urban's behest.[76]

But Pope Clement VII also had hopes for Doge Adorno's support. This papal rivalry, concentrated at this moment on Genoa, explains the dedicatory letter and Telesphorus's depiction of Clement VII as the legitimate pope and of Urban VI as the second Antichrist. With this pro-French treatise, Telesphorus clearly hoped to make his case for France's righteousness and predetermined role in ending the Great Schism. In fact, Franz Kampers places his treatise in the context of a "national battle of prophecies" and details the growing French influence in Lombardy.[77] For his cause of determining the origins of the Great Schism, Telesphorus brought together the traditions of the world emperor, the unleashing of Satan, and the reign of the Antichrist.

In the dedicatory letter, dated September 3, 1386, Telesphorus evokes past kingdoms and lists the books he scrutinized for his prophecies, notably those by Joachim of Fiore, the historian Orosius, and Saint Augustine.[78] For reasons we cannot know, he does not mention Jean de Roquetaillade, to whom he owes a great deal. He concludes his letter with a clear exhortation to Adorno: alluding to the "last schism" in which Frederic I supported Pope Alexander III,[79] Telesphorus moves on to the "present Schism," which Adorno is in an excellent position to "remove"—in fact, this is his duty (tolli debere). Telesphorus recommends that public opinion and vulgar prattle be ignored (popularium et vulgarium garulitas despicias; pp. 290–91), for the truth rarely resides in the common people. Rather, Adorno should turn to the eternal truth of Telesphorus's Libellus, which emanates not from himself but from prophetic authorities, whose "obscure sayings" (obscura loquentium; p. 291) he will elucidate, so that Adorno can become a worthy arbiter in the conflict of the Schism.

As we just saw, at the beginning of the text proper Telesphorus presents his work as a divinely inspired research project: the angel that appeared to him on Easter morning 1386 exhorted him to scrutinize the works of previous prophets, to transcribe their findings and disseminate them. Faithful to this charge, Telesphorus delivers a veritable bibliography of Joachimite and

---

76. Adam Easton was the only one of the captives to be liberated due to the intervention of the English king. On this horrific episode, see Valois, La France, 2:113–16.

77. Kampers, Kaiserprophetieen, p. 167.

78. Edited by Donckel, "Studien," pp. 282–91.

79. That is, the schism of 1159; see Chapter 1. Quotations from the letter in Donckel, "Studien," p. 290.

pseudo-Joachimite literature.[80] His own scheme is based on the appearance of the nefarious "king from the North," Frederick III from the poisonous breed of the Hohenstaufen, the same house condemned by Jean de Roquetaillade. Next to Frederick will stand the "Antipope from the German Nation" (Antipapa, qui erit ex natione Alemannus). Together they will form alliances with the Turks, the Saracens, and the Greeks to bring about the ruin of the church. They will vanquish and imprison the French king, who will subsequently be miraculously liberated. Then the true "Angelic" pope will crown him emperor after having taken away the German electors' right to vote. The true pope and the French emperor will then reform the church and lead a last successful crusade.

Much of this scheme is indebted to the *Liber de Flore,* a pro-French tract written in the milieu of the Spiritual Franciscans in the early fourteenth century.[81] Here Telesphorus found some of his animal symbolism, notably the opening line "Tempore colubri leene filii" (in the time of the sons of the viper and lioness; p. 36) and the idea of a succession of Angel Popes, also a feature of the Pope Prophecies, as we saw above. Herbert Grundmann has studied in detail the contemporary problems this text works out for the late thirteenth and early fourteenth centuries in the context of the struggle of the Spiritual Franciscans with various popes and the emperor.[82] Telesphorus's redeployment of a prophecy anchored in the political reality of the period of its composition is thus a prime example of prophetic activity at the time of the Great Schism; older prophecies were refurbished and updated to fit current events. Thus, we find the familiar scheme of Antichrist–World Emperor–Angel Pope(s) interspersed with references to the Great Schism.

Chapter one announces that the Schism, predicted by many prophets as well as the Holy Spirit over many years, has arrived as a punishment for the sins of clerics and the Christian people. Detailing the vices of the Roman church, Telesphorus shows no surprise at the serious punishment God meted out. The mendicants' sins—that is, succumbing to the desire for property and abandoning the ideal of pure evangelical poverty—are paradigmatic of the sins of the clergy and the Catholic church as a whole. Therefore, in 1365 Satan was unleashed, as predicted in Revelation 20:7 (though without a precise date!), and thirteen years later the Great Schism began: "In the year of our Lord 1378

---

80. See Rusconi, *L'attesa della fine,* p. 172. For a detailed list of the sources, see Donckel, "Studien." See also Reeves, *Influence,* pp. 423–28.

81. See Kurze, "Nationale Regungen in der spätmittelalterlichen Prophetie," p. 9. On the *Liber de Flore,* see Grundmann, "Liber de Flore." The parenthetical page number refers to this article.

82. On these problems, see most recently Burr, *Spiritual Franciscans.*

Satan seduced the clerics, the Emperor and kings and princes and other people to a Schism and Wars."[83] This traumatic event is depicted in manuscript illuminations as a kind of group haunting: black-winged demons hover and interact with humans representing different groups of society, though in this particular image no churchmen are present (fig. 10). Paola Guerrini points out that in several manuscripts each demon is in charge of one of the groups of society that have been mentioned as having been "seduced" by Satan: an emperor, a king, a prince, a cleric, and a layman. Guerrini, in her figure 16, reproduces an image from Vatican MS Reg. lat. 580 (fol. 21v) that shows a larger crowd but where the emperor, with his characteristic pointy German beard, a crowned king, two cardinals with their hats, several monks in brown habits, and some laymen, two with lawyers' hoods, can be discerned.[84] While the cardinals alone were usually blamed for the origin of the Schism, the people in this illustration represent the major groups that were involved in the subsequent development of the Schism. The emperor's German-style beard conforms to Telesphorus's claim that in 1365 the Mystical Antichrist was born in Germany to be crowned by a "false German pope as Frederick III."[85] This *pseudo pontifex sive antipapa* (pseudo-pope or antipope) will have been elected through the maliciousness of this Frederick.[86]

　　In an image from MS BnF fr. 9783, a fifteenth-century French translation of the *Libellus* (fig. 11), we see a false prophet (falsus propheta) from whose mouth emerge toads, illustrating Revelation 16:13–14, quoted in Telesphorus's text: "And I saw three unclean spirits like frogs come out of the mouth of the dragon, and out of the mouth of the beast, and out of the mouth of the false prophet.[87] For they are the spirits of devils, working miracles, which go forth unto the kings of the earth and of the whole world, to gather them to the battle of that great day of God almighty" (RSV). The "seduction" depicted here, while still assigning some human responsibility for the beginning of the Schism, also implies a higher force, that of the "loosened Satan" of the Apocalypse and his minions, who are the necessary forerunners of the Last Times. The conceptualization of the Schism is thus completely removed from the "real" circumstances of the double election and the political wrangling that both preceded and succeeded it. It is integrated into the apocalyptic scheme of

---

83. MS Modena, Biblioteca Estense lat. 233, folio 14v.

84. Guerrini, *Propaganda politica*, p. 29.

85. McGinn, *Antichrist*, p. 178.

86. MS Modena, Biblioteca Estense lat. 233, folio 27v. Note here the term "antipope," which puts these events into the context of the Schism.

87. The charge of being a false prophet was the very one leveled against Telesphorus by Heinrich of Langenstein, as we saw above.

FIG. 10 Winged demons "seduce" prelates and rulers to the Schism. The *Libellus* of Telesphorus of Cosenza. Paris, Bibliothèque nationale de France, lat. 11415, folio 131v

the Book of Revelation and presented as a divine punishment. The iconography of its beginnings is that of demonic possession.

Telesphorus's third chapter predicts that in 1394 the truth of the Schism will be known. Roberto Rusconi highlights the contradictions and confusions in Telesphorus's scheme for the end of times, which is indebted to the tradition of the Seven Ages as well as to the Joachimite tradition of the three ages.[88] Following Joachim of Fiore and Jean de Roquetaillade, Telesphorus repeats the idea that there will be several Antichrists, the third identified with Gog, though

88. According to Rusconi, this precise date is a feature of a second redaction. See *L'attesa*, p. 176. However, in line with Spence (as in note 74, above), the idea of a second redaction does not survive closer scrutiny, and it is not necessary for Rusconi's arguments. Kampers also observes that Telesphorus's prophecies get more and more confused, especially toward the end: "There were just too many prophecies that the good Telesphorus had to pass through his sieve" (*Kaiserprophetieen*, p. 170).

FIG. 11 Toads emerge from the mouth of the false prophet. From a French translation of the *Libellus* of Telesphorus of Cosenza. Paris, Bibliothèque nationale de France, fr. 9783, folio 9r.

Telesphorus, as did his predecessors, does not take the one thousand years of his reign literally but rather sees it as a perfect number.[89]

Before the beginning of the Great Schism an Angel Pope and his army would appear to defeat the Mystical Antichrist Frederick III, only to face the Magnus Antichristus, who in 1378 would be responsible for the beginning of the Schism. For our purposes these are the most interesting passages, dealing as they do with the actual events of the Schism; the death of Pope Gregory XI coincides with the arrival of the Second (or Magnus) Antichrist, Pope Urban VI. Here we find a reference to the *Liber de Flore* and to the noncanonical election of a heretic supported by Frederick III, who through his errors will infect the church, for many will listen to his errors and adhere to them. This will lead to the Schism.[90] On the other side, an Angel Pope will appear, followed by three other Angel Popes. These figures have strong affinities, both iconographically and ideologically, with the Pope Prophecies we considered above.[91]

89. Rusconi, *L'attesa*, p. 177. See also Lerner, "Joachim of Fiore's Breakthrough," 507 n. 42.
90. MS Modena, Biblioteca Estense lat. 233, folio 31r.
91. Telesphorus's text and the Pope Prophecies often appear in the same manuscripts.

The Angel Pope will crown the French king Charles as emperor. Telesphorus's account of a succession of schisms resolved by the French king puts him squarely into the pro-French polemical context of the Schism. The French kings, states Telesphorus, were always on the side of the true pope, and the present Schism will also be ended by the French between 1391 and 1393. Yet, the French emperor Charles will abdicate in Jerusalem before the arrival of the final Antichrist, Gog, in 1433. Another messianic era, a time of peace and joy, will follow the defeat of this last Antichrist. As Marjorie Reeves points out regarding this last era: "Here the only surviving institutions seem to be the papacy whom all the world will obey and the *Ecclesia contemplativa* of Joachim's vision."[92] Without going into the more and more confused predictions at the end of the treatise, we can conclude with Bernard McGinn that "this scenario, with its odd triple Antichrist, used both Joachite and imperial apocalypticism in attempting to locate the crisis of the schism within God's total plan for history."[93]

Telesphorus certainly was the most popular prophet of the Great Schism, the one prophetic writer whose entire work was focused on this one burning problem. Through his depiction of the Schism as fulfilling predictions from the Book of Revelation, he reassured his audience that there was some sense— and also hope for an eventual resolution—in this seemingly intractable situation. Of course, as time went on none of the specific prophecies came true,[94] enough of a reason for Heinrich of Langenstein to use Telesphorus as the paradigmatic example of the false prophets so prevalent in his time.

We do not know how, except for his text, Telesphorus may have attempted to spread his message. But there are some indications that prophets engaging in partisan politics did circulate in the region of Genoa, the contested site for papal rivalry in 1386. The story recounted by the chronicler Gobelinus Person in the eighty-first chapter of *Cosmidromius* provides an atmospheric backdrop to Telesphorus's *Libellus*.[95]

Gobelinus, a cleric who had come to Genoa with Urban VI—and the above-mentioned captive cardinals—in 1385, tells us that on March 5, 1386, a false (se simulans; p. 116) prophet, full of himself (tumidus) and audaciously sacrilegious, appeared in that city. Of large stature, dressed in a black habit, with a

---

92. Reeves, *Influence*, p. 327.
93. McGinn, *Antichrist*, p. 178.
94. This did not prevent his text from having an active afterlife. See Beaune, "De Telesphore à Guillaume Postel."
95. See Rusconi, *L'attesa*, pp. 169–71. The hypothesis that this prophet was in fact Telesphorus himself has been refuted. Parenthetical references will be to the edition by Weber (in the bibliography, see Gobelinus Person, *Cosmidromius*).

black beard and deep-set, serious eyes, he directs himself toward the papal palace, where Pope Urban VI, undoubtedly alerted to the approach of this strange personage, had surrounded himself with a number of prelates. Admitted to the pope's presence, the prophet announces that he wants to proclaim—in French, being ignorant of Latin—a number of divine revelations granted to him during his fifteen years of contemplation in his hermitage: "I perceived through divine revelation that Clement is the true supreme pontiff and vicar of Christ and that you are the pseudo-pope. Therefore, in the interest of the union of the church and your own salvation you must resign the papacy" (p. 117). Urban, asking for visible signs or scriptural testimony to support the prophet's assertions, is told only that the prophet does not fear torture to affirm the correctness of his prophetic insights. It is not surprising that Urban calls these revelations "pretense" and further unmasks the prophet by asking about his precious ring, a non-hermit-like accessory. The prophet admits that he received this jewel from Pope Clement VII and is in fact his and the French king's emissary. Thrown into jail and under torture the prophet also confesses to diabolical inspiration (suggestionem diabolicam magis esse confessus est; p. 117). Rather than punishing him more severely, however, Urban decides, after the intercession of some French prelates, to have the prophet's beard cut off, to have him recant his previous statements and affirm that Urban is the only true pope, and to send him back to France.

If true—and even if not true—this story sheds some intriguing light on the use of prophets and prophecy by the various factions during the Great Schism. The prophet-authors we considered so far were not explicitly commissioned by one pope or the other to create their texts—as were many of the authors of polemical treatises—though their partiality is often very obvious. The Genoa "prophet," rather than disseminating prophecies in writing (scriptis), chose to do so by oral proclamation (voce), exposing himself to considerable risks. We saw earlier that these two means of spreading prophecies were often mentioned in conjunction, yet each has different characteristics. Compared with the more often than not obscure written prophecies, this oral one is of an almost breathtaking simplicity: Urban is called a pseudo-pope and is warned that the salvation of his soul is in danger unless he abdicates. Given that in 1386 the Schism had already lasted for eight years without any notable signs of progress toward resolution, one can only surmise that the fact of the pope's "exile" in Genoa had encouraged Pope Clement VII and his advisers to devise this strange scenario. In any case, this episode provides another piece of the *imaginaire* of the Great Schism: the idea that what amounted essentially to a theatrical performance could possibly resolve a problem that had proved resistant to any number of diplomatic interventions.

Closing the Circle: Hildegard of Bingen, Heinrich of Langenstein, and Pierre d'Ailly

Bernard Guenée suggests that in order to be able to understand the political problems of the late Middle Ages we have to understand the prophecies that circulated at the time.[96] The prophecies we have considered so far were created outside the strictly clerical or university milieu that also saw the creation of a large number of treatises suggesting solutions to the Schism. But within the circles of clerics committed to ending the Schism we also find a strong interest in prophecy. They, as well, wanted to know where the Schism fit into the schemes of the coming of the Antichrist and the end of times. Among these scholars two—Heinrich of Langenstein, whom we just encountered as Telesphorus of Cosenza's adversary, and Pierre d'Ailly (1350–1420)—stand out for their intense conciliarist activities and for their interest in prophecies emerging from the works of Hildgard of Bingen, a fact that allows us to close the circle with regard to our Twelfth-Century Prelude.

In 1383 and 1384, while at the abbey of Eberbach between his university posts at Paris and Vienna, Heinrich penned two letters to his friend the bishop of Worms, Eckard von Ders, of which the first in a number of manuscripts received the subtitle *Epistola de scismate* (Letter on the schism).[97] Both letters forcefully describe the current tribulations of the schismatic church and draw on the prophecies of Hildegard of Bingen in order to integrate the Schism into a larger scheme of apocalyptic thought.

Hildegard's prophecies circulated most widely in the version assembled by Gebeno of Eberbach in 1220, the so-called *Pentachronon* (The five ages) or *Mirror of Future Times*.[98] Residing at the very abbey where Heinrich of Langenstein more than 160 years later consulted the text, Gebeno assembled excerpts from Hildegard's books having to do with the coming of the Antichrist and the end of times. He argued that for most readers Hildegard's books are too obscure and difficult—as is the case for most prophets—and that therefore such a compendium would be extremely useful.[99] And indeed, knowledge of Hildegard's thought throughout the Middle Ages was mostly limited to the ideas

96. Guenée, *Histoire et culture historique*, p. 333.
97. See Sommerfeldt, "Die Prophetien der hl. Hildegard von Bingen in einem Schreiben des Magisters Heinrich von Langenstein," p. 45. This article also contains the edition of the two letters. Parenthetical page references will be to this edition.
98. On Gebeno, see Kerby-Fulton, *Reformist Apocalypticism*, pp. 28–29, and Gouguenheim, *La Sibylle du Rhin*, pp. 169–73. There is no edition of the *Pentachronon*, only the chapter headings and a brief summary given by Pitra in Hildegard of Bingen, *Analecta Sanctae Hildegardis*, pp. 483–86.
99. Pitra in *Analecta Sanctae Hildegardis*, pp. 484–85.

Gebeno had collected from her various lengthy works. Far from wanting to stir up apocalyptic anxieties, Gebeno intended to show that according to Hildegard the arrival of the Antichrist was still far away. He was not destined to appear until the fifth and last age in her scheme that assigned an animal figure to each age. In our context the first age, that of the fiery hound, is the most significant since it was predicted to last until a great schism appeared (durabit usque ad magnum schisma).[100] This is one of the phrases that reappears in Heinrich's 1383 letter (p. 52), and one can understand how applicable he found this idea to be for his own age. The Schism had already lasted five years, and it must have seemed to Heinrich that indeed "the bishops and clerics will be expelled from their living places and their communities" (p. 52); here he uses the exact words Gebeno had extracted from Hildegard's *Liber divinorum operum*. Although he does not state this explicitly, his readers would see Heinrich himself as a prime example of this expulsion, having been forced to leave his Parisian university post. And was not Hildegard's prediction that "the church would generate its own downfall"[101] amply fulfilled through the cardinals' double election, which had split the church in two? Furthermore, Heinrich linked the Schism and the coming of the Antichrist, two events that are separated by several ages in the *Pentachronon*. But for Heinrich it was enough that Hildegard had said that before the coming of the Antichrist the church would undergo "many tribulations" (p. 307). This was clearly the current age, and for this accuracy Heinrich, like John of Salisbury centuries earlier, lauded the saintly woman as a "Teutonic Sibyl" (p. 47).

Sylvain Gouguenheim in his 1996 study of Hildegard, *La Sibylle du Rhin*, titles the chapter on her afterlife and Gebeno's role in it "La prophétesse trahie" (The prophet betrayed). Looking at the vagaries of medieval prophecies in the present chapter, it is hard to speak of betrayal in the context of any prophetic activity. Prophecies were rewritten and adapted in all time periods; no prophet was exempt. Heinrich found consolation and confirmation of his ideas in Hildegard's writings, however fragmentary or even distorted they came down to him. For him the Great Schism was made to fit into a scheme of the five ages, and because we are only at the end of the first, no immediate apparition of the Antichrist need to be feared.

One of the most striking proponents of linking the Schism and the Antichrist is our second Hildegard aficionado, the theologian and onetime chancellor of the University of Paris, Pierre d'Ailly, whom we encountered in Chapter 3 as the champion of the canonization of the boy-bishop Pierre de

---

100. Pitra in *Analecta Sanctae Hildegardis*, p. 485. See Kerby-Fulton, *Reformist Apocalypticism,* pp. 49–50, for a table laying out this scheme.
101. Kerby-Fulton, *Reformist Apocalypticism,* p. 33.

Luxembourg.[102] Pierre, like Heinrich of Langenstein an early supporter of the conciliar idea, was preoccupied with the Great Schism for most of his life. But unlike Gerson, for example, who also authored a vast number of texts relating to the Schism, Pierre, like the prophets considered above, placed the Schism into various schemes related to the end of times. Together with Heinrich he thus brings together the different milieus and textual genres that tried to deal with the trauma of the Great Schism.

Pierre d'Ailly experimented with various forms for his writings on the division of the church. An intriguing example is his *Epistola diaboli Leviathan* (The letter from the devil Leviathan) of 1381, in which he has Leviathan address the prelates and rulers to "bid them break up the unity of peace and to preserve the stability of the schism against the church of Christ." The division between the Urbanist and Clementist factions makes the devil rejoice; he delights in the "city torn asunder, . . . his seamless tunic torn asunder."[103] He argues against a general council because such an event would mend the rifts in Christendom and deprive him of his joy in seeing discord and mutual destruction. The involvement of the devil in the Schism Pierre posits here confirms that he "originally did view the Schism as a sure sign that Antichrist's reign was imminent."[104] To place this view into a proper context, Pierre appealed to a host of previous prophets, such as Hildegard of Bingen and Joachim of Fiore. Like Jean de Roquetaillade, he cites 2 Thessalonians 2:3–4 and interprets is as follows: "Before the day of the Lord, it says, there will be a certain dissension or division of the church of God, as an immediate preamble to the Antichrist."[105] In the early years of the Schism, Pierre became more and more convinced that the Antichrist's arrival was close and that the Schism was a sign of the end of times.

In a penetrating analysis, Laura Smoller has shown how Pierre revised this view in the years after 1400, becoming more and more confident that human efforts could avert the feared imminent disasters and resolve the Schism.[106] Enlisting astrology, Pierre figured out that the Apocalypse was still a long way off. Hope was now the watchword, a hope for reconciliation that Pierre saw realized at the Council of Constance.

In 1418, once Christendom had been reunited, Pierre composed his *De persecutionibus ecclesie* (On the persecutions of the church), in which he placed

102. On his life, see Guenée, *Between Church and State,* chap. 3.
103. Pierre d'Ailly, *Epistola,* pp. 185–89. On the context of Pierre's views on a general council, see Oakley, *Political Thought of Pierre d'Ailly;* on the *Epistola,* see esp. p 158.
104. Smoller, *History,* p. 85.
105. Translated from his *Sermon on St. Bernard* by Smoller, *History,* pp. 97–98. On this theme, see also Pascoe, "Pierre d'Ailly: Histoire, Schisme, Antéchrist."
106. Smoller, *History,* chap. 6.

the Schism into the scheme of the persecutions predicted by the Book of Reve-
lation. He is of the opinion that Saint John must have predicted this dire event
somehow, given that "it is said that the venerable abbot Joachim and Saint
Hildegard predicted much about this Great Schism" (venerabilis abbas
Joachim ac S. Hildegardis de hoc Magno Scismate multa predixisse legantur).[107]
For Pierre the fifth vision in the Book of Revelation fits the bill: the whore rid-
ing the apocalyptic beast "represented the schismatic church, while the city of
Babylon referred to Rome and the entire schismatic obedience. The beast of
the seven heads and ten horns stood for the temporal powers that supported
the schismatic church."[108]

Several ideas from this text will allow us to tie together the beginning and
the end of the Schism. Hildegard, as we saw in the "Twelfth-Century Prelude"
was concerned with the schism of her own time but not in the burning and
apocalyptic way that the prophets of the Great Schism were. It is in later periods that prophetic writers, like Heinrich of Langenstein and Pierre d'Ailly,
appeal to her as one of those illuminated people who had predicted the disaster
of 1378. The whore and the city of Babylon take us back to Petrarch, whose
indictment of Avignon as Babylon on the Rhone may have contributed to the
papacy's return to Rome. We can also evoke the eighth of the combined Pope
Prophecies (fig. 1), which depicts Pope Clement V's (1304–14) departure for
Avignon as his abandonment of his spouse, the woman from Babylon who
remains behind as if she were a widow.[109] The prophecy indicates that he left
her behind because she was abominable to him, as abominable as was the
whole schismatic Roman obedience—figured by the city of Babylon—to Pierre
d'Ailly. As for apocalyptic beasts, we saw that they were plentiful in the figura-
tions of the Great Schism.

Thus, Pierre brings together in his post–Council of Constance text a number of ideas and images that were woven into the very fabric of the *imaginaire*
of the Great Schism. Unlike the earlier prophets we dealt with in this chapter,
Pierre eventually abandoned the connection he had established between the
Great Schism and the end of times. But his imagery remained indebted to the
Book of Revelation, which as the universal prophetic key could be applied to
every crisis at hand. Once the Great Schism was over, other disasters would
strike, among them one of the greatest schisms of all: the Reformation.[110]

---

107. Valois, "Un ouvrage inédit de Pierre d'Ailly," p. 571.
108. Smoller, *History*, p. 112.
109. *Vide hic mulieris Babiloniae sponsum fugientem sponsam suam sibi abhominabilem, quasi vid-
uatam relinquens* (ed. in Schwartz and Lerner, "Illuminated Propaganda," p. 189).
110. In this context, the Pope Prophecies reappeared and were exploited in anti-Catholic propaganda. See the interesting dissertation by Heffner, "Eyn Wunderliche Weyssagung."

CONCLUSION

Pierre d'Ailly, with whom we ended our last chapter, appeared at the Council of Constance in November 1414 with a retinue of no fewer than forty-four people. Altogether, more than 2,200 official participants slowly gathered on Lake Constance for the three and a half years the council was to last. About half of them were lay nobles and freemen; the other half consisted of prelates, abbots, heads of ecclesiastical corporations, curial officials, envoys of universities, secular lords, and representatives of towns.[1] The goal of this enormous meeting was the union of the church and its reform. While the first goal was achieved, the second was not a complete success.[2]

The initiative for this council came from the emperor Sigismund, who began planning it in the wake of the Council of Pisa in 1409, which, rather than resolving the Schism, had created a tricephalic church.[3] The three popes and

1. See Stump, *Reforms*, p. xiii n. 3. See also Miethke, "Die Konzilien." For Pierre d'Ailly, see Delaruelle et al., *L'Eglise*, 1:171 n. 14; pp. 167–200 offer an excellent concise history of the council and are my major source for the remarks here. For a new and comprehensive study, see Brandmüller, *Das Konzil von Konstanz*.
2. On the reforms, which cannot be treated here, see Stump, *Reforms*.
3. In the second version of Pierre Salmon's *Dialogues* (1412–15), Sigismund is depicted as the "imperial Antechrist," a sign that not everyone had confidence in his ending the Schism. In any case, throughout this conflict Sigismund had been on the opposing side of the French, which explains this unflattering image! (See Roux, *Les Dialogues de Salmon et de Charles VI*, p. 121, and color plate xivb from ms BnF fr. 165.)

representatives of the different nations involved in the Schism were invited to the Council of Constance, but as in Pisa not all of them came. The most notable absence was that of Pope Benedict XIII, who was still in Perpignan. Pope Gregory XII, in his refuge in Rimini, was eventually persuaded to abdicate in 1415, which he did with dignity; he became again Angelo Correr, bishop of Porto. His cardinals joined the unionist efforts at Constance. He died in 1417 before the end of the council. John XXIII agreed to attend the council but wanted to lead it, a decision that did not sit well with the organizers.

Cardinal Zabarella, one of the foremost conciliar theorists, read the opening decree on November 1, 1414. Most of that year had been spent in preparations, full of misgivings and suspicions on the part of many invitees. Pope John XXIII finally came in late October, and on his arrival compared the city to a trap for foxes.[4] This attitude did not bode well. Indeed, the council's threefold accusation and call to abdication did not make any distinction between the three popes, all of them equally designated as usurpers. John XXIII, faced with deposition, reacted by fleeing from Constance with a group of supporters. This absence left the council itself as the major authority. It then "enacted its now most famous decree,"[5] stating that council received its authority directly from God. This decree allowed them to continue their work without the presence of any of the three popes.

Sigismund pursued John XXIII, brought him back to the gates of Constance, made him a prisoner, and deposed him as "unworthy, useless, and harmful."[6] This left Benedict XIII. The emperor decided to travel to Perpignan to get the last of the three popes to abdicate. In the summer of 1415 Sigismund traveled with a number of representatives from France, England, Savoie, and Navarre to the pope's abode. Benedict played his last trump card: because he was the only cardinal still alive who had been appointed by the pre-Schism Pope Gregory XI, he asserted, this made him ipso facto the only legitimate person to elect a pope. It is not surprising that Sigismund rejected Benedict's offer to come up with a new supreme pontiff, but this time the emperor was not defeated by the wily old pope. He assembled representatives of the Iberian kingdoms and of the remaining areas that still were loyal to Benedict and persuaded them to sign an accord to abandon Benedict. The Aragonese clergy was now obliged to send delegates to Constance, and it fell to Saint Vincent Ferrer to proclaim this decree. Thus, before a huge crowd, he denounced the pope he

4. Delaruelle et al., *L'Eglise*, 1:169. The chronicler Ulrich von Richental reports that John XXIII, when he saw the city of Constance from a distance, said, "Sic capiuntur volpes" (Thus, foxes will be caught). Ed. Feger, p. 160.

5. Stump, *Reforms*, p. xiv. Stump (p. xiv n. 7) shows that John Figgis in 1916 called this decree "probably the most revolutionary document in the history of the world."

6. Delaruelle et al., *L'Eglise*, 1:181.

had served for so many years—a tragic moment for Vincent.[7] While Benedict still believed himself to be pope, hardly anyone else did at this point.[8]

The Council of Constance now could proceed to elect a new pope. But the longer the council lasted the more tension and discord emerged. The various European crises, such as the conflict between the Armagnacs and Burgundians in France and the continuing Hundred Years War (the French defeat at Agincourt occurred in 1415, the first full year of the council), were mirrored in the acrimonies in Constance.

These problems were exacerbated by the creation of only four nations for the purpose of voting: France; England with Wales and Ireland; Italy with Crete and Cyprus; and the Empire with the Netherlands and the Swiss, as well as Dalmatia, Croatia, Hungary, Poland, Bohemia, and the Scandinavian countries.[9] Eventually the Spanish kingdoms constituted a fifth nation. Getting them to send their delegates proved to be "a huge task, accompanied by infinite nuisances, delays, and truly incredible unpleasantness," according to one of the representatives Sigismund had sent to Castille.[10]

Now the question arose (prefiguring the prelude to the French Revolution) whether one should vote by head or by nation, a serious problem because each nation had a widely divergent number of representatives. Finally, Pierre d'Ailly proposed a voting system that included a variety of participants. Fifty-three voters were designated, coming from different nations and groups: the cardinals plus thirty "nationals," six from each nation.[11] On Saint Martin's Day 1417 they elected Ottone Colonna, who in honor of that day took the name Martin V (1417–31). All the bells in Constance began ringing, and after thirty-nine years the Great Schism was finally over: the church again had only one papal husband![12]

---

7. Delaruelle et al., *L'Eglise*, 1:185. Gerson generously credited Vincent with having ended the Schism with this move (Fages, *Histoire de Saint Vincent Ferrier*, 2:111). See also above, Chapter 3, for more on this scene.

8. Nonetheless, successors to Benedict appeared after his death in 1423. See above, the end of Chapter 5. And for Nicolas de Clamanges the Schism still persisted in 1425, as one can see from a passage in his commentary on Isaiah (see Coville's remarks in his edition of Clamanges's *Traité de la ruine de l'Eglise*, p. 99).

9. For details on the problems this division caused, see Finke, "Die Nation in den spätmittelalterlichen allgemeinen Konzilien."

10. Quoted by Delaruelle et al., *L'Eglise*, 1:187.

11. Delaruelle et al., *L'Eglise*, 1:199.

12. This unified state was not to last for very long, however. From 1439 to 1449 there was another schism with the antipope Felix V. This schism, according to Fossier, did not "excite historiographers" ("Rapports Eglise-Etat," p. 28). The Council of Basel dragged on for many years and gave rise to its own polemical literature. According to Jonathan Beck the problems related to this council contributed to the birth of political theater in France. See Beck, ed., *Le "Concil de Basle" (1434)*. In this play the council itself is a character, and Eglise complains to him about the slowness of the proceedings!

Throughout this book we encountered various metaphors likening the Great Schism and the divided church to the concepts of marriage, adultery, and even rape. As a final example of this imagery—and its happy resolution—we can contemplate two illustrations from Antonio Baldana's poem about the Great Schism, which he wrote for the new pope Martin V in 1419. The beginning of the Schism, an image already evoked earlier in this book, is shown as an act of violence against a woman—that is, the personified church; the Avignon cardinals rip off her veil while capturing the keys of Saint Peter from Urban's tiara with a lasso. The circular city is split down the middle. The caption reads "The first act of the Schism" (primus actus scismatis) (fig. 12). In fitting contrast, Martin V's accession is shown as a marriage ceremony in which the emperor Sigismund joins the hands of the as yet tiara-less Ottone Colonna and the personified Church. She is gently pushed by the cardinals in the direction of her new spouse (fig. 13). The city, featuring two churches, as in figure 12, is now reunited and enclosed by a single wall. Harmony and unity have been restored.

This harmony, the council members realized, could not be disturbed by futile recriminations. Therefore the most important thing that was *not* done at Constance was the determination which of the two papacies had been in the right. As Noël Valois put it, the question of who had been the legitimate popes remained "un mystère ténébreux" (a dark mystery).[13] Only in the sixteenth century, when new popes began to take the same names the Avignon popes had chosen during the Schism (for example, Clement VII [1523–34]), was an implicit judgment made that only the Roman line had been legitimate.[14] But in Constance this claim was never put forward—and with good reason, because otherwise all the actions of a whole series of popes would have become invalid.

Later medieval and early modern historians for the most part also gloss over these questions, either by not addressing the different popes' legitimacy at all or by calling everyone of them a false pope. In the hugely popular *Nuremberg Chronicle* from the late fifteenth century, for example, we see four popes from the Great Schism peacefully united in a single frame (fig. 14). None of them has a caption of antipope. But a somewhat earlier German woodcut (1475) does call each Avignon pope *antipapa*, although, as we saw, they were not designated as such by the council.[15] Thus, there were a number of partisan

---

13. Valois, *La France,* 4:502.

14. On these questions, see Fink, "Zur Beurteilung des grossen abendländischen Schismas."

15. In the copy of the *Nuremberg Chronicle* from my own collection used here, the misprint "Clemens sextus" was corrected in contemporary brown ink to "Clemens septimus." Laura Smoller is preparing a study of the post-Constance iconography. The German woodcut I mention here was part of her presentation titled "Two-Headed Monsters and Chopped-Up Babies: Re-Imagining the Schism after the Council of Constance."

FIG. 12 The Avignon cardinals pull away the Church's veil and capture Pope Urban VI's papal keys with a lasso. The manuscript caption reads *Primus actus schismatis* (the first act of the Schism). From Antonio Baldana. *De magno schismate* (1419). Parma, Biblioteca Palatina, MS 1194, folio 2r

FIG. 13 Pope Martin V weds the reunited church at the Council of Constance. The emperor Sigismund officiates. From Antonio Baldana, *De magno schismate* (1419). Parma, Biblioteca Palatina, MS 1194, folio 13v

interpretations—which could be the subject of another book. In any case, at this point the interpretation of the Schism had begun, but as a true historiographical subject the Schism came into being only in the seventeenth century.[16] By the twentieth century the literature on the Great Schism had become immense.

Looking back at the large cast of characters we encountered in this book, we can now ask: So how *did* they see the Schism? How did they conceptualize this crisis and how was an *imaginaire* of the Schism created? How did they respond to the divided church both emotionally and practically? For Catherine of Siena

16. See Fossier, "Rapports Eglise/Etat."

FIG. 14 Four popes of the Schism years peacefully united in one frame. Clockwise: Urban VI, Clement VII, Benedict XIII, and Boniface IX. From Hartmann Schedel, *The Nuremberg Chronicle.* Nuremberg, 1493, folio 232v

every other disaster—be it war, dishonor, or any other tribulation—paled in comparison with the Schism. Her passionate engagement in trying to find solutions to the Schism marked the last two years of her life. For Honoré Bovet as well, the Schism was at the very top of the tree of battles: above the Hundred Years War and various civil wars. Far from being a problem for the papacy only, the Schism created political and spiritual fissures throughout Europe, causing deep anxiety for many Christians of all classes; to eradicate it was our protagonists' sacred mission. For Eustache Deschamps, as we saw, the unity of the church was a requirement reflected in the very structure of the universe—a cosmic divine command, as it were.

But whose fault was the division of the church? Throughout this study we were faced with a multiplicity of explanations reflecting the multiple and often contradictory roles the church was assigned in this period. All along the church was monster and victim; mutilated mother and double-headed dragon; a persecuted innocent woman and the embodiment of moral failure. Eustache Deschamps's poems, for example, showed us the church as a victim of polygamy and marital rape (thus the popes were to blame) as well as a bicephalic mythic monster (expressing the corruption of the church herself). In many of the versions of the Pope Prophecies, Pope Urban VI appeared as the fiery dragon of the Apocalypse, thus suggesting an indictment of the Roman side. For Constance de Rabastens and fr. Pedro of Aragon there was simply no question who was at fault: their divine revelations indicted the Avignon pope without the slightest doubt. Vincent Ferrer and Marie Robine equally firmly believed the opposite—until they were disillusioned and gave up their belief in Benedict XIII, either rapidly and completely, like Marie, or reluctantly and painfully, as was the case for Vincent. Two generations later, the author of Ursulina of Parma's *Vita* still saw the Schism as a struggle between good and evil, and the identity of the true pope—the Roman one—as divinely ordained. For Bovet the Schism was a battle between papal armies as well as an attack of children against their beloved mother. For Christine de Pizan the Schism was simultaneously part of a series of disasters attributable to Fortune; a horrible illness of the body politic; and the consequence of a rational political decision by King Charles V—whose guilt was nonetheless confirmed in the allegory of the *Advision,* in which Christine blames Fraud for creating the Schism. In each work and each genre, Christine conceptualized the Schism differently, reflecting the many currents of thought that swirled around this intractable problem. For our prophets, especially Telesphorus of Cosenza, the Schism was part of a complicated historical and apocalyptic scheme that involved the coming of the world emperor, the unleashing of Satan, and the

arrival of the Antichrist. For Telesphorus the division of Christendom was initiated by evil demons that came to possess secular and religious leaders (see
fig. 10).

Especially fascinating for our study of the *imaginaire* was the confluence of
dramatic imagery surrounding the Schism in quite different contexts. Aside
from the more current images of the church as a sinking ship, for example, we
found a lot of smoke. Smoke was a major sign of the confusion and trouble
created by the Schism in the visions of Constance de Rabastens, who saw
Clement VII in a smoky temple; in Bovet's apocalyptic interpretation of the
Schism in his *Arbre des batailles,* where smoke rose from the abyss; and in
Philippe de Mézières's fantastic vision of Pope Urban VI in Genoa, who
seemed to the Old Pilgrim a person "made out of smoke." Another instance is
the stumbling or limping pope, seen by Constance de Rabastens and, in both a
real and a symbolic manner, by Saint Colette. As for the suffering caused by the
Schism, people as diverse as Catherine of Siena, Honoré Bovet, Christine de
Pizan, and Telesphorus of Cosenza all describe the same state of depression
and even painful physical manifestations.[17] Thus, people in different time periods and areas created imagery and depicted emotions that were quite similar
and that expressed their anguish and uncertainty in the face of multiple popes.

But what kind of solutions did our protagonists propose? Given the double
perspective of the church as victim and monster, different types of solutions
should have been proposed. If the church is seen as a morally corrupt beast,
only reform from the inside can heal the Schism; and certainly there were
plenty of calls for church reform during the Schism years. If the church is a victim help must come from the outside, and this help is not necessarily related to
the shape the Schism took in people's imagination. Indeed, in the texts and
visions we studied in this book we find a most interesting contrast between the
often fantastical or apocalyptic frameworks used for thinking about the Schism
(just picture the Old Pilgrim's mad journey from pope to pope, or Telesphorus's vision of the pre-Schism Antichrist) and the actual proposals for ending
this crisis that can be derived from these texts. Thus, we find no calls for the
exorcism of schismatic demons, for example, but rather rational analyses of
what needs to be done. Catherine of Siena is a good example of this rational
approach, for although in her letters she often integrated the Schism into a
scheme of perdition and salvation, she never lost sight of the realities of the
double election and the political expediency that motivated the cardinals'

---

17. Although some of these descriptions could qualify as literary topoi in the Boethian tradition,
they are nonetheless united and historicized by their relationship to the Schism.

actions. For her and for many later authors and visionaries it was clear that either one or both popes had to abdicate or that a general council had to be called. These solutions presupposed that the Schism was a man-made crisis that required man-made diplomatic interventions. Bovet's *Somnium* of the Schism came closest to combining the emotional mode of lamentation with concrete suggestions for ending the Schism: Bovet's alter ego personally encountered the suffering Ecclesia but then went on a multitude of diplomatic missions whose allegorical aspects did not disguise their essential reasonableness. Had the rulers done what Bovet asked them to do at this point (1394) the Schism could have been over twenty years earlier.

As we saw especially in the chapters on visionaries, the Schism served as a catalyst for seers to speak out. The period of the Schism coincided with the increasing codification of the process of the discernment of spirits.[18] In the politically charged climate of the Schism years, visionary interventions like those of Marie Robine or Constance de Rabastens were welcomed less and less by the church hierarchy; in fact, they could land the seer in jail. We saw that Ursulina of Parma was even accused of being a witch or sorceress by the Avignon cardinals who were less than happy with her visits to Pope Clement VII urging him to abdicate. The charismatic Jean de Varennes, a forceful critic of Benedict XIII, disappeared from the scene and probably died in prison. And fr. Pedro of Aragon's repeated visions in favor of Pope Urban VI did not sit well with the Aragonese king, who by then favored Clement VII. Rulers, both secular and religious, seemed to listen to their visionaries only when it suited their purposes. Certainly the increasing distrust of visionaries and especially of "mystical activists"—men or women—was closely related to the unstable situation of the church. If churchmen could not control the unity of their own institution, at least they attempted to control those who presumed to tell them what to do!

Some of our protagonists lived to see the Council of Constance, others did not. One can venture to say that all of those who died before the union of the church would have been gratified and relieved by the events of 1414–17. Of those who survived until that date, Saint Vincent Ferrer and Pierre d'Ailly were most actively involved in this event, the former less joyfully than the latter. For Vincent saw the pope to whom he had been loyal for many years deposed and had to acknowledge in sorrow his illegitimacy. Pierre d'Ailly, by contrast, felt vindicated; his proposals had come to fruition, and he was one of the leading men at Constance. Saint Colette went about her business of reforming the

---

18. As Elliott shows in *Proving Woman*, both the inquisition and the discernment procedures (which are in fact two sides of the same coin) were fixed in this period.

Franciscan order, skillfully navigating between multiple popes. Other sur-
vivors, like Christine de Pizan, waited out the French civil war in seclusion, and
it is not clear how quickly she was informed of the council's actions. But the
majority of our many passionate advocates of ending the Schism died before
the church could be united.

We saw that, as the years wore on, frustration with the popes who had
divided the church grew. Some people became resigned and stagnant, while
others tried every means to exert pressure on the popes. The period that saw
the greatest visionary, poetic, and prophetic activity was the early one, particularly before 1400. The two major types of efforts to unite the church we
encountered again and again in this study—to force the popes to abdicate and
the call for a general council—continued to be the subjects of countless polemical and theoretical texts throughout the Schism era, but political allegories
and visions directly related to the Schism petered out. The Schism became
entrenched, and the nonclerical voices of protest faded, more and more aware
of their futility perhaps. Nonetheless, eventually a number of pieces of advice
proffered by our characters came to fruition at Constance.

Even if their voices were not heeded they were heard. We moderns can hear
their anguish and frustration and admire the ingenuity with which they
expressed themselves. Clothing their thoughts in political allegories, revelatory
visions, stunning images, or prophetic pronouncements, they still speak to us.
Still divided by political and religious crises, we should be touched by these
people who tried to find consolation and offer solutions through their spirituality and their artistic endeavors.

BIBLIOGRAPHY

Primary Sources

Alfonso of Jaén. *Informaciones.* See Jönnson.

Arnaud-Gillet, Claude, ed. *Entre Dieu et Satan: Les visions d'Ermine de Reims (+1396) recueillies et transcrites par Jean le Graveur.* Florence: Galluzzo, 1997.

Baluze, Stéphane. *Vitae paparum avenionensium.* 4 vols. New ed. Georges Mollat. Paris: Letouzey, 1928.

Beck, Jonathan. *Le "Concil de Basle" (1434): Les origines du théâtre réformiste et partisan en France. Edition, introduction, glossaire et notes critiques. Préface de Daniel Poirion.* Studies in the History of Christian Thought 18. Leiden: Brill, 1979.

Birgitta of Sweden. *Revelaciones IV.* Ed. Hans Aili. Stockholm: Almqvist & Wiksell, 1992.

———. *Revelaciones VII.* Ed. Birger Bergh. Uppsala: Almqvist & Wiksell, 1967.

———. *St. Bridget's Revelations to the Popes: An Edition of the So-Called "Tractatus de summis pontificibus."* Ed. Arne Jönsson. Lund: Lund University Press, 1997.

Bovet, Honorat. *Medieval Muslims, Christians, and Jews in Dialogue: The "Apparicion maistre Jehan de Meun."* Ed. and trans. Michael Hanly. Tempe: Arizona Center for Medieval and Renaissance Studies, 2005.

Bovet (Bonet, Bouvet), Honoré. *L'Apparicion Maistre Jehan de Meun et le Somnium super materia scismatis.* Ed. Ivor Arnold. Paris: Les Belles Lettres, 1926.

———. *L'Arbre des batailles.* Ed. E. Nys. Brussels: Librairie Europénne, C. Muquardt, Merzbach & Falk, 1883.

———. *The Tree of Battles.* Trans. G. W. Coopland. Cambridge: Harvard University Press, 1949.

Catherine of Siena. *The Dialogue.* Trans. Suzanne Noffke. New York: Paulist Press, 1980.

———. *Epistolario.* Ed. Eugenio Dupré Theseider. Rome: Tipografia del senato, 1940.

———. *Lettere di Santa Caterina.* Ed. Niccolò Tommaseo. Presentazione di Gabriella Nodal. Rome: Bibliotheca Fides, 1973.

———. *The Letters of St. Catherine of Siena.* 2 vols. Suzanne Noffke. Tempe: Arizona Center for Medieval and Renaissance Studies, 2000.

Christine de Pizan. *The Book of Deeds of Arms and Chivalry.* Trans. Sumner Willard. Ed. Charity Cannon Willard. University Park: The Pennsylvania State University Press, 1999.

——. *Lavision-Christine*. Ed. Mary Louise Towner. Washington, D.C.: Catholic University of America Press, 1932.

——. *Le Chemin de longue étude*. Ed. and trans. Andrea Tarnowski. Paris: Livre de poche, 2000.

——. *Le Ditié de Jehanne d'Arc*. Ed. and trans. Angus J. Kennedy and Kenneth Varty. Oxford: Society for the Study of Mediaeval Language and Literature, 1977.

——. *Le Livre de l'advision Cristine*. Ed. Christine Reno and Liliane Dulac. Paris: Champion, 2001.

——. *Le Livre de la mutacion de Fortune*. 4 vols. Ed. Suzanne Solente. Paris: Picard, 1959–66.

——. *Le Livre de la paix*. Ed. Charity Cannon Willard. The Hague: Mouton, 1958.

——. *Le Livre des fais et bonnes meurs du sage roy Charles V*. 2 vols. Ed. Suzanne Solente. Paris: Société de l'Histoire de France, 1936–40.

——. *Le Livre du corps de policie*. Ed. Angus J. Kennedy. Paris: Champion, 1998.

——. *Les oeuvres poétiques de Christine de Pisan*. 3 vols. Ed. Maurice Roy. Paris: Firmin Didot, 1886–96.

——. *The Selected Writings of Christine de Pizan*. Ed. R. Blumenfeld-Kosinski. Trans. R. Blumenfeld-Kosinski and Kevin Brownlee. New York: W. W. Norton, 1997.

——. *Les Sept psaumes allégorisés of Christine de Pisan: A Critical Edition from the Paris and Brussels Manuscripts*. Ed. Ruth Ringland Rains. Washington, D.C.: Catholic University of America Press, 1965.

Constance de Rabastens. *Les Révélations*. Ed. A. Pagès and Noël Valois in "Les Révélations de Constance de Rabastens et le Grand Schisme d'Occident." *Annales du Midi* 8 (1896): 241–78.

Dante Alighieri. *Inferno*. Ed. and trans. Charles Singleton. Princeton: Princeton University Press, 1970.

Deschamps, Eustache. *Oeuvres complètes*. 11 vols. Ed. Marquis Queux de Saint-Hilaire and Gaston Raynaud. Paris: Société des anciens textes français, 1878–1904.

Du Boulay, César Egasse. *Historia Universitatis Parisiensis*. Paris, 1665–73. Reprint, 1966.

Elisabeth of Schönau. *The Complete Works*. Trans. Anne L. Clark. Preface by Barbara Newman. Mahwah, N.J.: Paulist Press, 2000.

——. *Die Visionen der hl. Elisabeth und die Schriften der Aebte Ekbert und Emecho von Schönau*. Ed. F. W. E. Roth. Brünn: Verlag der Studien aus dem Benediktiner- & Cistercienser-Orden, 1884.

Evrard de Trémaugon. *Le Songe du vergier*. Ed. M. Schnerb-Lièvre. 2 vols. Paris: CNRS, 1982.

Froissart, Jean. *Chroniques*. Ed. Le Baron Kervyn de Lettenhove. 28 vols. Brussels: Devaux, 1867–77.

Gautier de Châtillon. *Moralisch-Satirische Gedichte Walters von Châtillon*. Ed. Karl Strecker. Heidelberg: Carl Winter, 1929.

Gerson, Jean. *Oeuvres complètes*. 10 vols. Ed. Palémon Glorieux. Paris: Desclée, 1960–73.

Gobelinus Person. *Cosmidromius Gobelini Person und Processus translacionis et reformacionis monasterii Budecensis*. Ed. Max Jansen. Münster: Aschendorff, 1900.

Heinrich of Langenstein. *Heinrich von Langensteins "Unterscheidung der Geister": Texte und Untersuchungen zu Übersetzungsliteratur der Wiener Schule*. Ed. Thomas Hohmann. Zurich: Artemis Verlag, 1977.

——. *Liber adversus Thelesphori eremitae vaticiniae de ultimis temporibus*. Cols. 507–64 in Bernhard Pez, ed., *Thesaurus anecdotorum novissimus*, vol. 1, part 2. Augsburg: Veith, 1721.

Hildegard of Bingen. *Analecta Sanctae Hildegardis*. Ed. Joannes Baptista Pitra. *Analecta sacra* 8. Montecassino, 1882.

——. *Epistolarium*. 3 vols. Ed. Lieven van Acker and M. Klaes-Hachmöller. Corpus Christianorum, Continuatio Mediaevalis 91–91B. Turnholt: Brepols, 1991, 1993, 2001.

——. *The Letters of Hildegard of Bingen*. 2 vols. Trans. Joseph L. Baird and Radd K. Ehrman. New York: Oxford University Press, 1994, 1998.

——. *Liber divinorum operum*. Ed. Albert Delorez and Peter Dronke. Corpus Christianorum, Continuatio Mediaevalis 92. Turnholt: Brepols, 1996.

——. *S. Hildegardis Abbatissae Opera Omnia: Patrologiae latinae* 197. 1855.

[Jeanne-Marie de Maillé]. *Vita et processus canonisationis: Acta sanctorum*, March III.

Johannes de Rupiscissa. *Liber secretorum eventuum*. Ed. and trans. Robert Lerner and Christine Morerod-Fattebert. Specilegium Friburgense 36. Fribourg: Editions Universitaires, 1994.

John of Salisbury. *The "Historia pontificalis" of John of Salisbury*. Ed. and trans. Marjorie Chibnall. Oxford: Clarendon Press, 1986.

——. *The Letters of John of Salisbury*. 2 vols. Ed. W. J. Millor and C. N. L. Brooke. Oxford: Clarendon, 1979, 1986.

Jönnson, Arne. *Alfonso of Jaén: His Life and Works with Critical Editions of the "Epistola Solitarii," the "Informaciones," and the "Epistola Serui Christi."* Lund: Lund University Press, 1989.

Martin de Alpartil. *Cronica actitarum temporibus Benedicti XIII*. Ed. and trans. José Angel Sesma and María del mar Agudo Romeo. Saragossa, 1994.

——. *Cronica actitarum temporibus domini Benedicti XIII*. Ed. Franz Ehrle. Paderborn, 1906.

Nicolas de Clamanges. *Le Traité de la ruine de l'Eglise de Nicholas de Clamanges et la traduction française de 1564*. Ed. Alfred Coville. Paris: Droz, 1936.

Petrarca, Francesco. *Petrarch's Book Without a Name*. Trans. Norman P. Zacour. Toronto: Pontifical Institute of Mediaeval Studies, 1973.

Philippe de Mézières. *Letter to King Richard II: A Plea Made in 1395 for Peace Between England and France*. Ed. and trans. G. W. Coopland. New York: Barnes & Noble, 1976.

——. *Le Songe du Vieil Pelerin*. 2 vols. Ed. G. W. Coopland. Cambridge: Cambridge University Press, 1969.

Physiologus. Trans. Michael J. Curley. Austin: University of Texas Press, 1979.

Pierre d'Ailly. *Epistola diaboli Leviathan*. Trans. Irving W. Raymond. *Church History* 22 (1953): 181–91.

[Pierre de Luxembourg.] *Vita et processus canonisationis: Acta sanctorum*, July I.

Pintoin, Michel [Religieux de Saint-Denis]. *Chronique du religieux de Saint-Denys*. Ed. and trans. M. L. Bellaguet. 6 vols. Paris, 1842. Reprint, with a preface by Bernard Guenée. Paris: Editions du Comité des travaux historiques et scientifiques, 1994.

The Play of Antichrist. Trans. John Wright. Toronto: Pontifical Institute of Mediaeval Studies, 1967.

Quicherat, Jules, ed. *Procès de condamnation et de réhabilitation de Jeanne d'Arc, dite la Pucelle.* 5 vols. Paris: Jules Renouard, 1841–49.

Ranzanus, Petrus. *Vita de Vicente Ferrer: Acta sanctorum,* April I.

Raymond of Capua. *The Life of Catherine of Siena.* Trans. Conleth Kearns, O.P. Wilmington, Del.: Michael Glazier, 1980.

———. *Vita de Catherina da Siena: Acta sanctorum,* April III.

Richental, Ulrich von. *Chronik des Constanzer Conzils, 1414–1418.* Ed. Michael Richard Buck. Tübingen: Literarischer Verein Stuttgart, 1882.

———. *Das Konzil zu Konstanz: Kommentar und Text.* Ed. Otto Feger. Starnberg & Konstanz: J. Keller, 1964.

Rupert of Deutz. *Carmina de Sancto Laurentio.* Ed. H. Boehmer in *Monumenta Germaniae Historica: Libelli de lite* 3 (1896): 622–41.

Telesphorus of Cosenza. *Libellus.* Manuscript Estense Lat. 233. Biblioteca d'Este.

Tisset, Pierre. *Proces de condamnation de Jeanne d'Arc.*Vol. 3. Paris: Klincksieck, 1971.

Vincent Ferrer. *Oeuvres.* Ed. Henri Fages. 2 vols. Paris: Picard, 1909.

Zanacchi, Simone. *De beatae Ursulina Virgine: Acta sanctorum,* April I.

Secondary Sources

Ahlgren, Gillian T. W. "Visions and Rhetorical Strategy in the Letters of Hildegard of Bingen." Pp. 46–63 in Cherewatuk and Wiethaus, eds., *Dear Sister.*

Alphandéry, Paul. "Prophète et ministère prophétique dans le Moyen-Âge latin." *Revue d'Histoire et de Philosophie religieuses* 12 (1932): 334–59.

Anderson, Wendy Love. "Free Spirits, Presumptuous Women, and False Prophets: The Discernment of Spirits in the Late Middle Ages." Ph.D. dissertation, Divinity School, University of Chicago, 2002.

Arduini, Maria Lodovica. *Non fabula sed res: Politische Dichtung und dramatische Gestalt in den "Carmina" Ruperts von Deutz.* Rome: Edizioni di storia e letteratura, 1985.

Astell, Ann W. *Political Allegory in Late Medieval England.* Ithaca: Cornell University Press, 1999.

Badel, Pierre-Yves. *Le Roman de la Rose au XIVe siècle: Etude de la réception de l'oeuvre.* Geneva: Droz, 1980.

Batany, Jean. "Un Usbek au XIVe siècle: Le sarrasin juge des français dans *L'Apparicion Jehan de Meun.*" Pp. 43–58 in *Images et signes de l'Orient dans l'Occident médiéval: Senefiance* 11. Marseille: Editions Jeanne Laffitte, 1982.

Bautier, Robert-Henri. "Aspects politiques du Grand Schisme." Pp. 457–81 in Favier, ed., *Genèse et débuts.*

Beaune, Colette. "De Telesphore à Guillaume Postel: La diffusion du Libellus en France aux XIVe et XVe siècles." Pp. 196–208 in Gian Luca Potestà, ed., *Il profetismo gioachimita tra Quattrocento e Cinquecento.* Genoa: Marietti, 1991.

Bell, Dora M. *Etude sur le "Songe du Vieil Pelerin" de Philippe de Mézières (1327–1405). D'après le manuscrit français 22542: Document historique et moral du règne de Charles VI.* Geneva: Droz, 1955.

Bellitto, Christopher. *Nicolas de Clamanges: Spirituality, Personal Reform, and Pastoral Renewal on the Eve of the Reformation.* Washington, D.C.: Catholic University Press, 2001.

Benz, Ernst. *Die Vision: Erfahrungsformen und Bilderwelt.* Stuttgart: Ernst Klett Verlag, 1969.

Bernstein, Alan. *Pierre d'Ailly and the Blanchard Affair: University and Chancellor at the Beginning of the Great Schism.* Leiden: Brill, 1978.

Bertini, Ferruccio, et al., eds. *Medioevo al femminile.* Bari: Laterza, 1989.

Beyer, Rolf. *Die andere Offenbarung: Mystikerinnen des Mittelalters.* Bergisch Gladbach: Lübbe Verlag, 1989.

Bignami-Odier, Jeanne. *Etudes sur Jean de Roquetaillade.* Paris: Vrin, 1952.

———. "Jean de Roqutaillade." *Histoire littéraire de la France* 41 (1981): 75–240.

Bihlmeyer, Karl. "Die schwäbische Mystikerin Elsbeth Achler von Reute (+1420) und die Überlieferung ihrer Vita." Pp. 88–109 in Georg Baesecke and Ferdinand Joseph Schneider, eds., *Festgabe Philipp Strauch.* Halle: Max Niemeyer, 1932.

Blanchard, Joël. "Discours de la réformation et utopie à la fin du Moyen Age: Le 'Songe du Vieil Pelerin' de Philippe de Mézières (1389)." *Studi francesi* 32:3 (1988): 397–403.

Blanchard, Joël, and Jean-Claude Mühlethaler. *Ecriture et pouvoir à l'aube des temps modernes.* Paris: Presses Universitaires de France, 2002.

Bliemetzrieder, Franz. *Literarische Polemik zum Beginn des grossen abendländischen Schismas.* Publikationen des Österreichischen Historischen Instituts in Rom, vol. 1. Vienna: F. Tempksy; Leipzig: G. Freytag, 1909.

———. "Die zwei Minoriten Prinz Petrus von Aragon und Kardinal Bertrand Atgerius zu Beginn des abendländischen Schismas." *Archivum Franciscanum Historicum* 2 (1909): 441–46.

Bloch, Marc. *Les rois thaumaturges: Etude sur le caractère surnaturel attribué à la puissance royale particulièrement en France et en Angleterre.* 1924. New ed., preface by Jacques Le Goff. Paris: Gallimard, 1983.

Blumenfeld-Kosinski, Renate. "Christine de Pizan and the Political Life in Late Medieval France." Pp. 9–24 in Barbara Altmann and Deborah McGrady, eds., *Christine de Pizan: A Casebook.* New York: Routledge, 2003.

———. "Constance de Rabastens: Politics and Visionary Experience in the Time of the Great Schism." *Mystics Quarterly* 25:4 (1999): 147–68.

———. *Not of Woman Born: Representations of Caesarean Birth in Medieval and Renaissance Culture.* Ithaca: Cornell University Press, 1990.

———. "The Practice of Discerning Spirits: Raymond de Sabanac, preface to Constance de Rabastens, *The Revelations.*" In Miri Rubin, ed. *Medieval Christianity in Practice.* Princeton: Princeton University Press, forthcoming.

———. *Reading Myth: Classical Mythology and Its Interpretations in Medieval French Literature.* Stanford: Stanford University Press, 1997.

———. "The Scandal of Pasiphae: Narration and Interpretation in the *Ovide moralisé.*" *Modern Philology* 93 (1996): 307–26.

———. "Two Responses to Agincourt: Alain Chartier's *Livre des quatre dames* and Christine de Pizan's *Epistre de la prison de vie humaine.*" Pp. 75–85 in Angus J. Kennedy et al., eds., *Contexts and Continuities: Proceedings of the IVth International Colloquium on Christine de Pizan (Glasgow 21–27 July 2000), published in honour of Liliane Dulac.* 3 vols. Glasgow: University of Glasgow Press, 2002. Vol. 1.

Bogdanos, Theodore. "The Shepherd of Hermas and the Development of Medieval Visionary Allegory." *Viator* 8 (1977): 33–46.

Boland, Paschal. *The Concept of "discretio spirituum" in Jean Gerson's "De probatione spirituum" and "De distinctione verarum visionum a falsis."* Washington, D.C.: Catholic Press of America, 1959.

Bornstein, Daniel, ed. and trans. *Sister Bartolomeo Riccoboni: Life and Death in a Venetian Convent: The Chronicle and Necrology of Corpus Domini, 1395–1436.* Chicago: University of Chicago Press, 2000.

Boudet, Jean-Patrice, and Hélène Millet. *Eustache Deschamps en son temps.* Paris: Publications de la Sorbonne, 1997.

Boureau, Alain. *La papesse Jeanne.* Paris: Aubier, 1988.

Boutet, Dominique, and Armand Strubel. *Littérature, politique et société dans la France du Moyen Age.* Paris: Presses Universitaires de France, 1979.

Brandmüller, Walter. *Das Konzil von Konstanz, 1414–1418.* 2 vols. Paderborn: F. Schöningh, 1991–97.

———. *Papst und Konzil im Grossen Schisma (1378–1431): Studien und Quellen.* Paderborn: Ferdinand Schöningh, 1990.

Brettle, Sigismund. *San Vicente Ferrer und sein literarischer Nachlass.* Münster: Aschendorff, 1924.

Brownlee, Kevin. "Cultural Comparison: Crusade as Construct in Late Medieval France." *Esprit Créateur* 32:3 (1992): 13–24.

Burr, David. *The Persecution of Peter Olivi.* Philadelphia: American Philosophical Society, 1976.

———. *The Spiritual Franciscans: From Protest to Persecution in the Century After Saint Francis.* University Park: The Pennsylvania State University Press, 2001.

Bynum, Caroline Walker. *Holy Feast and Holy Fast: The Religious Significance of Food to Medieval Women.* Berkeley and Los Angeles: University of California Press, 1987.

Cabié, Robert. "Une mystique? Réflexions sur Constance de Rabastens." *La femme dans la vie religieuse du Languedoc (XIIIe–XIVe s.): Cahiers de Fanjeaux* 23 (1988): 37–54.

Caciola, Nancy. *Discerning Spirits: Divine and Demonic Possession in the Middle Ages.* Ithaca: Cornell University Press, 2003.

Capitani, Ovidio, and Jürgen Miethke, eds. *L'attesa della fine dei tempi nel Medioevo.* Bologna: Il Mulino, 1990.

Capitani, Ovidio, Claudio Leonardi, and Enrico Menestò, eds. *Conciliarismo, stati nazionali, inizi dell'umanesimo.* Atti del XXV convegno storico internazionale, Todi, 9–12 ottobre 1988. Spoleto: Centro Italiano di Studi sull'Alto Medieoevo, 1990.

Cardini, Franco. "L'idea di crociata in Santa Catarina da Siena." Pp. 57–87 in Maffei and Nardi, eds., *Atti del Simposio Internazionale Catariniano-Bernardiniano.*

Cavallini, Giuliana. "Le Dialogue de Sainte Catherine de Sienne et le Grand Schisme." Pp. 349–60 in Favier, ed., *Genèse et débuts.*

Charpentier, Hélène. "La fin des temps dans le *Livre des oraisons* de Gaston Fébus et les *Révélations* de Constance de Rabastens." Pp. 147–62 in *Fin des temps et temps de la fin dans l'univers médiéval: Senefiance* 33. Aix: CUERMA, 1993.

Cherewatuk, Karen, and Ulrike Wiethaus, eds. *Dear Sister: Medieval Women and the Epistolary Genre.* Philadelphia: University of Pennsylvania Press, 1993.

Clark, Anne L. *Elisabeth of Schönau: A Twelfth-Century Visionary.* Philadelphia: University of Pennsylvania Press, 1992.

Coakley, John. "Friars as Confidants of Holy Women in Medieval Dominican Hagiography." Pp. 222–46 in R. Blumenfeld-Kosinski and Timea Szell, eds., *Images of Sainthood in Medieval Europe.* Ithaca: Cornell University Press, 1991.

Colledge, Eric. "*Epistola solitarii ad reges:* Alphonse of Pecha as Organizer of Birgittine and Urbanist Propaganda." *Mediaeval Studies* 18 (1956): 19–49.

Combarieu du Grès, Micheline de. "Deschamps, poète de la fin du temps?" Pp. 163–85 in *Fin des temps et temps de la fin dans l'univers médiéval: Senefiance* 33. Aix: CUERMA, 1993.

Coote, Leslie, A. *Prophecy and Public Affairs in Later Medieval England.* Rochester, N.Y.: York Medieval Press, 2000.

Costello, Melanie Starr. "Women's Mysticism and Reform: The Adaptation of Biblical Prophetic Conventions in Fourteenth-Century Hagiographic and Visionary Literature." Ph.D. dissertation, Northwestern University, 1989.

Coville, A. *Recherches sur quelques écrivains du XIVe et du XVe siècle.* Paris: Droz, 1935.

Cramer, Thomas. "Bilder erzählen Geschichte: Die Illustrationen in Ulrich Richentals Chronik als Erzählung in der Erzählung." Pp. 327–49 in Harald Haferland and Michael Mecklenburg, eds., *Erzählungen in Erzählungen: Phänomene der Narration in Mittelalter und früher Neuzeit.* Forschungen zur Geschichte der älteren deutschen Literatur 19. Munich: Wilhelm Fink Verlag, 1996.

Cupples, Cynthia. "*Ames d'élite:* Visionaries and Politics in France from the Holy Catholic League to Louis XIV." Ph.D. dissertation, Princeton University, 1999.

Czarski, Carl. "The Prophecies of St. Hildegard of Bingen." Ph.D. dissertation, University of Kentucky, 1983.

Delaruelle, Etienne. "L'Antéchrist chez S. Vincent Ferrier, S. Bernardin de Sienne et autour de Jeanne d'Arc." Pp. 39–64 in Ermini, ed., *L'Attesa dell'età nuova.*

Delaruelle, Etienne, E.-R. Labande, and Paul Ourliac. *L'Eglise au temps du Grand Schisme et la crise conciliaire: 1378–1449.* 2 vols. Paris: Bloud & Gay, 1962–64.

Denis-Boulet, Noële M. *La carrière politique de Sainte Catherine de Sienne: Etude historique.* Paris: Desclée, de Brouwer & Cie., 1939.

Denizot-Ghil, Michèle. "Poétique de la discontinuité dans l'œuvre lyrique d'Eustache Deschamps." Ph.D. dissertation, New York University, 2000.

Dillon, Janet. "Holy Women and Their Confessors or Confessors and Their Holy Women? Margery Kempe and Continental Tradition." Pp. 115–40 in Rosalynn Voaden, ed., *Prophets Abroad: The Reception of Continental Holy Women in Late-Medieval England.* Cambridge: D. S. Brewer, 1996.

Dinzelbacher, Peter. *Heilige oder Hexen? Schicksale auffälliger Frauen in Mittelalter und Neuzeit.* Zurich: Artemis & Winkler, 1995.

———. *Mittelalterliche Frauenmystik.* Paderborn: Ferdinand Schöningh, 1993.

———. "Revelationes." Typologie des sources du Moyen Age occidental, fasc. 57. Turnhout: Brepols, 1991.

———. *Vision und Visionsliteratur im Mittelalter.* Stuttgart: Hiersemann, 1981.

Donckel, Emil. "Studien über die Prophezeiung des Fr. Telesforus von Cosenza, O.F.M. (1365–86)." *Archivum Franciscanum Historicum* 26 (1933): 29–104, 282–314.

Duby, Georges. "Histoire des mentalités." Pp. 937–66 in Charles Samaran, ed., *L'Histoire et ses méthodes*. Paris: Gallimard, 1961.

Duby, Georges, and Andrée Duby. *Les procès de Jeanne d'Arc*. Paris: Gallimard, 1973.

Dupré Theseider, Eugenio. "L'Attesa escatologica durante il periodo avignonese." Pp. 67–126 in Ermini, ed., *L'Attesa dell'età nuova*.

——. *I papi di Avignone e la questione romana*. Florence: Felice Le Monnier, 1939.

Dutton, Paul Edward. *The Politics of Dreaming in the Carolingian Empire*. Lincoln: University of Nebraska Press, 1994.

Elliott, Dyan. *Proving Woman: Female Spirituality and Inquisitional Culture in the Later Middle Ages*. Princeton: Princeton University Press, 2004.

——. "Seeing Double: John Gerson, the Discernment of Spirits, and Joan of Arc." *American Historical Review* 107 (2002): 26–54.

Emmerson, Richard Kenneth. *Antichrist in the Middle Ages: A Study of Apocalypticism in the Middle Ages*. Seattle: University of Washington Press, 1981.

Emmerson, Richard K., and Ronald B. Herzman. *The Apocalyptic Imagination in Medieval Literature*. Philadelphia: University of Pennsylvania Press, 1992.

Ermini, Giuseppe, ed. *L'Attesa dell'età nuova nella spiritualità della fine del medioevo, 16–19 ottobre 1960*. Todi: Presso l'Accademia Tudertina, 1962.

Fages, Henri (le Père). *Histoire de Saint Vincent Ferrier*. 2 vols. Paris: Maison de la Bonne Presse, 1892–94.

——. *Notes et documents de l'Histoire de Saint Vincent Ferrier*. Louvain: Uystpruyst, 1905.

Favier, Jean, et al., eds. *Genèse et débuts du Grand Schisme d'Occident*. Paris: Editions du Centre National de la Recherche Scientifique, 1975.

Fawtier, Robert. *La double expérience de Catherine Benincasa (Saint Catherine de Sienne)*. Paris: Gallimard, 1948.

——. *Sainte Catherine de Sienne: Essai de critique des sources*. 2 vols. Paris: E. de Boccard, 1921, 1930.

Ferrante, Joan. "Correspondent: 'Blessed Is the Speech of Your Mouth.'" Pp. 91–109 in Newman, ed., *Voice of the Living Light*.

Fink, Karl August. "Zur Beurteilung des Grossen abendländischen Schismas." *Zeitschrift für Kirchengeschichte* 73 (1962): 335–43.

Finke, Heinrich. "Die Nation in den spätmittelalterlichen allgemeinen Konzilien." *Historisches Jahrbuch* 57 (1937): 323–38.

——. "Drei spanische Publizisten aus den Anfängen des grossen Schismas: Matthäus Clementis, Nikolaus Eymerich, der hl. Vicente Ferrer." Pp. 174–95 in *Gesammelte Aufsätze zur Kulturgeschichte Spaniens*, ser. 1, vol. 1. Münster: Aschendorff, 1928.

Fleming, Martha H. *The Late Medieval Pope Prophecies: The "Genus nequam" Group*. Tempe: Arizona Center for Medieval and Renaissance Studies, 1999.

Fossier, François. "Rapports Eglise-Etat: Le Grand Schisme vu par les historiens du XIVe au XVIIe siècle." Pp. 23–30 in J.-Ph. Genet and B. Vincent, eds., *Etat et Eglise dans la genèse de l'état moderne*. Madrid: Casa Velázquez, 1986.

Fourier de Bacourt, Etienne. *Vie du Bienheureux Pierre de Luxembourg, 1369–1387*. Paris: Berche & Tralin, 1882.

Galbreath, Donald Lindsay. *Papal Heraldry*. 2d rev. ed. by Geoffrey Briggs. London: Heraldry Today, 1972.

Garganta, José M. de, O.P., and Vicente Forcada, O.P. *San Vicente Ferrer: Biografía y escritos.* Madrid: Biblioteca de Autores Cristianos, 1956.

Gilkaer, Hans Torben. *The Political Ideas of St. Birgitta and Her Spanish Confessor, Alfonso Pecha: Liber Celestis Imperatoris ad Reges, a Mirror of Princes.* Odense University Studies in History and Social Sciences 163. Odense: Odense University, 1993.

Goetz, Hans-Werner. "'Vorstellungsgeschichte': Menschliche Vorstellungen und Meinungen als Dimension der Vergangenheit." *Archiv für Kulturgeschichte* 61 (1979): 253–71.

Gössmann, Elisabeth. *Mulier Papa: Der Skandal eines weiblichen Papstes, Zur Rezeptionsgeschichte der Päpstin Johanna.* Archiv für philosophie- und theologiegeschichtliche Frauenforschung 5. Munich: Iudicium, 1994.

Gothic and Renaissance Art in Nuremberg, 1330–1550. New York: Metropolitan Museum of Art, 1986.

Gouguenheim, Sylvain. *La Sibylle du Rhin: Hildegarde de Bingen, abbesse et prophétesse rhénane.* Paris: Publications de la Sorbonne, 1996.

Graus, František. "Mentalität: Versuch einer Begriffsbestimmung und Methoden der Untersuchung." Pp. 9–48 in Graus, ed., *Mentalitäten im Mittelalter: Methodische und inhaltliche Probleme.* Sigmaringen: Jan Thorbecke Verlag, 1987.

———. *Pest—Geisler—Judenmorde: Das 14. Jahrhundert als Krisenzeit.* Göttingen: Vandenhoeck & Rupprecht, 1987.

Graziano, Fr. di Santa Teresa, O.C.D. "Tre sante nella chiesa del s. XIV." *Ephemerides Carmeliticae* 17 (1966): 174–81.

Grundmann, Herbert. "Die Papstprophetien des Mittelalters." *Archiv für Kulturgeschichte* 19 (1929): 77–138.

———. "Liber de Flore: Eine Schrift der Franziskaner-Spritualen aus dem Anfang des 14. Jahrhunderts." *Historisches Jahrbuch* 49 (1929): 33–91.

Guenée, Bernard. *Between Church and State: The Lives of Four French Prelates in the Late Middle Ages.* Trans. Arthur Goldhammer. Chicago: University of Chicago Press, 1991. [Originally published as *Entre l'Eglise et l'Etat.* Paris: Gallimard, 1987.]

———. *Histoire et culture historique dans l'Occident médiéval.* Paris: Aubier Montaigne, 1980.

———. *L'opinion publique à la fin du Moyen Age d'après la "Chronique de Charles VI" du Religieux de Saint-Denis.* Paris: Perrin, 2002.

———. *Un meurtre, une société: L'assassinat du duc d'Orléans, 23 novembre 1407.* Paris: Gallimard, 1992.

Guerra, Anna Morisi. "Il silenzio di Dio e la voce dell'anima: Da Enrico di Langenstein a Gerson." *Cristianesimo nella storia* 17 (1996): 393–413.

Guerrini, Paola. "Le illustrazioni nel *De magno schismate* di Antonio Baldana." Pp. 283–99 in Maria Chiabò et al., eds., *Alle origini della nuova Roma: Martino V (1417–1431).* Rome: Istituto Palazzo Borromini, 1992.

———. *Propaganda politica e profezie figurate nel tardo medioevo.* Naples: Liguori, 1997.

Hanly, Michael. "Courtiers and Poets: An International System of Literary Exchange in Late Fourteenth-Century Italy, France, and England." *Viator* 28 (1997): 305–32.

———. "Literature and Dissent in the Court of Charles VI: The Careers of the 'Courtier-Poets' Philippe de Mézières and Honorat Bovet." Pp. 273–90 in Nancy van Deusen, ed., *Tradition and Ecstasy: The Agony of the Fourteenth Century.* Claremont Cultural Studies. Ottawa: Institute of Mediaeval Music, 1997.

Harvey, Margaret. *Solutions to the Schism: A Study of Some English Attitudes, 1378 to 1409.* Erzabtei St. Ottilien: Eos Verlag, 1983.

Hasenohr, Geneviève. "Pierre de Luxembourg." *Dictionnaire de Spiritualité* 12:2, cols. 1612–14.

Hassig, Debra. *Medieval Bestiaries: Text, Image, Ideology.* Cambridge: Cambridge University Press, 1995.

Hedeman, Anne D. *Of Counselors and Kings: The Three Versions of Pierre Salmon's* Dialogues. Urbana: University of Illinois Press, 2001.

Heffner, David Todd. "'Eyn wunderliche Weyssagung von dem Babstumb': Medieval Prophecy into Reformation Polemic." Ph.D. dissertation, University of Pennsylvania, 1991.

Helbling, Hanno. *Katharina von Siena: Mystik und Politik.* Munich: Beck, 2000.

Hindman, Sandra L. *Christine de Pizan's "Epistre d'Othéa": Painting and Politics at the Court of Charles VI.* Toronto: Pontifical Institute of Mediaeval Studies, 1986.

Hiver-Bérenguier, J.-P. *Constance de Rabastens: Mystique de Dieu ou de Gaston Fébus?* Toulouse: Privat, 1984.

Hohmann, Thomas, and Georg Kreuzer. "Heinrich von Langenstein." Cols. 763–73 in *Deutsche Literatur des Mittelalters: Verfasserlexikon,* vol. 3, ed. Kurt Ruh and Gundolf Keil. Berlin: De Gruyter, 1980.

Huerga, Alvaro. "El 'Tratado del cisma moderno' de San Vicente Ferrer." *Revista española de teleogìa* 39–40 (1979–80): 145–61.

Ivars Andrés, P. "La 'indiferencia' de Pedro IV de Aragón en el Gran Cisma de Occidente." *Archivo ibero-americano* 29 (1928): 21–97, 161–86.

Jorga, Nicolas. *Philippe de Mézières, 1327–1405, et la croisade au XIVe siècle.* Bibliothèque de l'Ecole des Hautes Etudes 110. Paris: Emile Bouillon, 1896.

Kagan, Richard L. *Lucrecia's Dreams: Politics and Prophecy in Sixteenth-Century Spain.* Berkeley and Los Angeles: University of California Press, 1990.

Kaminsky, Howard. "The Great Schism." Pp. 674–96 in Michael Jones, ed., *New Cambridge Medieval History,* vol. 6. Cambridge: Cambridge University Press, 2000.

——. "From Lateness to Waning to Crisis: The Burden of the Later Middle Ages." *Journal of Early Modern History* 4 (2000): 85–125.

——. "The Politics of France's Subtraction of Obedience from Pope Benedict XIII, 27 July 1398." *Proceedings of the American Philosophical Society* 115, no. 5 (1971): 366–97.

——. *Simon de Cramaud and the Great Schism.* New Brunswick, N.J.: Rutgers University Press, 1983.

Kampers, Franz. *Kaiserprophetieen und Kaisersagen im Mittelalter: Ein Beitrag zur Geschichte der deutschen Kaiseridee.* Munich: H. Lüneburg Verlag, 1895.

Kerby-Fulton, Kathryn. "Hildegard and the Male Reader: A Study in Insular Reception." Pp. 1–18 in Rosalynn Voaden, ed., *Prophets Abroad: The Reception of Continental Holy Women in Late-Medieval England.* Cambridge: D. S. Brewer, 1996.

——. *Reformist Apocalypticism and "Piers Plowman."* Cambridge Studies in Medieval Literature 7. Cambridge: Cambridge University Press, 1990.

Kieckhefer, Richard. *Unquiet Souls: Fourteenth-Century Saints and Their Religious Milieu.* Chicago: University of Chicago Press, 1984.

Kleinberg, Aviad. *Prophets in Their Own Country: Living Saints and the Making of Sainthood in the Later Middle Ages.* Chicago: University of Chicago Press, 1992.

Kreuzer, Georg. *Heinrich von Langenstein: Studien zur Biographie und zu den Schisma-traktaten unter besonderer Berücksichtigung der Epistola pacis und der Epistola concilii pacis.* Paderborn: Ferdinand Schöningh, 1987.

Kruger, Steven F. *Dreaming in the Middle Ages.* Cambridge: Cambridge University Press, 1992.

Krynen, Jacques. *Idéal du prince et pouvoir royal en France à la fin du Moyen Age (1380–1440).* Paris: Picard, 1981.

Kurze, Dietrich. "Nationale Regungen in der spätmittelalterlichen Prophetie." *Historische Zeitschrift* 202 (1966): 1–23.

Lacassagne, Miren. "Eustache Deschamps: Discours et Société." Ph.D. dissertation, Washington University, 1994.

Ladner, Gerhart B. *Die Papstbildnisse des Altertums und des Mittelalters.* 3 vols. Rome: Pontificio Istituto di Archeologia Cristiana, 1941–84.

Lanahan, William, F. "The Speaking Voice in the Book of Lamentations." *Journal of Biblical Literature* 93 (1974): 41–49.

Landi, Aldo. *Il papa deposto (Pisa 1409): L'idea conciliare nel Grande Scisma.* Turin: Claudiana, 1985.

Lassabatère, Thierry. "Le bon gouvernement selon Eustache Deschamps." Mémoire de maîtrise, Université de Paris IV Sorbonne, 1992.

———. "Sentiment national et messianisme politique en France pendant la guerre de Cent Ans: Le thème de la fin du monde chez Eustache Deschamps." *Bulletin de l'Association des amis du Centre Jeanne d'Arc* 17 (1993): 27–56.

Laurie, I. S. "Eustache Deschamps: 1340(?)–1404." Pp. 1–72 in Sinnreich-Levi, ed., *Eustache Deschamps, French Courtier-Poet.*

Lee, Harold, Marjorie Reeves, and Giulio Silano. *Western Mediterranean Prophecy: The School of Joachim of Fiore and the Fourteenth-Century "Breviloquium."* Toronto: Pontifical Institute of Mediaeval Studies, 1989.

Le Goff, Jacques. "Les mentalités: Une histoire ambiguë." Pp. 76–93 in Le Goff and Pierre Nora, eds., *Faire de l'histoire.* 3 vols. Paris: Gallimard, 1974. Vol. 3.

Leonardi, Claudio. "Caterina, la mistica." Pp. 171–95 in Bertini et al., eds., *Medioevo al femminile.* Rome: Laterza, 1989.

Lerner, Robert E. "Antichrists and Antichrist in Joachim of Fiore." *Speculum* 60 (1985): 553–70.

———. "The Black Death and Western European Eschatological Mentalities." Pp. 77–105 in Daniel William, ed., *The Black Death: The Impact of the Fourteenth-Century Plague.* Binghamton, N.Y.: Center for Medieval and Early Renaissance Studies, 1982.

———. "Joachim of Fiore's Breakthrough to Chiliasm." *Cristianesimo nella storia* 6 (1985): 489–512.

———. *The Powers of Prophecy: The Cedar of Lebanon Vision from the Mongol Onslaught to the Dawn of the Enlightenment.* Berkeley and Los Angeles: University of California Press, 1983.

———. "Recent Work on the Origins of the 'Genus nequam' Prophecies." *Florensia* 7 (1993): 141–57.

———. "Refreshment of the Saints: The Time After Antichrist as a Station for Earthly Progress in Medieval Thought." *Traditio* 32 (1976): 97–144.

Lerner, Robert E., and Robert Moynihan. *Die Weissagungen über die Päpste (Vat. Ross. 374)*. 2 vols. Stuttgart: Hiersemann, 1985.

Lopez, Elisabeth. *Culture et sainteté: Colette de Corbie (1381–1447)*. Saint-Etienne: Publications de l'Université de Saint-Etienne, 1994.

———. *Petite Vie de sainte Colette*. Paris: Desclée de Brouwer, 1998.

Luongo, Thomas. "The Politics of Marginality: Catherine of Siena in the War of Eight Saints (1374–1378)." Ph.D. dissertation, University of Notre Dame, 1997.

Mack, Phyllis. *Visionary Women: Ecstatic Prophecy in Seventeenth-Century England*. Berkeley and Los Angeles: University of California Press, 1992.

Maffei, Domenico, and Paolo Nardi, eds. *Atti del Simposio Internazionale Catariniano-Bernardiniano, Siena, 17–20 aprile 1980*. Siena: Academia Senese degli Intronati, 1982.

Mannocci, Ildebrando. "Orsolina di Parma." *Bibliotheca sanctorum* 9 (1967): cols. 1271–73.

Marchello-Nizia, Christiane. "Entre l'histoire et la poétique: Le 'Songe politique,'" *Revue des sciences humaines* 55 (July–September 1981): 39–53.

Margolis, Nadia. "Culture vantée, culture inventée: Christine, Clamanges et le défi de Pétrarque." Pp. 269–308 in Eric Hicks, ed., with the collaboration of Diego Gonzalez and Philippe Simon, *Au champ des escriptures, IIIe colloque international sur Christine de Pizan, Lausanne, 18–22 juillet 1998*. Paris: Champion, 2000.

Martin, Victor. *Les origines du gallicanisme*. 2 vols. Paris: Bloud & Guay, 1939.

McGinn, Bernard. "Angel Pope and Papal Antichrist." *Church History* 47 (1978): 155–73.

———. *Antichrist: Two Thousand Years of the Human Fascination with Evil*. New York: Harper Collins, 1994.

———. *Apocalyptic Spirituality: Treatises and Letters of Lactantius, Adso of Montier-en-Der, Joachim of Fiore, the Spiritual Franciscans, Savonarola*. New York: Paulist Press, 1979.

———. "'Pastor Angelicus': Apocalyptic Myth and Political Theory in the Fourteenth Century." Pp. 221–51 in *Santi e santità nel secolo XIV*. Perugia: Università degli Studi di Perugia, 1989.

———. "'To the Scandal of Men, Women Are Prophesying': Female Seers of the High Middle Ages." Pp. 59–85 in Christopher Kleinhenz and Fannie J. Le Moine, eds., *Fearful Hope: Approaching the New Millennium*. Madison: University of Wisconsin Press, 1999.

———. *Visions of the End: Apocalyptic Traditions in the Middle Ages*. New York: Columbia University Press, 1998.

McGuire, Brian Patrick. *Jean Gerson and the Last Medieval Reformation*. University Park: The Pennsylvania State University Press, 2005.

McLaughlin, Elizabeth. "Women, Power, and the Pursuit of Holiness in Medieval Christianity." Pp. 99–130 in Rosemary Radford Ruether and E. McLaughlin, eds., *Women of Spirit: Female Leadership in Jewish and Christian Traditions*. New York: Simon & Schuster, 1979.

Meiss, Millard. *French Painting in the Time of Jean de Berry*. 2 vols. New York: George Braziller, 1974.

———. *Painting in Florence and Siena After the Black Death: The Arts, Religion, and Society in the Mid-Fourteenth Century*. Princeton: Princeton University Press, 1951.

Meyer, Paul, and Noël Valois. "Poème en quatrains sur le Grand Schisme (1381)." *Romania* 24 (1895): 197–218.

Miethke, Jürgen. "Die Konzilien als Forum der öffentlichen Meinung im 15. Jahrhundert." *Deutsches Archiv für Erforschung des Mittelalters* 37 (1981): 736–73.

Miller, Patricia Cox. *Dreams in Late Antiquity: Studies in the Imagination of Culture.* Princeton: Princeton University Press, 1994.

Millet, Hélène. "Comment mettre fin au Grand Schisme d'Occident? L'opinion des évêques et des chapitres de Normandie en 1398." Pp. 231–40 in *Chapitres et cathédrales en Normandie: Annales de Normandie, série Congrès et Sociétés Historiques et Archéologiques de Normandie,* vol. 2. Caen: Musée de Normandie, 1997.

——. "Ecoute et usage des prophéties par les prélats pendant le Grand Schisme d'Occident." *Mélanges de l'Ecole française de Rome, Moyen Age* 102:2 (1990): 425–55.

——. *"Il libro delle immagini dei papi": Storia di un testo profetico medievale.* Rome: Viella, 2002.

——. "Le cardinal Martin de Zalba (+1403) face aux prophéties du Grand Schisme d'Occident." *Mélanges de l'Ecole française de Rome, Moyen Age, temps modernes* 98 (1986): 265–93.

——. "Le Grand Schisme d'Occident." Pp. 729–35 in *Dictionnaire de la papauté,* ed. Philippe Levillain. Paris: Fayard, 1994.

——. "Le Grand Schisme d'Occident selon Eustache Deschamps: Un monstre prodigieux." Pp. 215–26 in *Miracles, prodiges et merveilles au Moyen Age: XXVe congrès de la S.H.M.E.S.* Paris: Publications de la Sorbonne, 1995.

——. *Le "Livre des prophéties des papes" de la Bibliothèque municipale de Lunel.* Lunel: Mairie de Lunel, 2004.

——. "Michel Pintoin, Chroniqueur du Grand Schisme d'Occident." Pp. 213–36 in Françoise Autrand, Claude Gauvard, and Jean-Marie Moeglin, eds., *Saint-Denis et la royauté: Etudes offertes à Bernard Guenée.* Paris: Publications de la Sorbonne, 1999.

Millet, Hélène, and Michael Hanly. "Les batailles d'Honorat Bovet: Essai de biographie." *Romania* 114 (1996): 135–81.

Millet, Hélène, and Dominique Rigaux. "Ascende calve: Quand l'historien joue au prophète." *Studi medievali,* ser. 3, 33 (1992): 695–719.

——. "Aux origines du succès des *Vaticinia de summis pontificibus.*" In *Fin du monde et signes des temps: Visionnaires et prophètes en France méridionale (fin XIIIe–début XVe siècle): Cahiers de Fanjeaux* 27 (1992): 129–56.

——. "Un double mal: Images de schismes dans les prophéties sur les papes." Pp. 145–72 in Nathalie Nabert, ed., *Le mal et le diable: Leurs figures à la fin du Moyen Age.* Cultures et christianisme 4. Paris: Beauchesne, 1996.

——. "Un puzzle prophétique dans le manuscrit 6213 de la Biblioteca Nacional de Madrid," *Revue Mabillon,* n.s. 3 (= 64) (1992): 139–77.

Möhring, Hannes. *Der Weltkaiser der Endzeit: Entstehung, Wandel, und Wirkung einer tausendjährigen Weissagung.* Stuttgart: Jan Thorbecke Verlag, 2000.

Mollat, Georges. "Grégoire XI et sa légende." *Revue d'histoire écclésiastique* 49 (1954): 873–77.

——. *Les papes d'Avignon.* 9th ed. Paris: Letouzey & Ané, 1950.

Mollat, Michel, and Philippe Wolff. *Les Révolutions populaires en Europe aux XIVe et XVe siècles.* Paris: Flammarion, 1993. [Originally published as *Ongles bleus, Jacques et Ciompi: Les révolutions populaires en Europe aux XIVe et XV siècles.* Paris: Calmann-Lévy, 1970.]

———. "Vie et sentiment religieux au début du Grand Schisme." Pp. 295–303 in Favier, ed., *Genèse et débuts.*

Mombello, Gianni. "Quelques aspects de la pensée politique de Christine de Pisan d'après ses oeuvres publiées." Pp. 43–153 in Franco Simone, ed., *Culture et politique en France à l'époque de l'Humanisme et de la Renaissance.* Turin: Accademia delle Scienze, 1974.

Montagnes, Bernard. "Prophétisme et eschatologie dans la prédication méridionale de S. Vincent Ferrier." In *Fin du monde et signes des temps: Visionnaires et prophètes en France méridionale (fin XIIIe–début XVe siècle), Cahiers de Fanjeaux* 27 (1992): 331–51.

Mooney, Catherine M., ed. *Gendered Voices: Medieval Saints and Their Interpreters.* Philadelphia: University of Pennsylvania Press, 1999.

Moreira, Isabel. *Dreams, Visions, and Spiritual Authority in Merovingian Gaul.* Ithaca: Cornell University Press, 2000.

Morrall, John B. *Gerson and the Great Schism.* Manchester: Manchester University Press, 1960.

Morris, Bridget. *Saint Birgitta of Sweden.* Woodbridge, N.Y.: Boydell Press, 1999.

Munz, Peter. *Frederick Barbarossa: A Study in Medieval Politics.* London: Eyre & Spottiswoode, 1969.

Newman, Barbara. *From Virile Woman to WomanChrist: Studies in Medieval Religion and Literature.* Philadelphia: University of Pennsylvania Press, 1995.

———. *God and the Goddesses: Vision, Poetry, and Belief in the Middle Ages.* Philadelphia: University of Pennsylvania Press, 2003.

———. "'Sibyl of the Rhine': Hildegard's Life and Times." Pp. 1–29 in Newman, ed., *Voice of the Living Light.*

———. *Sister of Wisdom: St. Hildegard's Theology of the Feminine.* Berkeley and Los Angeles: University of California Press, 1987.

———, ed. *Voice of the Living Light: Hildegard of Bingen and Her World.* Berkeley and Los Angeles: University of California Press, 1998.

———. "What Did It Mean to Say: 'I Saw'? The Clash Between Theory and Practice in Medieval Visionary Culture." *Speculum* 80 (2005): 1–43.

Niccoli, Ottavia. *Prophecy and People in Renaissance Italy.* Trans. Lydia G. Cochrane. Princeton: Princeton University Press, 1990.

Nyberg, Tore. "Birgitta, St." Pp. 246–47 in Strayer, ed., *Dictionary of the Middle Ages.* Vol. 2.

Oakley, Francis. *The Political Thought of Pierre d'Ailly: The Voluntarist Tradition.* New Haven: Yale University Press, 1964.

———. *The Western Church in the Later Middle Ages.* Ithaca: Cornell University Press, 1979.

Obermeier, Anita, and Rebecca Kennison. "The Privileging of *Visio* over *Vox* in the Mystical Experiences of Hildegard of Bingen and Joan of Arc." *Mystics Quarterly* 23 (1997): 137–67.

Ols, Daniel. "Sainte Catherine de Sienne et les débuts du Grand Schisme." Pp. 338–47 in Favier, ed., *Genèse et débuts.*

Ourliac, Paul. "Les lettres à Charles V." Pp. 173–80 in Maffei and Nardi, eds., *Atti del Simposio Internazionale Cateriniano-Bernardiniano.*

Ouy, Gilbert. "Une maquette de manuscrit à peintures (Paris, BN Lat. 14643, ff. 269–283 v°), Honoré Bouvet, *Somnium prioris de Sallano super materia Scismatis,* 1394." Pp. 44–51 in *Mélanges d'histoire du livre et des bibliothèques offerts à monsieur Frantz Calot.* Paris: Librairie d'Aregences, 1960.

Palmer, J. J. N. "England and the Great Western Schism, 1388–1399." *English Historical Review* 83, no. 328 (1968): 516–22.

Pascoe, Louis. "Pierre d'Ailly: Histoire, Schisme et Antéchrist." Pp. 615–22 in Favier, ed., *Genèse et débuts.*

Perroy, Edouard. *L'Angleterre et le Grand Schisme d'Occident: Etude sur la politique religieuse de l'Angleterre sous Richard II (1378–1399).* Paris: Monnier, 1933.

Petzold, Andreas. "'Of the Significance of Colours': The Iconography of Colour in Romanesque and Early Gothic Book Illumination." Pp. 125–34 in Colum Hourihane, ed., *Image and Belief: Studies in Celebration of the Eightieth Anniversary of the Index of Christian Art.* Princeton: Princeton University Press, 1999.

Picherit, Jean-Louis G. *La Métaphore pathologique et thérapeutique à la fin du Moyen Age.* Beihefte zur Zeitschrift für Romanische Philologie 260. Tübingen: Niemeyer, 1994.

Pleij, Herman. *Colors Demonic and Divine: Shades of Meaning in the Middle Ages and After.* Trans. Diane Webb. New York: Columbia University Press, 2004.

Pomian-Turquet, Joanna. "Philippe de Mézières: Carnaval Romain ou révolte de Cola di Rienzo?" *Médiévales* 4 (1983): 123–31.

Pommerol, Marie-Henriette de. "Jean de Roquetaillade." Pp. 843–45 in Geneviève Hasenohr and Michel Zink, eds., *Dictionnaire des Lettres francaises: Le Moyen Age.* Paris: Fayard, 1992.

Pou y Martí, J. M. *Visionarios, beguinos y fraticelos catalanes.* Vich, 1930; 2d ed. Presentation by A. Abad Pérez. Introductory study by J. M. Arcelus Ulibarrena. Madrid: J. Vicente, 1991.

———. *Visionarios, beguinos y fraticelos catalanes (Siglos XIII–XV).* With a preliminary study by Albert Hauf i Valls. Alicante: Instituto de Cultura "Juan Gil-Albert," 1996.

Prouvost, Yveline. "Les miracles de Pierre de Luxembourg (1387–1390)." *Hagiographie et culte des saints en France méridionale (XIIIe–Xve siècle): Cahiers de Fanjeaux* 37 (2002): 481–506.

Quaglioni, Diego. "La tipologia del 'somnium' nel dibattito su scisma e concilio." Pp. 97–117 in Capitani et al., eds., *Conciliarismo.*

Quillet, Jeannine. "Herméneutique et discours allégorique dans le *Songe du Vieil Pelerin* de Philippe de Mézières." Pp. 1084–93 in *Sprache und Erkenntnis im Mittelalter.* Miscellanea Medievalia. Veröffentlichungen des Thomas-Instituts der Universität Köln, vol. 13/2. Berlin: De Gruyter, 1981.

———. "Songes et songeries dans l'art politique du XIVe siècle." *Les Etudes Philosophiques* 3 (1975): 327–49.

Rathmann, Thomas. *Geschehen und Geschichten des Konstanzer Konzils: Chroniken, Briefe, Lieder, und Sprüche als Konstituenten eines Ereignisses.* Munich: Wilhelm Fink Verlag, 2000.

Raymond, J. W. "D'Ailly's *Epistola Diaboli Leviathan.*" *Church History* 22 (1953): 181–91.

Reeves, Marjorie. *The Influence of Prophecy in the Later Middle Ages: A Study in Joachimism.* Oxford, 1969. New ed. University of Notre Dame Press, 1993.

———. "Some Popular Prophecies from the Fourteenth to the Seventeenth Centuries." Pp. 107–34 in G. J. Cuming and Derek Baker, eds., *Popular Belief and Practice.* Cambridge: Cambridge University Press, 1972.

———. "The *Vaticinia de summis pontificibus:* A Question of Authority." Pp. 145–56 in Lesley Smith and Benedicta Ward, eds., *Intellectual Life in the Middle Ages: Essays Presented to Margaret Gibson.* London: Hambledon Press, 1992.

Rehberg, Andreas. "Der 'Kardinalsorakel-Kommentar' in der 'Colonna'-Handschrift Vat. Lat. 3819 und die Entstehungsumstände der Papstvatizinien." *Florensia* 5 (1991): 45–112.

Reno, Christine. "The Preface to the *Avision-Christine* in ex-Phillips 128." Pp. 207–27 in Earl Jeffrey Richards, ed., *Reinterpreting Christine de Pizan.* Atlanta: University of Georgia Press, 1990.

Richter, Reinhilt. "La tradition de l'Arbre des Batailles par Honoré Bonet." *Romanica Vulgaria* 82 (1983): 129–41.

Rohr, J. "Die Prophetie im letzten Jahrhundert vor der Reformation als Geschichtsquelle und Geschichtsfaktor: Ein Beitrag zur Geschichte der öffentlichen Meinung." *Historisches Jahrbuch* 19 (1898): 29–56.

Rollo-Koster, Joëlle. "*Castrum Doloris:* Rites of the Vacant See and the Living Dead Pope in Schismatic Avignon." Pp. 245–77 in Rollo-Koster, ed., *Medieval and Early Modern Ritual: Formalized Behavior in Europe, China, and Japan.* Leiden: Brill, 2002.

———. "The Politics of Body Parts: Contested Topographies in Late-Medieval Avignon." *Speculum* 78 (2003): 66–98.

Roth, Cornelius. *Discretio spirituum: Kriterien geistlicher Unterscheidung bei Johannes Gerson.* Würzburg: Echter, 2002.

Rouse, Richard H. "Bostonus Buriensis and the Author of the *Catalogus Scriptorium Ecclesiae,*" *Speculum* 41 (1966): 471–99.

Rousset, Paul. "Sainte Catherine de Sienne et le problème de la croisade." *Revue Suisse d'histoire* 25 (1975): 499–513.

Roux, Brigitte. *Les Dialogues de Salmon et de Charles VI: Images du pouvoir et enjeux politiques.* Geneva: Droz, 1998.

Ruh, Kurt. *Geschichte der abendländischen Mystik.* 4 vols. Munich: C. H. Beck, 1990–99.

Rusconi, Roberto. *L'attesa della fine: Crisi della società, profezia ed Apocalisse in Italia al tempo del grande scisma d'Occidente.* Rome: Istituto storico italiano per il medio evo, 1979.

———. "Eschatological Movements and Millenarism in the West (13th–Early 16th Centuries)." Pp. 29–44 in Vauchez, ed., *L'attente des temps nouveaux.*

———. "Il presente e il futuro della Chiesa: Unità, scisma, e riforma nel profetismo tardomedievale." Pp. 195–220 in Capitani and Miethke, eds., *L'attesa della fine dei tempi nel Medioevo.*

———. "Vicent Ferrer e Pedro de Luna: Sull'iconografia di un predicatore fra due obbedienze." Pp. 213–33 in Capitani et al., eds., *Conciliarismo.*

Sahlin, Claire L. *Birgitta of Sweden and the Voice of Prophecy.* Rochester, N.Y.: Boydell Press, 2001.

———. "Preaching and Prophesying: The Public Proclamations of Birgitta of Sweden's Revelations." Pp. 70–96 in Mary A. Suydam and Joanna E. Ziegler, eds., *Performance and Transformation: New Approaches to Late Medieval Spirituality.* New York: St. Martin's Press, 1999.

Salembier, Louis. *The Great Schism of the West.* Trans. "M.D." London: Kegan Paul, 1907.

Schäfer, Lucie. "Die Illustrationen zu den Handschriften der Christine de Pizan." *Marburger Jahrbuch für Kunstwissenschaft* 10 (1937): 119–208.

Schrader, Marianna, and Adelgundis Führkötter. *Die Echtheit des Schrifttums der Heiligen Hildegard von Bingen.* Cologne: Böhlau Verlag, 1956.

Schwartz, Orit, and Robert E. Lerner. "Illuminated Propaganda: The Origins of the 'Ascende calve' Pope Prophecies." *Journal of Medieval History* 20 (1994): 157–91.

Scott, Karen. "'Io Caterina': Ecclesiastical Politics and Oral Culture in the Letters of Catherine of Siena." Pp. 87–121 in Cherewatuk and Wiethaus, eds., *Dear Sister.*

———. "St. Catherine of Siena, 'Apostola.'" *Church History* 61 (1992): 34–46.

Scribner, Robert W. *For the Sake of Simple Folk: Popular Propaganda for the German Reformation.* Cambridge: Cambridge University Press, 1981.

Seckendorff, Eleonore Freiin von. *Die kirchenpolitische Tätigkeit der heiligen Katharina von Siena unter Papst Gregor XI (1371–1378): Ein Versuch zur Datierung ihrer Briefe.* Abhandlungen zur mittleren und neueren Geschichte 64. Berlin: Rothschild, 1917.

Seidlmayer, Michael. *Die Anfänge des grossen abendländischen Schismas.* Spanische Forschungen der Görresgesellschaft, 2d ser., vol. 5. Muenster: Aschendorff, 1940.

———. "Die spanischen 'Libri de Schismate' des Vatikanischen Archivs." *Gesammelte Aufsätze zur Kulturgeschichte Spaniens* 8 (1941): 199–262.

Seiferth, Wolfgang S. *Synagogue and Church in the Middle Ages: Two Symbols in Art and Literature.* Trans. Lee Chadeayne and Paul Gottwald. New York: Frederick Ungar, 1970.

Sieben, Hermann Josef. *Traktate und Theorien zum Konzil, vom Beginn des Grossen Schismas bis zum Vorabend der Reformation (1378–1521).* Frankfurter Theologische Studien 30. Frankfurt: Josef Knecht, 1983.

Sinnreich-Levi, Deborah M. *Eustache Deschamps, French Courtier-Poet: His Work and His World.* New York: AMS Press, 1998.

Smoller, Laura Ackerman. *History, Prophecy, and the Stars: The Christian Astrology of Pierre d'Ailly, 1350–1420.* Princeton: Princeton University Press, 1994.

———. "St. Vincent Ferrer and the Miracle of the Chopped-Up Baby: Creating the Image of a New Saint in the Fifteenth Century." Paper presented at the conference "Signs, Wonders, Miracles: Representations of Divine Power in the Life of the Church." University of Exeter, 2003.

———. "Two-Headed Monsters and Chopped-Up Babies: Re-Imagining the Schism After the Council of Constance." Paper presented at the Annual Meeting of the Medieval Academy of America, Seattle, 2004.

Sommerfeldt, Gustav. "Die Prophetien der hl. Hildegard in einem Schreiben des Magisters Heinrich von Langenstein (1383), und Langensteins Trostbrief über den Tod eines Bruders des Wormser Bischofs Eckard von Ders (um 1384)." *Historisches Jahrbuch* 30 (1909): 43–61, 297–307.

Spence, Richard. "Manuscript Syracuse University von Ranke 90 and the *Libellus* of Telesphorus of Cosenza." *Scriptorium* 33 (1979): 271–74.

Strayer, Joseph R., ed. *Dictionary of the Middle Ages*. 13 vols. New York: Charles Scribner's Sons, 1982–89.

Stroll, Mary. *The Jewish Pope: Ideology and Politics in the Papal Schism of 1130*. Leiden: Brill, 1987.

Strubel, Armand. "Le *Songe du Vieil Pelerin* et les transformations de l'allégorie au XIVe siècle." *Perspectives médiévales* 6 (1980): 54–74.

Stump, Philip. *The Reforms of the Council of Constance*. Leiden, New York: E. J. Brill, 1994.

Swanson, R. N. *Universities, Academics, and the Great Schism*. Cambridge: Cambridge University Press, 1979.

Szittya, Penn R. *The Antifraternal Tradition in Medieval Literature*. Princeton: Princeton University Press, 1986.

Tanz, Sabine. *Spätmittelalterliche Laienmentalitäten im Spiegel von Visionen, Offenbarungen und Prophezeiungen*. Frankfurt: Peter Lang, 1993.

Tarnowski, Andrea. "Unity and the *Epistre au roi Richart*": *Medievalia et Humanistica*, n.s. 26 (1999): 63–77.

Tierney, Brian. *Foundations of the Conciliar Theory: The Contributions of the Medieval Canonists from Gratian to the Great Schism*. Cambridge: Cambridge University Press, 1955.

Tobin, Matthew. "Une collection de textes prophétiques du XVe siècle: Le manuscrit 520 de la Bibliothèque municipale de Tours." Pp. 127–33 in André Vauchez, ed., *Les textes prophétiques et la prophétie en Occident (XIIe–XIVe siècle)*. Rome: Ecole française de Rome, 1990.

——. "Le 'Livre des Révélations' de Marie Robine (+1399): Etude et édition." *Mélanges de l'Ecole française de Rome, Moyen Age, temps modernes* 98:1 (1986): 229–64.

——. "Les visions et révélations de Marie Robine d'Avignon dans le contexte prophétique des années 1400." In *Fin du monde et signes des temps: Visionnaires et prophètes en France méridionale (fin XIIIe–début XVe siècle). Cahiers de Fanjeaux* 27 (1992): 309–29.

Töpfer, Bernhard. *Das kommende Reich des Friedens: Zur Entwicklung chiliastischer Zukunftshoffnungen im Mittelalter*. Berlin: Akademieverlag, 1964.

Torrell, Jean-Pierre. *Recherches sur la théorie de la prophétie au Moyen Age, XIIe–XIVe siècles: Etudes et textes*. Fribourg: Editions Universitaires Fribourg, 1992.

Trexler, Richard C. "Rome on the Eve of the Great Schism." *Speculum* 42 (1967): 489–509.

Tuchman, Barbara W. *A Distant Mirror: The Calamitous Fourteenth Century*. New York: Alfred A. Knopf, 1978.

Tucoo-Chala, Pierre. *Gaston Fébus et la vicomté de Béarn, 1343–1391*. Bordeaux: Imprimerie Bière, 1959.

Ullmann, Walter. *The Origins of the Great Schism: A Study in Fourteenth-Century Ecclesiastical History*. 1948. Reprint, Hamden, Conn.: Archon Books, 1967.

———. *A Short History of the Papacy*. 1972. 2d ed. With a new introduction by George Garnett. New York: Routledge, 2003.

Valerio, Adriana, ed. *Donna, potere e profezia*. Naples: M. D'Auria, 1995.

Valois, Noël. *La France et le Grand Schisme d'Occident*. 4 vols. Paris: Picard, 1896–1902.

———. "Jeanne d'Arc et la prophétie de Marie Robine." Pp. 452–67 in *Mélanges Paul Fabre: Etudes d'Histoire du Moyen Age*. Paris: Picard, 1902.

———. "Un ouvrage inédit d'Honoré Bonet, Prieur de Salon." *Annuaire-Bulletin de la Société de l'Histoire de France* 17 (1890): 193–215.

———. "Un ouvrage inédit de Pierre d'Ailly: Le *De persecutionibus Ecclesiae*." *Bibliothèque de l'Ecole des chartes* 65 (1904): 557–74.

Van Engen, John H. *Rupert of Deutz*. Berkeley and Los Angeles: University of California Press, 1983.

Vauchez, André, ed. *L'attente des temps nouveaux: Eschatologie, millénarisme et visions du futur du Moyen Age au XXe siècle*. Turnhout: Brepols, 2002.

———. *The Laity in the Middle Ages: Religious Beliefs and Devotional Practices*. Ed. and with an introduction by Daniel Bornstein. Trans. Margery J. Schneider. Notre Dame: University of Notre Dame Press, 1993.

———. "Un réformateur religieux dans la France de Charles VI: Jean de Varennes (+1396?)." Pp. 1111–30 in *Académie des Inscriptions et Belles-Lettres, Comptes rendus*. Paris: Bocard, 1998.

———. "Saint Brigitte de Suède et Sainte Catherine de Sienne: La mystique et l'Eglise aux derniers siècles du Moyen Age." Pp. 229–48 in *Temi et problemi nella mistica femminile trecentesca, 14–17 ottobre 1979*. Rimini: Maggioli, 1983.

———. *La sainteté en Occident aux derniers siècles du Moyen Age d'après les procès de canonisation et les documents hagiographiques*. Rome: Ecole française de Rome, 1981.

———. "La sainteté mystique en Occident au temps des papes d'Avignon et du Grand Schisme." Pp. 361–68 in Favier, ed., *Genèse et débuts*.

———. "Les théologiens face aux prophéties à l'époque des papes d'Avignon et du Grand Schisme." Pp. 199–207 in *Saints, prophètes et visionnaires: Le pouvoir surnaturel au Moyen Age*. Paris: Albin Michel, 1999.

Voaden, Rosalynn. *God's Words, Women's Voices: The Discernment of Spirits in the Writings of Late Medieval Women Visionaries*. Rochester, N.Y.: York Medieval Press, 1999.

Voci, Anna Maria. "Giovanna I d'Angiò e l'inizio del Grande Scisma d'Occidente. La doppia elezione del 1378 e la proposta conciliare." *Quellen und Forschungen aus italienischen Archiven und Bibliotheken* 75 (1995): 178–255.

Vogt, Kari. "'Becoming Male': A Gnostic and Early Christian Metaphor." Pp. 172–87 in Kari E. Børresen, ed., *Image of God and Gender Models in Judaeo-Christian Tradition*. Oslo: Solum Forlag, 1991.

Wagner, Barbara, "Tradition or Innovation? Research on the Pictorial Tradition of a Miniature in the *Mutacion*: 'Le Plus Hault Siège.'" Pp. 855–72 in Angus J. Kennedy et al., eds., *Contexts and Continuities: Proceedings of the IVth International Colloquium on Christine de Pizan (Glasgow 21–27 July 2000), published in honour of Liliane Dulac*. 3 vols. Glasgow: University of Glasgow Press, 2002. Vol. 3.

Walter, Christopher. "Papal Political Imagery in the Medieval Lateran Palace." *Cahiers archéologiques fin d'Antiquité et Moyen Age* 20 (1970): 155–76, and 21 (1971): 109–36.

Walters, Lori J. "The Royal Vernacular: Poet and Patron in Christine de Pizan's *Charles V* and *Sept psaumes allégorisés*. Pp. 145–82 in Renate Blumenfeld-Kosinski, Duncan Robertson, and Nancy Warren, eds., *The Vernacular Spirit: Essays on Medieval Religious Literature*. New York: Palgrave, 2002.

Warner, Marina. *Joan of Arc: The Image of Female Heroism*. Berkeley and Los Angeles: University of California Press, 1981. Paperback ed., 2000.

Warren, Nancy Bradley. "Monastic Politics: St. Colette of Corbie, Franciscan Reform, and the House of Burgundy." *New Medieval Literatures* 5 (2001): 203–28.

Whitman, Jon. *Allegory: The Dynamics of an Ancient and Medieval Technique*. Cambridge: Harvard University Press, 1987.

Widmer, Bertha. *Heilsordnung und Zeitgeschehen in der Mystik Hildegards von Bingen*. Basel: Helbing & Lichtenhahn, 1955.

Wilckens, Leonie von. "Die Prophetien über die Päpste in deutschen Handschriften: Zu Illustrationen aus der Pariser Handschrift Lat. 10834 und aus anderen Handschriften der ersten Hälfte des 15. Jahrhunderts." *Wiener Jahrbuch für Kunstgeschichte* 28 (1975): 171–80.

Willard, Charity Cannon. *Christine de Pizan: Her Life and Works*. New York: Persea, 1984.

Williams-Krapp, Werner. "Fifteenth-Century German Religious Literature in Its Social Context." *Etudes Germano-Africaines* 15–16 (1997–98): 113–20.

Williamson, Joan B. "Ysangrin and Hellequin's Horde in *Le Songe du Vieil Pelerin*." *Reinardus* 1 (1988): 175–88.

Wojcik, Jan, and Raymond-Jean Frontain, eds. *Poetic Prophecy in Western Literature*. London: Associated University Presses, 1984.

Wood, Charles T. *Joan of Arc and Richard III. Saints, Sex, and Government in the Middle Ages*. New York: Oxford University Press, 1988.

INDEX

and popes' return to Rome, 38, 43
as prostitute, 129
as rape victim, 5
as ship, 50, 66, 75, 209
as victim, 125, 127, 141, 208–9
Clamanges, Nicolas de, 5, 7, 66–67, 104
Tractatus de ruina Ecclesiae (Treatise on
the ruin of the church), 116
Clark, Anne L., 27, 29
Clement IV (1265–68), pope, 44
Clement V (1304–14), pope, 31, 200
Clement VII (1378–94), Avignon pope, 4, 37,
48, 70, 75, 190, 195, *207*
as bear, 175
and Bovet, 135
and Christine de Pizan, 157
and Constance de Rabastens, 65–68, 70,
139, 209
death of, 9, 78, 86, 88, 119; and Bovet, 140,
145
in Deschamps, 122, 126
endorsed by Pierre de Luxembourg, 77
as leper, 67
and Marie Robine, 81, 85
in Mézières' *Songe du Vieil Pelerin*, 107,
109, 111, 120
and Ursulina of Parma, 87–89
Clement VII (1523–34), pope, 204
Clement VIII (1423–29), antipope, 161
Colette, saint, 16, 93–95, 209–10
color symbolism
red, 65, 112, 139
yellow, 112–13
confessors, and holy women, 72
Constance de Rabastens, 11, 82, 92–93, 139,
208–9
accused of being crazy, 72
compared to Elisabeth of Schönau, 27
and miraculous literacy, 70
Révélations, 61–75
visions of, 34–35, 39, 61–75
Coopland, G. W., 109, 110, 134
Corsini, cardinal, Saint Catherine's letter to,
50–51
Cossa, Baldassare. *See* John XXIII
Council of Constance, 8, 17, 100, 149, 162,
201–4
and election of Martin V, 161, 203–4
and post-Constance period, 76, 89
and Saint Colette, 94–95
Council of Paris
first (1395), 82

second (1396), 82
third (1398), 9, 127
Council of Pavia, 20
Council of Pisa, 10, 94, 160, 201
results of, 11
Correr, Angelo. *See* Gregory XII
Cramaud, Simon de, 10, 104, 116
crusade, 37, 160–61, 188
proposed by Catherine of Siena, 43, 53, 54,
70 n. 18
proposed by Constance de Rabastens, 74
proposed by Eustache Deschamps, 130
proposed by Philippe de Mézières, 69, 118
Cyprus, king of (Jacques I), 143

Dante, *Divine Comedy*, 1, 100
Delachenal, Robert, 53
Denis-Boulet, Noële, 50
Denizot-Ghil, Michèle, 122
Deschamps, Eustache (Eustache Morel), 16,
69, 119, 150, 162, 208
ballades, 121–29, 139, 174, 178
biography of, 104–5
Complainte de l'Eglise (Complaint of the
Church), 104, 122, 129–31
Dietrich of Niem, chronicler, 4, 10
Dillon, Janette, 68
discernment of spirits, 34 n. 11, 64, 210
Dominic, saint, 79, 80
dream visions, 15, 15 n. 53, 189
in Bovet, 140–47
and politics, 97–101, 159
and Telesphorus of Cosenza, 189
Duby, Georges, 13
Dupin, Louis Ellies, 2

Ecclesia. *See* church
Echecs amoureux (Chess game of love), 97–98
Easton, Adam, cardinal, 190 n. 76
Eckard von Ders, bishop of Worms, 197
Ekbert of Schönau, 27, 28
Elisabeth of Schönau, 16, 19, 22, 27–29
Liber viarum Dei (Book of the ways of
God), 27
Elliott, Dyan, 89
Elsbeth Achler von Reute, 47 n. 53
emperor, last. *See* world emperor
England, and Great Schism, 14–15, 119–20, 129,
145
Ermine de Reims, 29, 35, 89–91, 93
Eucharist, vision of, 84
Eugene III (1145–53), pope, 21, 23